THE FLAVOR OF WAVERLY

THE FLAVOR OF WAVERLY

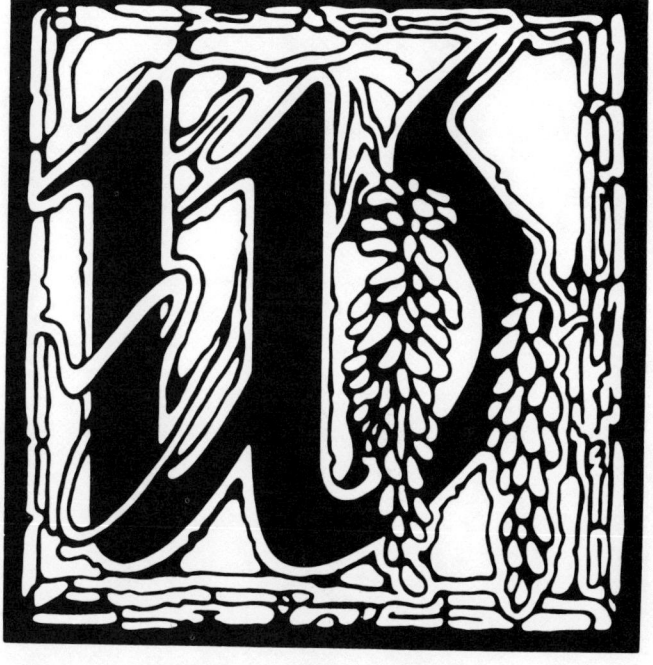

Author   Rosamond Peck
Editor   Susan S. Belin

Published by Waverly Community House, Inc.

First published 1986
© 1986 Waverly Community House, Inc.

Library of Congress Catalog Card Number: 86-50234
ISBN 0-9616433-0-7

Published by Waverly Community House, Inc.
Waverly, PA 18471

All rights reserved. No part of this publication may be reproduced, stored in a retrieval system or transmitted in any form or by any means electronic, mechanical, photocopying, recording or otherwise, without the prior permission of the copyright holder.

Culinary Editors Pat Atkins and Jean Colombo

This book was designed and produced by
The Lavelle-Miller Group
436 Spruce Street
Scranton, PA 18503

Art Director/Illustrator Helen Lavelle-Miller
Production Assistant/Researcher Mari Murrin

Artists
William Chickillo
Peter Hoffer
Karl Neuroth
Ed Parkinson
Gretchen Dow Simpson

Maps Rosamond Peck

Typography ComCom, Inc.
Color Separations Art Print Company
Manufactured by Haddon Craftsmen, Inc.

Library of Congress Cataloging-in-Publication Data

Peck, Rosamond, 1934-
  The flavor of Waverly.

  Bibliography: p.
  Includes index.
  1. Waverly (Penn.)—History. 2. Cookery, American—Pennsylvania. I. Belin, Susan S., 1943-
II. Title.
F159.W295P43   1986   974.8'36   86-50234
ISBN 0-9616433-0-7

Introduction

The idea of our book was born in the spring of 1983 when the Special Activities Committee of the Waverly Community House Board of Trustees decided a cookbook would be a worthwhile fundraising project. The initial idea of the ubiquitous spiral-bound collection of recipes evolved to encompass a decidedly more ambitious publication.

After months of meetings and lively discussions, the Book Committee envisioned a more distinct and distinguished book. We wanted to celebrate the unique spirit of the Community House and to highlight the beauty of our seasons and our seasonal gastronomic traditions.

We wanted to explore the wonderful patchwork of our varied experiences and to express the quality of our lives here, which is distinguished by a strong bond of caring for each other that bridges generations and ethnic distinctions. In short, we sought to capture the many flavors of life in our village. We hope we have achieved these goals in *The Flavor of Waverly*.

Working with the idea of our initial charge, we have incorporated community-wide recipes as the heart of our book. The sharing of good food and good cooking among friends is one of life's greatest pleasures. We celebrate the joy and camaraderie of such occasions, from the well-orchestrated to the impromptu; the elegant dinner to the community supper.

We have combined our wonderfully diverse and personal recipes into seasonal menus reflecting the annual rhythms of our life style. Our social patterns mirror our four seasons. Our activities are dictated by our weather, and the foods we eat are determined by the bounty of our local gardens. We recognize that our lives in Waverly are greatly enriched by the changing of the seasons.

To capture the drama and beauty of Mother Nature's handiwork on our landscape, we have incorporated the paintings of local artists. Depicting the four seasons, they are as integral to the message of our book as the seasons are to our lives. While the cover invites you to step inside to share the natural beauty of our Northeastern Pennsylvania landscape, the four seasonal paintings are as strong and varied as the moods of our changing weather. All are as rich and colorful as our lives here.

The threads that weave the book together with historical perspective and personal anecdotes are the narratives which graciously introduce each season and menu. Carefully researched and beautifully written, they reflect a deep understanding and love for the quality of life in Waverly.

Through these historical vignettes we get to know the eighteenth century pioneers who settled the Abington hillsides and we come to understand and appreciate the strong characters who molded the values and traditions of our community. We enjoy the tales of the changing village scenes in the nineteenth and twentieth centuries and see how the Waverly Community House evolved as the vital, central hub of activity for all of us, whatever age or background.

The illustrations throughout the book depicting local scenes were carefully chosen to complement the narratives and the menus.

We hope that *The Flavor of Waverly* will enhance the lives of you who read it and enjoy the recipes. And we hope it will contribute to a deeper appreciation for community bonds, for seasonal beauty and for friendships that are shared and celebrated when we break bread together.

Acknowledgements   x
Perspective   xii

Spring

Spring Celebration   7
Lenten Dinner   15
Cocktail Party   22
Graduation Brunch   32

Summer

Memorial Day Barbeque   49
Take-It-With-You Picnic   55
Fourth of July Salute   63
Intimate Summer Dinner   72
Kids In The Kitchen   79

Fall

Antiques Show Luncheon   97
Harvest Supper   107
Waverly Women's Club Luncheons   117
Dutch Treat Supper For Election Night   127

Winter

Grandma's Kitchen   144
Dinner Before The Christmas Dance   158
Newcomers' Coffee   171
Mid-Winter Blues Chasers   180
Cross Country Ski Supper   193

Table of Contents

Pot Pourri

Soup and Salad	212
Pasta	216
Poultry	220
Meat	225
Fish	234
Vegetables	239
Baked Goods	245
Desserts	248
Illustration Notes and References	255
Index	259

Acknowledgments

OUR THANKS . . .
To the Trustees of the Waverly Community House for their support throughout our project.

For the magnificent talents donated by our artists: Gretchen Dow Simpson for her inviting cover scene and William Chikillo, Peter Hoffer, Karl Neuroth and Ed Parkinson for their evocative seasonal paintings.

For the generous contributions of Mary C. Belin, Constance R. Belin, Mary Benjamin, Margaretta B. Chamberlin, Margery B. Clarke, Sally Marquardt, Gerald B. Payne, Rosemary Trane and Rhoda Warren.

To the Book Committee: Rosamond Peck for her delightful narratives that capture so beautifully the spirit and traditions of our community; Pat Atkins and Jean Colombo for their masterful menu-making and recipie analysis; Jane Bovard for her work and wise counsel.

To our eagle-eye recipe reviewers Martha Adams, Jean Hennessy, Ellie Hyde and Gail VanHorn and proof readers Cindy Neubert, Laura Frieder, Hallie Houck, Jody Sorrell, Abby Warman and Janet Wrightnour. To Rhoda Bernstein, Nancy Hemmler, Rebecca Peterson and Lou Roth for their narrative critiques and Peg Strom and Wendy Burns for narrative proof reading. To Janice Patterson for her thorough indexing and Marie Barycki for her skilled word processing.

For the advice and assistance of our friends John Clancy and Teri Stahller.

That our "book by committee" could be whipped into shape by Helen Lavelle-Miller and Mari Murrin. We've appreciated their unfailing good humor and their ability to transform our copy into a beautiful and creative design.

For the services of Haddon Craftsmen, Inc. and Art Print Co.

For three years of understanding and support from family and friends.

And finally, for the generosity of our community's creative and talented cooks. They have shared with us a delightful, delicious and diverse collection of recipes that truly reflect the many flavors of Waverly.

Susan S. Belin

Susan S. Belin
May, 1986

Perspective

Hundreds of millions of years have built this unique space on the surface of planet Earth which we call home. Seas have risen and retreated, continental plates have migrated and the earth crust has heaved up, folded and cracked into mountain barriers and notched passes. Dinosaurs and giant ferns have lain down in swamps to emerge in our time as the hardest coal of all, anthracite. Several times, a cooling climate froze millions of gallons of water into mile-thick mantles of ice. This frigid cap ground peaks into shoulders, scoured lowlands into lakes, bored the earth's largest pothole and gouged a southwestering valley before dropping its freight of boulders as it melted in retreat.

In the 25,000 years since then, evolution has developed now familiar flora and fauna in specialized varieties. Eroding water has left its marks. Hundreds of small, clear lakes dapple the pockets between gently rolling hills clad in maple, hickory, beech and oak. Dark hemlock and shiny mountain laurel climb steep stream banks, tenaciously anchored in shallow clay soil, amid shelves of Pennsylvania bluestone.

North America's first men came across the land bridge from Asia over 20,000 years ago. The native peoples developed many distinct cultures in response to the varied demands of the land and climate. In the 14th century they were living with a crude, but harmonious, Stone Age technology when Gothic cathedrals were rising in Europe, Ming Dynasty artisans were creating the Forbidden City with its porcelain treasures, and Tamerlane was ruling from fabulous Samarkand.

The Renaissance and the great voyages of exploration brought Judaeo-Christian white men to the New World, and they began to press inward from the coast. The Iroquois Confederacy included the area from the St. Lawrence River to Tennessee, governing the clans and tribes by concensus in a representative form of government. The Abington hills region was set aside by the Confederacy as a hunting preserve for all to use. A small group of Lenni-Lenape lived in the meadows beside the Lackawanna River. Nanticokes, Susquehannocks and others regularly traveled from the Delaware River to the Susquehanna along a well-worn path. This scene was sharply altered by the advent of firearms, liquor and devastating epidemics of measles and smallpox.

Northeastern Pennsylvania received a slow, but steady flow of Connecticut and Rhode Island settlers, moving west from crowded coastal villages. This migration had been delayed by a variety of factors. Pennsylvanians from the south bumped into Yankees coming from Connecticut. Dispute of jurisdiction led to the small, but serious Yankee-Pennamite Wars in the mid 1700's. Tories and Iroquois fought the Yankees who, in turn, fought the Pennsylvanians. Settlers were killed and their cabins and fields burned in successive raids that were caught up in the larger issues of the ensuing Revolutionary War.

After the Battle of Wyoming and its horrifying massacre in 1778, the Continental Congress authorized General Sullivan to march against the Iroquois allies of the British. In the summer of 1779, villages and crops were burned and many Indians killed in a sweep up the Susquehanna Valley that drove the survivors far to the west. The War for Independence had pitted Tory Pennsylvanians against Rebel Yankees, as well as the British Regulars and various Indian tribes involved.

The War ended in 1781 and the Articles of Confederation were adopted. A commission was established to examine the conflicting claims of Connecticut and Pennsylvania. The Trenton Decision of 1783 awarded jurisdiction to the Commonwealth of Pennsylvania, but honored the titles of all who were in occupancy of disputed lands at the time of the settlement. A new survey was authorized and settlement began again. Since the land of the Abingtons was heavily wooded and rocky, it was not as desirable as the fertile river flat lands of the Wyoming and Lackawanna valleys which were claimed and farmed by the first comers.

When the settlers finally came, it was with determination to build a first class community. They established churches and schools, formed a militia and opened a Post Office. By 1819, Turnpike Fever had spread here, and the Philadelphia-Great Bend Turnpike was chartered from Philadelphia through Easton to Mount Pocono. This toll road continued past Tobyhanna, Moscow, Dunmore, Providence, Chinchilla, Clarks Green, Waverly, Fleetville, Lennox, Glenwood and Harford, to Great Bend. Completed in 1826, it was a major thorough-fare, linking farmers to markets and making these hinterlands accessible to new settlers. Abington Center, or Waverly, developed into a trading village with inns, merchants and mechanics to serve the farm community, as well as the turnpike traffic of stage coaches, wagons and drovers traveling to more distant markets.

No sooner was the Turnpike open to traffic, than the Iron Horse snorted its first steam-driven locomotion. Aware of the potential, Dr. Andrew Bedford of Abington made the long trek to Harrisburg in 1832. There the legislature granted him a charter for the Leggett's Gap Railroad, one of the very first railroad charters in the nation. Bedford, Thomas Smith and William Clark accompanied the engineers on their surveys, paid all the expenses and urged their neighbors in Luzerne and Susquehanna counties to join them in this new venture. They renewed the charter every five years as they looked for support, and finally, in 1850, it received the needed impetus.

A significant battle in the Industrial Revolution in America was being waged in the Lackawanna Valley during the 1840's. The Scrantons built a furnace, brought together iron, limestone and coal, and produced the rails needed by the Erie Railroad for their line from Port Jervis to Binghamton. This ended America's dependence on English iron. It simultaneously built the foundation for a booming iron-anthracite-manufacturing center in Scranton for the better part of the next century.

Thwarted by vested transportation interests in Wilkes-Barre and Carbondale, the Scranton capitalists were happy to buy the Leggett's Gap Railroad charter from the Abington men in 1850. They consolidated with the Cobb's Gap Railroad, running to the Delaware River; and the Delaware, Lackawanna and Western Railroad was ready to transport raw materials, finished products, coal and passengers for the boomtown of Scranton and its satellite towns in the valley.

Bedford's hope that the railroad would come through Waverly across the village end of Carbondale Road was dashed by the engineer's elevation studies. Bypassed by modern transportation, the trading village of Waverly lost competitive edge and commercial vitality. By 1900 it was distinguished as a good place to live because of pure air and water and a healthful environment.

In the Lackawanna Valley, mining entrepreneurs saw right through the land to what could be taken from it. The extractive and processing industries that prospered there exploited earth and workers alike, and exhausted them both. The appeal of the unspoiled landscape of the Abington hills was magnified by the sharp contrast to the despoiled valley. Those who could afford to sought the refreshment of living in an area where man thrived by cooperating with the rhythms and forces of nature. Industrialists from Scranton came to summer and stayed on year-round, commuting on the D.L.&W. via the Glenburn station.

The Abingtons became accessible to middle class commuters with the advent of the Northern Electric Street Railroad in 1907. Since November, 1886, Scranton had been enjoying the nation's first scheduled electric trolley system to run on tracks. It made sense to extend the service out of the valley and into the Abington hills so that more could enjoy the possibilities of recreation and residence there. The Northern Electric ran from Scranton and Providence, through the Notch to Chinchilla, Clarks Summit, Dalton, and Factoryville, then to either Lake Winola or Montrose. A large brick building north of Dalton housed the generating plant for the line. The dark green trolleys ran at least hourly during the day and used most of the power generated. But at night, there was now plenty of surplus electricity to light the lamps in Abington households.

As the number of these households grew throughout the region, more local autonomy was sought to deal with the changing problems faced by governments. By 1900, the original Abington Township had been cut up by numerous political subdivisions. These had formed the boroughs of Dalton, Clarks Summit, Clarks Green and Waverly, and the townships of North, South and West Abington, Glenburn, Greenfield, LePlume Scott and Benton.

In 1916, Waverly Borough's faded commercial section was burned in a raging fire which left only four buildings standing on the front half of the block, between Clinton and Church Streets. This devastation set the scene for a unique phoenix to rise from these ashes. A living memorial to one of Waverly's first summer citizens was built on this site. Henry Belin, Jr.'s wife and his son, Paul, purchased the whole half of the square between Main Street and Foundry Alley, razed the remaining buildings and built a handsome brick community center designed by George Lewis, fresh out of architecture school. Owned by the township, but supported by contributions and gifts rather than taxes, this was a pioneering idea in community facilities. The Waverly Community House provides a focus which is very unusual in twentieth century suburbia. It is a place of many activities, both daily and special. It contributes a center, physical and symbolic, to the village.

In the following years, through the Depression and World War II to the present, families continued to leave the city in order to live "in the country." Waverly's cornfields, orchards and pastures are filling up with houses, driveways and swing sets. Lawnmowers whine on lawns, while tricycles and skateboards careen over hard top. The children of Scranton's captains of industry and immigrant laborers have joined the children of Abington's Yankee farmers on playing fields, tennis courts, and school boards, as well as in committee rooms and at dinner tables.

Waverly has evolved from a clearing on a path, an assortment of isolated cabins, a pause for traffic along a busy turnpike, a bustling trading and manufacturing center for area farmers, a rural backwater, a summer residential retreat, to today: home in 1986 to 1,487 residents of Northeastern Pennsylvania; a postmark on millions of pieces of cheerfully, personally handled mail; an exit on a convenient network of intersecting interstate highways; a handsome brick and white building welcoming people to a gracious square, with a sense of order and concern; an intersection bright with donated tulips, geraniums and TLC; country roads, edged with beautiful stone walls and shaded by sheltering maples; a school, four churches, a grocery, an antique shop, a handful of offices, several hundred well kept houses.

But over all other considerations, it is Home: Home to thousands of past as well as present residents; Home, by virtue of its qualities of heart, offering rest and security; Home, because of effort spent with love; Home, because of the extra touch in the kitchen or in the committee meeting that says, "You're worth the trouble"; Home, with values from the past, like a bayleaf in the stew, enriching the flavor, even though invisible; Home, where we all are comfortable in expressing love in a hundred familiar, friendly and flavorful ways.

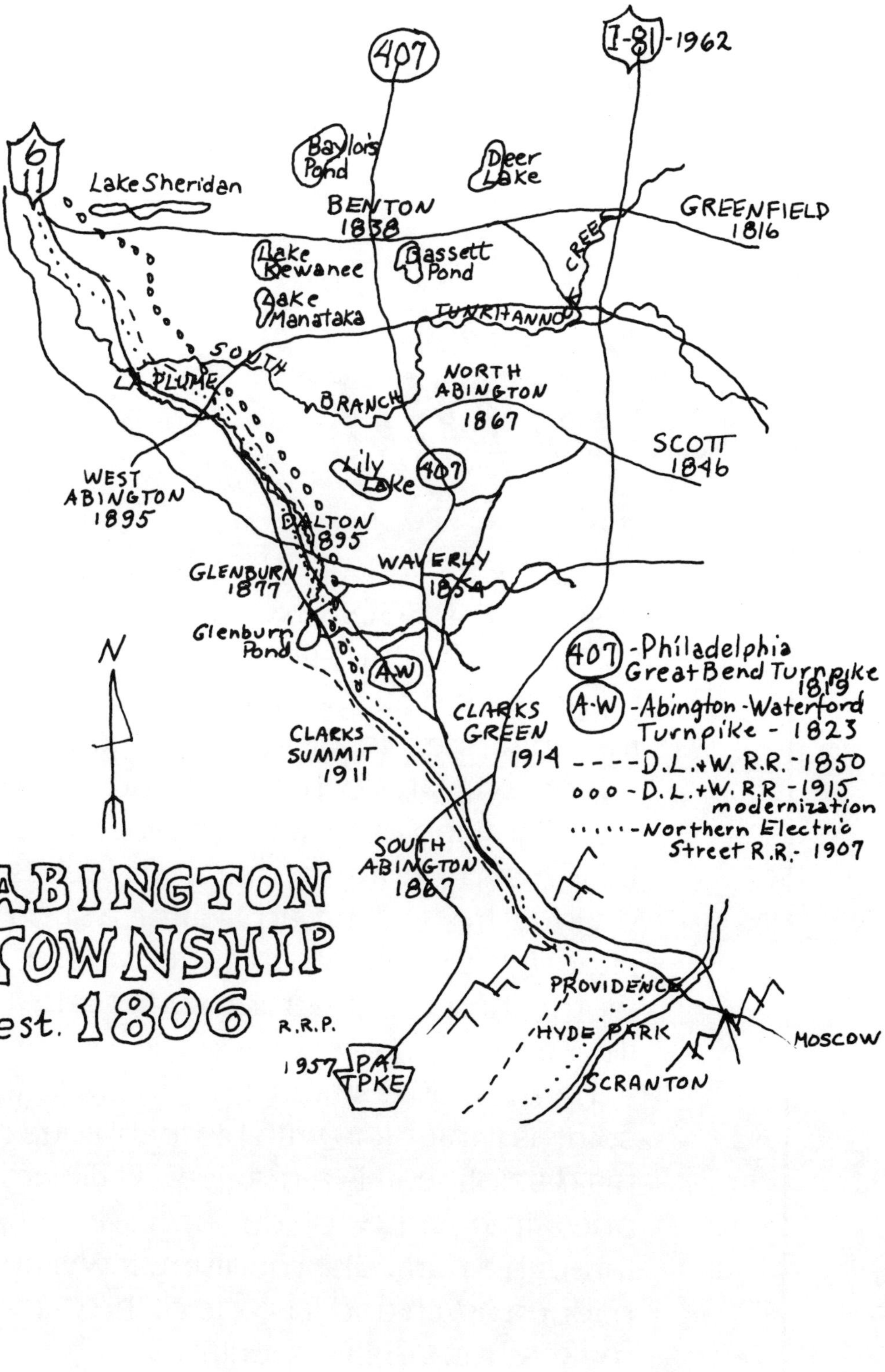

407
I-81 -1962
6
11
Lake Sheridan
Baylors Pond
Deer Lake
BENTON 1838
GREENFIELD 1816
Lake Kewanee
Bassett Pond
Lake Manataka
CREEK
TUNKHANNOCK
SOUTH BRANCH
LA PLUME
NORTH ABINGTON 1867
SCOTT 1846
Lily Lake
407
WEST ABINGTON 1895
DALTON 1895
WAVERLY 1854
GLENBURN 1877
Glenburn Pond
A-W
N
CLARKS GREEN 1914
CLARKS SUMMIT 1911
407 -Philadelphia Great Bend Turnpike 1819
A-W -Abington-Waterford Turnpike - 1823
----D.L.+W. R.R. -1850
ooo -D.L.+W. R.R -1915 modernization
......-Northern Electric Street R.R.- 1907
SOUTH ABINGTON 1867
ABINGTON TOWNSHIP
est. 1806
R.R.P.
1957 PA TPKE
PROVIDENCE
HYDE PARK
SCRANTON
MOSCOW

Spring

"SPRING IS THE END OF THE END AND THE BEGINNING OF THE BEGINNING." Bill Chickillo, speaking of his painting and its subject, mentions that the artist tries to develop a sixth sense which will guide his eye and hand in rendering the essence of a place in time. Like a symphony, a painting depicts individual trees, a thread of light, a streak of shadow, the patterns of the breeze, the warm thrust of fragrant spring air; and they interact in the composition to render a harmonious statement of the artist's spirit as it interacts with his technique and his discipline. It is a magical distillation of one time, one place and one spirit through a particular medium. It will never happen again and it is one of the gifts that makes human life special.

We all have the power to consecrate our lives by bringing our unique talents and vision to bear on the day and the place at hand. We may focus physical energy into a cake, a tennis game, the

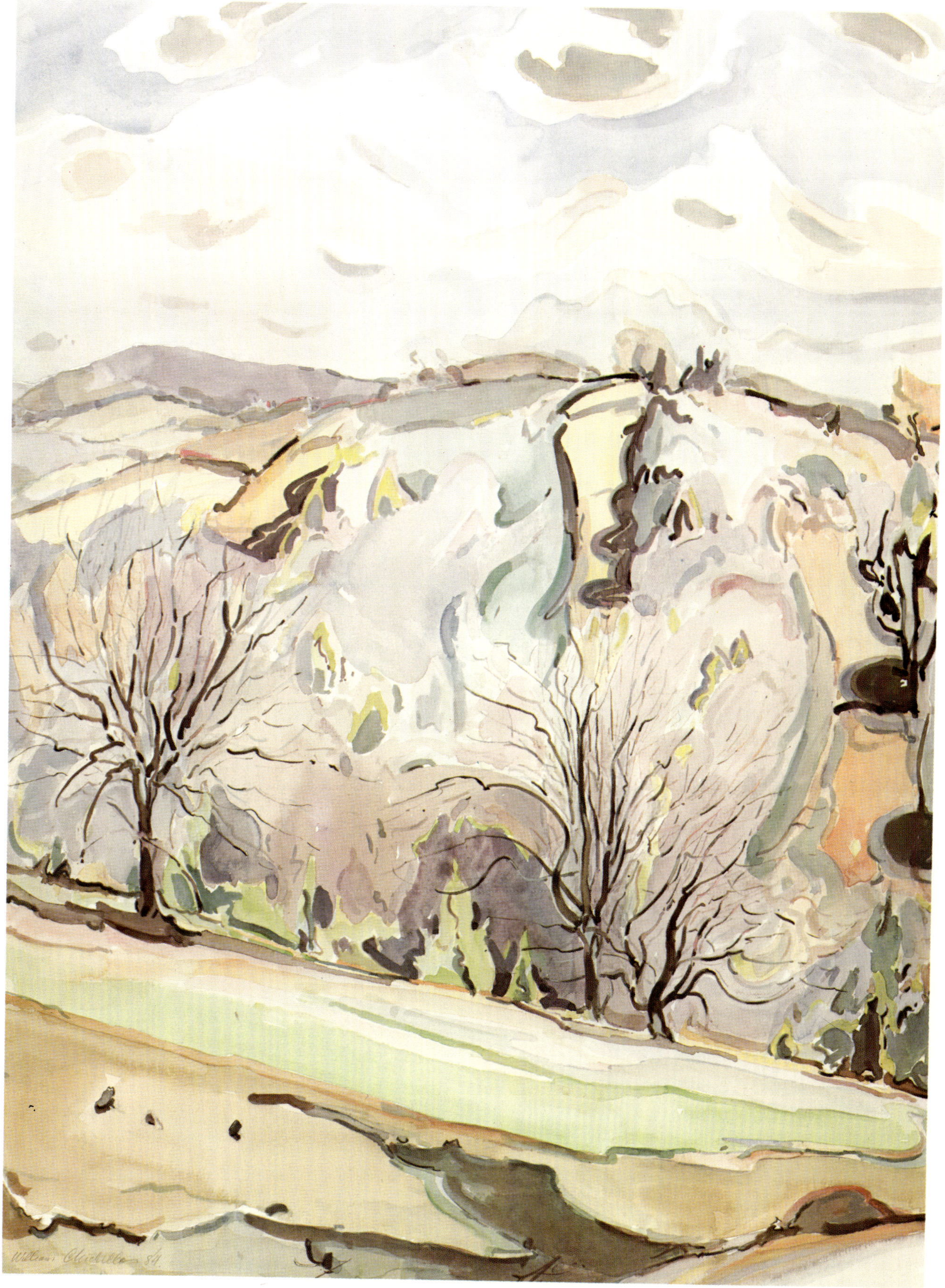

woodpile, or the garden; mental energy into reading, writing or problem solving; spiritual energy into hugging, praying, hearing a friend, or inviting our soul into a moment of quiet; we can all become artists, striving to make each of our days a masterpiece, uniquely ours and blessed by our attention.

Spring is a marvelously inspiring time. Who has not thrilled to the indomitable Canada geese as their cries lift our eyes and our hearts to the sight of the skeins, unravelling overhead, but never faltering in the northerly progress, adjusting to a succession of leaders wedging through the skies to lakes, thousands of miles north of their winter homes? The red-winged blackbirds unerringly return from the South to raucously claim the marshlands while the robins lay claim to all lawns and the worms beneath. The pussy willows are the first to keep the promise of soft new life, followed by buds, leaves, and blossoms in a dazzling profusion of colors and scents. As Waverly lawyer and columnist Horatio Nicholson eloquently noted in the Scranton *Herald* in May of 1853, "the hillsides have put on their finest and richest emerald robes; birds are abroad; apple trees and peach gardens, flinging the gauntlet at Jack Frost, yet hanging, I fear, about window eaves and cold fence corners, put out their best dress in promise of a beautiful harvest."

Water is one of spring's abundant gifts. We can hear it dripping from leaves and eaves; popping and trickling through the warming earth when we lay our ear to the ground; and gurgling in urgent streams under icy edges along the roadsides, inviting children to stay and dam.

Water becomes a relentless problem for neighborhoods where roof and pavement present their water-proof surfaces to the rain. Absorbent soil, protected from eroding rain by multiple canopies of buffering grasses and leaves, can catch and keep most rain where it falls. With the exchange of the natural cover for roofs and driveways, water now gains quantity and momentum, difficult to resist or divert; guttered, piped and sluiced away from one property, it rages over another. The problems come up at almost every supervisors' meeting. Robert Frost knew good fences could not make good neighbors; good ditches and swales could help. And when that's taken care of, let's get the canoe and head for Tunkhannock Creek or the Delaware, Lehigh or Susquehanna for some lively paddling.

Water, pure and abundant, was one of the appealing assets of the Abingtons in the mid-1800's. As the anthracite mines drove deep under the Lackawanna Valley, they disrupted the aquifers which provided water for the many backyard wells. The water, precious in the well, became a nuisance in the underground tunnels, and pumps were emplaced to carry the water off and away. Soon, most wells were dry.

Thirsty residents installed cisterns to catch rain water and sought mountain springs for drinking water. It was then that Scranton's water company developed its beautiful and profitable network of reservoirs. With watershed lands to protect them, this system provided a reliable water supply for the population of the valley.

Abington could still offer delicious water, readily available to a well digger. Many windmills stood tall on the landscape, sailing their circles, pumping water out of the wells for the houses and livestock. In the last half of the twentieth century we are all faced with many knotty problems connected with water, its quantity and quality, where it comes from and where it goes, in springtime and all year long.

Open the window and hear the peepers — a joyous, deafening din as the swamps surge with life. Some of this life drew the attention of Elder John Miller in his early nineteenth century journal, where he noted "plenty of gnats, mosquitoes and large ox flies in the air. These insects in this part of the year asserted their rights and insisted that their demands should be speedily satisfied and nothing was current with them, but blood and blood it must be; and the more they obtained the more impertinent and exacting they became." The situation is painfully familiar. The descendants of "these insects" still join us for spring gardening and evening cookouts. It's a price we pay for the welcome arrival of spring.

And all of our pleasures do exact their tolls. There is no such thing as a free lunch, whether describing ecology or domestic engineering. To build a house we buy lumber, hardware and furniture with money and mortgages. To make a home, we deal in the currency of caring; in the shop of love, we can only spend time and pay attention. And preparing food is a splendid way to do both.

Spring Celebration

Waves of applause from the auditorium, exhilarated smiles of the cast and back stage crew, heat from the lights, the smell of makeup, and the curtain falls on another Abington Players production. The same euphoria and excitement surround the Waverly grade school presentations like "Rip Van Winkle," the Minstrel Shows of the Sportsmen's Club and the Cassandra Devine Dance Recital. These feelings were present at the Rink, halfway up Academy Street, when local talent collaborated to present shows like "Ten Nights in a Barroom" in 1887, or when a traveling troupe of professionals came to town to share its repertoire in Factoryville, Fleetville, Waverly and other rural villages. The same elation lifted the "Waverly Milkmaids" for their recitations at the Methodist Church in the 1870's, as well as Nancy Light's Choral Readers in the 1940's.

The Understudies certainly relished the enthusiasm for their shows at the Comm which, in the 1950's, were tucked in between the school year and the start of summer jobs. Rita LaSorsa led a vigorous mixed chorus line of high school and college students, Janet Healy sang Betty Boop to David Niles, Myrna Gritman danced provocatively among a cluster of balloons, and Tony Mayer even swallowed a live goldfish, all for the Roaring Twenties or Showboat fun of it. That some money was raised for the Community House was the cherry on the sundae.

When the Belin family presented the Waverly Community House to the town in 1920, it was as a living memorial to their husband and father, Henry Belin, Jr. Pennsylvania Governor William C. Sproul and Judge George W. Maxey spoke at the dedication ceremony where Mrs. Henry Belin, Jr. turned over the deeds to the house and grounds to William Smith, president of the Waverly Borough Council.

This square brick building occupied the whole front half of the block facing Main Street, back to

Foundry Alley. It housed the Post Office, council chambers, an auditorium complete with a stage, dressing rooms and a moving picture projection booth, a town nurse's office, a barber shop, a women's clubroom with enclosed sun porch, and a canteen with a soda fountain and cigar and candy cases. On the second floor there was an apartment for the supervisor, a library, and a balcony which overlooked the tennis court and playgrounds. On the third floor there was a maid's room. The basement housed the fire-fighting equipment for the town, two bowling alleys, two billiard tables, men's dressing rooms and shower baths, a Boy Scout room, rooms for the pump and pressure tank, the boiler, coal and ice storage, and last, but not least, the village lock-up!

With all these wide-ranging provisions for community activities, there was opposition from some citizens who objected to a building "to be set aside for dancing, pool playing, and kindred other worldly amusements." In spite of this dissent, the Waverly Community House quickly filled with Grange meetings, sessions of the Women's League for Political Education, and a crowd of enthusiastic children enrolled in the first summer playground program.

And if life is characterized by change, the Community House has always been, definitely, alive. Ten years later, the still new building was changed by the addition of the two wings. These housed the Kindergarten and scout room at either end, with meeting rooms in between and an enlargement of the auditorium/gymnasium. The back half of the square was acquired at this time, and the whole property was landscaped to enhance the handsome edifice.

The villagers came to meetings and square dances, and the whole community came together for the Annual Fair and Agricultural Show, which raised the operating funds for the institution. Pony rides and a dunking tub, prize squashes and roses, shadow plays, children's parades and fashion shows, bountiful dinners provided by the ladies of the Baptist and Methodist Churches — this grand cooperative venture brought town and (evening) gown (of "summer folk") together. By 1937, the Fair had become so ambitious that its direction was too big a job for a volunteer, so an annual spring Maintenance Fund drive was instituted in its place.

The thirties and forties saw the Community House offering a focal point and activities which fostered the growing-together of the old families and the new "summer people." One of the most remarkable creations was Frances Andrews' Waverly Orchestra. She was the music teacher at the Waverly School and she built this orchestra from scratch, offering a place, with instrument and instructions, to any interested residents, providing they had never played their chosen instrument before. Every Monday night rehearsal sounds escaped through the open windows of the Scout room as Glennie Smith, Arch Brooks, Helen Von Storch, Betty Simpson, Mary Kennedy and other stalwarts produced "Pop Goes the Weasel" on unfamiliar violins, cellos, clarinets and tuba. They actually gave three or four performances and even had a guest conductor from Penn State!

But then, Waverly had some tradition of homegrown music. In 1867 the Urica String band met in the room over Wall's store, on Main Street, and in 1876 the Waverly Cornet Band built the Band Room on Church Street for their practices and performances. In 1896 the Baptist Church hosted a musical convention with a chorus of 60 voices and a 6 piece orchestra. Now the Community House is able to offer space for such pleasures for the whole community.

Still changing, in 1948, the Community House Board composed and adopted by-laws providing for an elected board of Trustees, nominated by the township as well as the Belin family. These by-laws stated: "The Waverly Community House is designed to give educational, recreational and social opportunities to the residents of this locality and to promote a sense of friendship, security and integrity."

These goals require more than a generous community and a dedicated Board of Trustees. A professional director sets the tone and pace of the atmosphere and the activities of the Community House. The very first Director was Mrs. George Peck, the wife of the pastor of Elm Park Church. The next year, 1921, Miss Gertrude Coursen took over the post and guided Comm and kindergarten with a genteel and diplomatic hand until 1937. The next thirty years were directed by the firm and friendly veteran, Bob Dixon. In 1967, Edgar "Special Delivery" Jones brought a genial coach's perspective to the Director's office until Jim Vanston, dapper and affable, took over in 1974. The office's many and varied responsibilities were assumed, in 1979, by Judy Dixon, whose gracious and even-tempered ways charm all who work with her or benefit from her friendly attention. As different as these directors have been, they have all been part of the give and take between the forces of change and preservation that characterize the dynamics of community, institution and goals.

To further enhance the function of the building, in 1958 F. Lammot Belin, as a memorial to his wife, Frances Jermyn Belin, expanded the bowling alleys, added a large and lovely room behind the stage and improved the lighting and seating for the auditorium. Soon there was a concert series, developed by Ray Cramer: brass ensembles, string quartets, folk singers and pianists filled the auditorium with song several times a season. On warm summer evenings, band concerts and strawberry festivals were enriched by paintings and sketches strung along the fences of the tennis court. Changing still, in 1985 the bowling alleys made way for Sylvia Jenkins' nursery school — evolution in action.

In 1964 the family of F. Lammot Belin established an Arts Scholarship in his name. Administered by a Committee appointed by the Board of Trustees, the scholarship provides a generous gift each year to an artist chosen by the selection committee. The fact that preference is given to local applicants provides nourishment for the arts in Northeastern Pennsylvania.

The Community House auditorium resonates with concerts and recitals, comes alive with Abington Players' Productions and embraces successful art shows and craft fairs. In addition, we all have the benefit of the company of artists in our midst; this helps us to sharpen our vision and appreciation of our surroundings, deepen our inner resources and hone our responses to music, art and ideas. When we can have a cup of coffee with a neighbor who is trying to develop his skills and focus his imagination and taste with discipline, we are stimulated to do the same. We can realize artistry in our sewing or our skiing, our sales skills or our sautéing, our mothering or our befriending, as well as the more traditional art forms. To do this we need inspiration and encouragement. Family and friends can be a wonderful source of these gifts. So invite them over to share a good meal and a regenerative potion of fellowship.

Spring Celebration

OSSO BUCCO MILANESE

RISOTTO

PURÉE OF PEAS IN ARTICHOKE BOTTOMS

CAULIFLOWER WITH SALSA VERDE

CERISES au PORT

OSSO BUCCO MILANESE

- 1 cup finely chopped onion
- ⅔ cup finely chopped carrot
- ⅔ cup finely chopped celery
- ¼ cup butter
- 1 teaspoon finely chopped garlic
- ½ cup vegetable oil
- ¾ cup flour
- 2 shanks of veal, cut into 8 pieces about 2 inches long.
- 1 cup dry white wine
- 1½ cup meat stock or broth, approximately
- 1½ cup canned plum tomatoes coarsely chopped, with juice
- 1 bay leaf
- Black pepper, freshly ground
- ¼ teaspoon dried thyme

Gremolada:
- ½ cup chopped fresh parsley, Italian if possible
- ¼ teaspoon finely minced garlic
- Grated rind of one lemon
- 2 anchovy filets, mashed
- Salt
- Pepper

Pre-heat oven to 350°F. Choose a heavy casserole with a tight fitting lid, that is large enough to contain veal pieces in a single layer, and is suitable for top of range cooking. Put in the onion, carrot, celery and butter, and saute over medium heat until the vegetables soften. Add the chopped garlic and cook a moment longer. Remove from heat.

Heat the oil in a skillet over medium-high heat. Turn the pieces of veal in the flour, coating well. Brown the veal pieces, on all sides. Arrange side by side on top of vegetables in the casserole. Remove fat from skillet, leaving behind the brown bits in the bottom of the pan. Pour in the wine and boil briskly about 3 minutes, scraping the skillet. Pour over the veal pieces in the casserole. In the same skillet bring the broth to a simmer and pour into the casserole. Add tomatoes, thyme, bay leaves, and pepper. The liquid should come up to the top of the veal pieces. If it does not, add more stock. Bring contents of the casserole to a simmer on top of the stove, cover tightly and place in lower third of the oven. Cook about 2 hours, basting and turning the veal occasionally. Ten minutes before the veal is done mix together ingredients for Gremolada and sprinkle on the veal, stirring to distribute through the sauce. Add salt and pepper to taste.

yield: 6 servings
JEAN COLOMBO

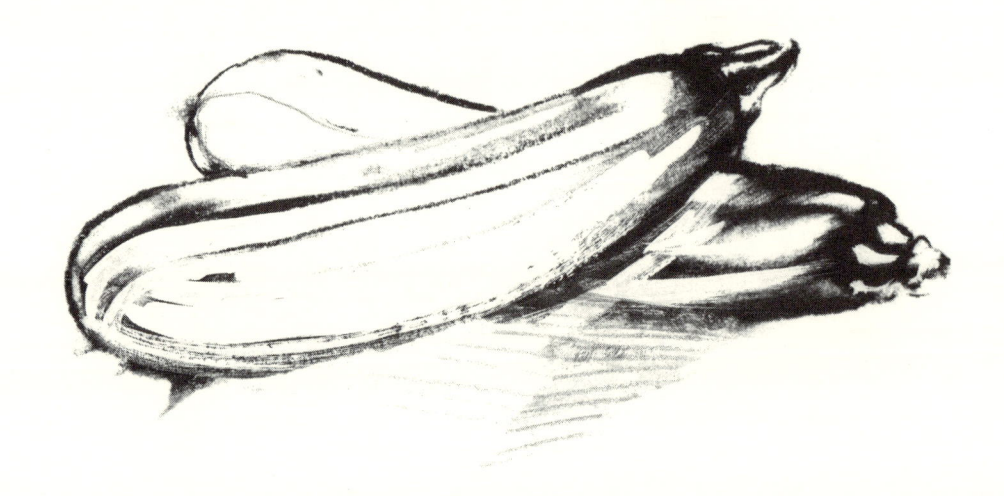

RISOTTO

1	medium onion, chopped
4	tablespoons butter
1	cup Arborio rice
4	cups chicken broth, kept warm
½	cup heavy cream
	Parmesan cheese for garnish

Optional Additions:
	A generous pinch of Saffron for Risotto Milanese style
3-4	tablespoons chopped cooked spinach for Risotto Verde
½	cup cooked peas or sauteed mushrooms

Sauté onions in butter until golden. Add the uncooked rice and stir over low heat until rice begins to take on a little color, stirring frequently. Add about a cupful of broth, stirring frequently. Add more broth as it is absorbed by the rice. After rice has been cooking about 15 minutes, add the cream. Stir well and continue cooking, adding broth as needed until the rice is tender. Add one of the optional ingredients just before serving. Sprinkle with Parmesan cheese.

yield: 4-6 servings
MARILYN WOLK

PURÉE OF PEAS WITH ARTICHOKE BOTTOMS

1	7½-ounce can of artichoke bottoms, rinsed and dried
1	10-ounce package frozen peas, cooked and drained
1	tablespoon butter
¼	cup heavy cream
	Salt and pepper
2	tablespoons melted butter

Pre-heat oven to 350°F. Put peas in food processor or blender with butter. With machine running, add heavy cream and process until smooth. Add salt and pepper to taste. Pipe puree decoratively in artichoke bottoms. Brush with melted butter. Bake for 15 minutes.

yield: 8 servings
MARGARETTA B. CHAMBERLIN

CAULIFLOWER WITH SALSA VERDE

- 1 large cauliflower
- ½ pound fresh spinach leaves, rinsed and dried
- 1 cup olive oil
- ¼ cup lemon juice
- 2 tablespoons capers
- 2 tablespoons chopped parsley
- 2 tablespoons chopped watercress
- 2 tablespoons minced black olives
- 2 tablespoons chopped pimento
- 1 teaspoon salt
- Dash Cayenne pepper

Steam whole cauliflower until crisp-tender. Remove from saucepan while still firm. Place head down, in rounded bowl with weight on top. Cover and refrigerate overnight. Except for spinach, combine remaining ingredients. Arrange spinach on platter. Invert cauliflower on spinach. Spoon some sauce over cauliflower and spinach. Serve the rest of sauce in separate bowl.

yield: 6 servings
MARILYN COSTA

CERISES AU PORT

- 1 3-ounce package black cherry gelatin
- 1 1-pound can pitted black cherries
- 1 cup port wine
- ½ cup heavy cream
- 1 tablespoon powdered sugar

Drain cherries and reserve liquid. Add water to the cherry liquid to equal one cup, and bring mixture to a boil. Pour over gelatin and stir until completely dissolved. Stir in port wine. Refrigerate until slightly thickened. Fold in cherries, put in mold and refrigerate until firmly set. Whip cream with the sugar until soft peaks form. Unmold jello and top decoratively with whipped cream. Jello can be made one or two days in advance. Unmold and decorate shortly before serving.

yield: 6 to 8 servings
RHODA WARREN

Lenten Dinner

The Word of God was carried into early Abington by circuit riders. These indomitable pioneers on horseback threaded the narrow tracks to small cabins or door-yard clearings crowded with settlers eager for inspiration. From their saddlebags, they drew worn Bibles for lessons; and from the convictions won by their own and their fathers' religious struggles, they drew inspiration for their preaching. And they moved on, leaving behind nuclei of new churches. These churches would foster preachers to serve their members and to ride out into the surrounding countryside on small circuits of their own.

In this manner, Reverend Samuel Sturdevant came to the log cabin home of William Clark in 1802 and formalized the organization of the First Abington Baptist Church with the Clarks, Deans, Gardners, Halls, Lewins and Millers. And in 1818 the Reverend George Peck established the first appointment for Methodist preaching at Leach's Flats. This parent church soon became five churches: the West Abington Church near Factoryville; the North Abington Church which met in the Aylesworth Schoolhouse in 1830; the Abington Center Church which met in the new schoolhouse on the Turnpike in 1832 and which produced its own offshoot as the Bailey Hollow Church begun in 1865 in what is now Dalton.

John Miller became the Elder for the Abington Baptist Church and in the first year he performed six weddings uniting families whose names are familiar in the Abingtons almost two centuries later: Ezra Dean and Amy Gardner; Sheldon Wall and Eunice Capwell; James Dean and Catherine Tripp; Henry Hall and W. Reynolds; George Capwell and Mary Gardner; Daniel Reynolds and Mercia Hall. It would not take long for a settlement or a church to grow with that kind of cooperation. During his 50-year ministry, Elder Miller baptized almost 2,000 converts, officiated at 1,800 funerals and married 457 couples. This activity covered a territory from Tunkhannock to Northmoreland, and from Pittston to Carbondale.

In 1821, Elder Miller donated an acre of land on the hilltop above his home on the crest now occupied by the Hickory Grove Cemetery. There the Baptist congregation built the New Salem Meeting House. In 1849, when they outgrew this building, they built a handsome church on the corner of the Turnpike and Carbondale Road, with sheds behind for carriages, wagons and horses during services.

By this time the Methodists had built their own church overlooking the Turnpike on the south side of the trading center of Abington. In 1842, Reverend Samuel Griffin and his initial group of worshippers, Owen Wight and his wife, Nehemiah Tinkham and his wife with Mrs. Elvira Whaling, Mrs. Samuel Griffin and Anne Evans had grown to a church building strength. This church was struck by lightning in 1878 and 1890 and promptly repaired; in 1899, the church building was turned to face Church Street and raised for a furnace; then, on the morning of March 13, 1921, the church burned to the ground. That afternoon, the church members came together, formed a plan for a new building and raised $1,000 toward that end. The cornerstone was laid on June 21st and the new church was dedicated on December 9, 1921. This diligence and dedication were part of a pay as you go tradition exemplified by an 1869 rule of the Methodists that no house of worship would be dedicated to God until it was entirely paid for.

In 1850 the First Presbyterian Church was organized by five members, and in 1859 it moved into a new building on Beech Street. Ten years later they sold this to the Waverly School and moved to newly built, elegant quarters across Carbondale Road from the Baptist Church. The interior boasted a beautiful pulpit and woodwork of finely worked, natural chestnut and walnut. But the population of Waverly was declining, and the Presbyterians closed their church until it was sold in 1892 to the Free Methodists.

The Waverly Free Methodist Church, organized in 1872, met in members' homes for the first six years. It moved to the Beech Street Church vacated by the Waverly School, and in 1892 it moved to the handsome Carbondale Road church building of the Presbyterians.

The fifth church in Waverly Borough was the African Methodist Episcopal Church, built in 1854. The community of slaves who escaped on the underground railroad had been attending Sunday School in the Schoolhouse on the Turnpike since 1844. After ten years, they had the numbers and committment to raise their own church. Of classically simple proportions, it stood on Carbondale Road looking across the field to Madison Academy. It housed regular meetings of a literary society as well as a Sunday school, and the Sunday services were lively, spontaneous and well attended.

The fact that there were five churches for a population of about 300 people set the scene for a controversy in 1895. George Stevenson, a school director, sought an injunction from County Court Judge Gunster to restrain Waverly Public School Principal, F.C. Hanyon, from reading the Bible in public schools. School directors Dr. N.C. Mackey, T.F. Stone, John Hall and Lester Stone all joined the Principal as co-defendants. Principal Hanyon said, "This is a Christian community and I feel that the reading of the Bible in school meets with its approval." The Scranton *Republican* of April 13, 1895, reports: "Not so long ago Mr. Stevenson, though known to be an agnostic, or at least an infidel, was fairly popular in the community. Now he is universally execrated and wherever one goes, he hears him condemned in good, flexible, vigorous Anglo-Saxon. There never was a time when quiet little Waverly was so stirred up."

Director D. M. Vail pointed out that, of 507 schools in Lackawanna County, the Bible is read in 193, and not read in 314; he supported Mr. Stevenson and stressed the clarity of the law against things of a sectarian nature in a school supported by tax-paying people. But he admitted there were only four men in town who sympathized with George Stevenson.

A few years earlier, Mrs. Mahoney, the only Roman Catholic in town, had objected to her children having to attend the reading of the Bible at the opening of each school day. The issue was settled then by excusing her children until 9:15, when the reading had been concluded. This time, the court was involved, and the village in an uproar. On September 7, 1898, three years later, Judge H.M. Edwards dismissed the complaint and dissolved the injunction granted in 1895.

There are other tensions which strain our institutions in the twentieth century. Waverly proper now has four churches. Many inhabitants drive to other villages nearby to satisfy their religious committments. In the Abington area in the 1980's, there are over twenty churches for almost 20,000 residents. There are many worshippers in many sacred halls, and many hours of Bible study, counselling, praying and feasting together. But there is also the force of materialism and secularism to lure attention away from church life. One observation, celebrated across sectarian boundaries, is the Lenten season. It is a time to admit we are tempted and to address those temptations which make us complacent, ignorant or less than we might be; to restrain our appetites and acknowledge our hungers. Abington's early settlers knew this realm. Organized religions have formalized the recognition of these basic human traits. Fasting in the Lenten Season can be a tool to remind us of this truth.

Lenten Dinner

FILET OF SOLE DUGLERÉ
ASPARAGUS CAESAR
ELEGANT AND SIMPLE VEGETABLES
CARROT TIMBALES
CHILLED LIME SOUFFLÉ

FILET OF SOLE DUGLERÉ

4	filets of sole, Gray, Dover or Flounder
	Lemon juice, salt, pepper
	Butter
3	peppercorns
1	small bay leaf
1	slice onion
¾	cup dry white wine
¼	cup water
3	firm, ripe tomatoes
3	tablespoons butter
3	tablespoons flour
	Salt
	Cayenne pepper
½	cup light cream
2	tablespoons chopped parsley
	Parmesan cheese

Pre-heat oven to 350°F. Wash sole in lemon juice and water and dry well with towels. Season skin side with salt and pepper. Put tiny dots of butter on filets and fold over. Place in oven-proof dish and scatter peppercorns, bay leaf, and onion over top. Pour on wine and water. Poach 15 minutes. Remove fish. Place in warmed serving dish. Reserve liquid in oven-proof dish.

Peel and seed tomatoes, saving the seeds and pulp. Cut tomatoes into ¼" wide shreds. Puree pulp and seeds in blender or food processor, then strain through fine sieve. Set aside. Melt butter in pan; off heat stir in flour, salt, pepper. Strain in fish stock. Add strained tomato pulp. Stir over heat until sauce thickens. Add cream and bring to boil carefully. Mix in shredded tomatoes and parsley. Carefully mask fish on serving dish with sauce. Sprinkle top with Parmesan cheese and some melted butter. Glaze under hot broiler before serving.

yield: 4 servings

This recipe looks difficult but is not. The result is one of the more beautiful and more delicious productions. The most discriminating guest will enthuse about it - unless of course, said guest dislikes seafood, or fish.

CONSTANCE R. BELIN

ASPARAGUS CAESAR

2	15-ounce cans white asparagus
¼	pound melted butter
3	tablespoons lemon juice
½	cup freshly grated Parmesan cheese
	Dash paprika

Pre-heat oven to 400°F. Place drained asparagus in baking dish. Pour melted butter over and drizzle on lemon juice. Sprinkle with cheese and paprika. Bake 15 minutes. Serve on thinly-sliced toast.

yield: 4 to 6 servings
MARY S. HOUCK

ELEGANT AND SIMPLE VEGETABLES

Place frozen peas in boiling water with the spring onions. When water resumes boil, remove from heat and add cucumber slices, and simmer. After 5 minutes drain and place in serving dish. Add lemon juice, salt and ground pepper to taste. Add butter and/or chopped parsley.

yield: Whatever amount desired
SALLY PREATE

Frozen peas, bright green, 4 ounces per person
Cucumber, thinly sliced, 8 slices per person
Spring onion, chopped, ½ onion per person
Lemon juice
Salt
Pepper
Butter
Parsley

CARROT TIMBALES

Pre-heat oven to 375°F. Place carrots in saucepan with water to cover and salt. Cook until tender. Drain. Process in food processor using steel blade. Mixture should retain some texture. Put in bowl. Blend eggs with cream in bowl. Add carrots along with seasonings. Butter a 4 cup charlotte mold or 6 ramekins. Line bottom with waxed paper. Butter paper. Pour carrot mixture into mold or ramekins. Place mold or ramekins in baking pan. Add hot water to 1½ inches. Bake 45 minutes for mold or 20 minutes for individual ramekins.

yield: 6 servings
CAROL PATTERSON

1½	pounds carrots, peeled and cut in 2 inch lengths
½	teaspoon salt
3	eggs
½	cup heavy cream
⅛	teaspoon nutmeg
	Pepper

CHILLED LIME SOUFFLÉ

Sprinkle gelatin over cold water to soften. In top of double boiler, mix egg yolks with ½ cup sugar, lime juice and salt. Cook over simmering water wisking until slightly thickened. Add gelatin and lime rind, stirring until gelatin is completely dissolved. Cool. Beat egg whites until soft peaks form, add remaining sugar slowly until mixture is stiff. Fold in lime mixture and whipped cream. Pour into 1½ quart oiled souffle dish with foil collar extending above rim. Chill until set. Garnish with lime slices, whipped cream and candied violets.

yield: 6 to 8 servings
PAT ATKINS

1	envelope plain gelatin
¼	cup cold water
4	egg yolks, lightly beaten
1	cup sugar
½	cup lime juice
1	tablespoon grated lime rind
½	teaspoon salt
6	egg whites
1	cup whipped cream

Cocktail Party

In June, 1871, "a revolting sight was witnessed in the village Monday. Six hard looking cases.... were on exhibition at the tavern door in a state of intoxication. A crowd of citizens gathered about the corners and looked upon the shameful scene, and exchanged remarks with regard to the party who is responsible for this outrage upon the moral sense of the entire community."

In November, 1872, Reverend S.S. Kennedy continued to write his "Waverly News" for *The Republican* in Scranton ". . . monthly temperance meetings have a peculiar interest and are well attended by our people, both old and young, most of whom have signed the pledge. As a result, the temperance sentiment is strong and radical in this community, and keeping a tippling house among us is not looked upon as a very honorable business... The few habitual drinkers among us do the best they can to make the rum business a success, but they fail for lack of capacity. They can hold but a quart, and would fain drink a gallon. When they are gone, and many are going fast, we hope they will have no successors."

Grain was grown on every farm in early Abington; wheat, rye, barley, and corn provided nourishment for man and beast alike. The extra became a source of cash. But it was bulky and the farmer and miller fast realized that if it were converted into whiskey, a seller would have to make only a third as many tedious trips to market. A bushel of wheat could be converted into a gallon of whiskey in a still anyone could build and operate. It did add a certain something to a gathering and most haying, barn raising or other communal endeavors included a jug of John Barleycorn to wet the whistle.

However, Abington was settled by upright men, earnest Baptists and Methodists, and it was not long before Dr. Andrew Bedford and Lemuel Stone supervised the haying on their fields without benefit of whiskey! It was unusual enough to be noticed and applauded. Taking encouragement from this success, in 1850 they formed an alliance, the Band of Hope. "Temperance is a very fine virtue" was the motto and those who took the pledge and joined this Band foreswore "the use of spirituous liquors as a beverage, tobacco in every form and profanity."

By 1854, Bedford and Stone, joined by Leonard Batchelor, John Fell and Alvah Parker built a Temperance House and went into the hotel business on the southwest corner of the Turnpike and Clinton Street. Soon named the Waverly Hotel, it never attracted enough business from drivers and stage passengers. In ten years it was sold out to "parties from abroad" who abandoned the temperance policies with the results observed by S.S. Kennedy, above. Temperance may have been a good idea, but it was not a profitable business policy.

In 1870 the temperance forces in Waverly gathered additional ammunition. They were reading *Arts of Intoxication: The Aims and The Results* by Reverend J.T. Crane, D.D. It contained a comprehensive brief statement of various intoxicating drugs used in different parts of the world at the same and different times; their common and also specifically different effects. It was divided into discussions of history; an analysis of the nature of man and addiction; coca; thornapple; betel nut; tobacco; hemp; opium; with alcohol dominating the second half of the book. Wouldn't the Band of Hope be interested to observe the work at Waverly's Marworth Treatment Center?

Temperance forces finally prevailed on the national level and effected the Prohibition era. In 1920, Amendment 18 and the Volstead Act outlawed the manufacture, sale or transportation of intoxicating liquors in the United States and its territories. Intoxicating liquors were defined as any containing one-half of one percent of alcohol by volume. It was a controversial measure and, by many, more honored in the breach than in the observance. Repeal in 1933 seemed to justify those breaches and a cocktail party enjoyed a stamp of approval from the legal majority. It still offered the age old appeal of relaxation and escape. Some humans have indulged in drink or drugs since the first encounter with a mushroom or a fermented berry.

The cocktail party can bring together a large group of friends and offer them a dazzling array of finger foods, both decorative and delicious. So we may eat well, drink less and still be merry.

Cocktail Party

MENU I
HOT ARTICHOKE DIP
SALMON MOUSSE
BAKED BRIE
SPINACH BALLS
CRAB CASSEROLE
PALMER'S EDAM DIP
SHRIMP BALLS
COCKTAIL DIP FOR SHRIMP

MENU II
RED CHICKEN WINGS
MEXICAN LAYERED DIP
BAKED ARTICHOKE HEARTS
CHEESE DREAMS
CLAM BALLS
HOT CRAB DIP
SAUSAGE & BEEF APPETIZER
CURRIED CHICKEN TID BITS

MENU I

HOT ARTICHOKE DIP

- 1 cup Parmesan cheese
- 1 cup mayonnaise
- 2 cups artichoke hearts, chopped and drained
- 1 cup Tuscan peppers, chopped
- Garlic and salt to taste

Pre-heat oven to 350°F. Combine ingredients. Pour into 2-quart casserole. Bake 10 minutes or until hot through. Serve with crisp crackers.

yield: 20 servings
NORA FOX

SALMON MOUSSE

excellent

- 1 1-pound can salmon
- 2 envelopes gelatin softened in ½ cup cool water
- 1 envelope chicken broth dissolved in ½ cup boiling water
- ½ cup mayonnaise
- ½ cup sour cream
- 1 medium onion or 1 bunch scallions, chopped
- 1 teaspoon dill
- Juice of one large lemon
- Dash of soy sauce, Tabasco, Worcestershire & paprika

Skin and bone salmon and crumble. Put softened gelatin into hot broth to dissolve. Combine all ingredients in a blender a little at a time until all are blended smoothly together. Lightly grease 4 or 5 cup fish mold with mayonnaise. Pour salmon mixture into mold. Refrigerate until ready to use. Can be made 2-3 days ahead. Serve with party rye.

yield: 20 servings
PATTI SCHRECKENGAUST

BAKED BRIE

- 1 wheel Brie, about six pounds
- Walnuts or pecans, chopped
- Brown sugar

Place Brie on an oven-proof platter. Skim thin layer of white crust off the top with a cheese cutter. Spread chopped nuts over top of Brie. Put brown sugar over nuts and Brie to cover top. Place on platter in middle of a cold oven. Heat at 350°F. until Brie softens, but is still firm, 10-15 minutes. Broil top slightly to give brown sugar a toasted look and flavor, 3-5 minutes. Serve hot with lots of crackers.

yield: 50-60 servings

I served this for a cocktail party for 60. "They ate the whole thing!"

CHERYL ROSE-WEAVER

[order form overlay:]

You may order
The Flavor of Waverly from:

The Waverly Community House, Inc.
Waverly, Pa. 18471

Please enclose $18.95 plus
$1.50 for postage and handling
for each copy. Pa. residents
add 6% sales tax ($1.14 per copy)

Make Checks payable to The
Waverly Community House, Inc.

- - - - - - - - - - -

Send me _____ copies of
The Flavor of Waverly. Enclosed
is my check or money order for _____.

Name _____
Address _____
City _____
State _____ Zip _____

Proceeds from the sale of this book
benefit The Waverly Community House.

...together. Form into walnut sized ...well greased cookie sheet and ...en, remove and store in a plastic ...to serve bake at 350°F. straight ...r 20–25 minutes, or until firm but

yield: 60 servings
FAY GUNSTER

...350°F. Blend mayonnaise and ...remaining ingredients. Mix well. ...dish and bake for 30–35 minutes. ...dish with crackers or cocktail

yield: 10 servings
PAULA LOWE

...inch slice off the top of the Edam ...out the cheese, including the top. ...owed shell and top. Chop cheese ...d beer, butter, caraway seeds, dry ...salt. Mix lightly with fork and let ...temperature for one hour. Add in-...nder or food processor a little at a time until all is blended. Fill cheese shell and refrigerate. You will have enough to fill the shell twice. Remove from refrigerator about ½ hour before serving to allow to soften.

yield: 20 servings

Tastes best if you make it a day or two before serving. This is named for Jane Havey Palmer, who grew up in Waverly.

MARY JOY HAVEY

SPINACH BALLS

- 2 packages chopped spinach, cooked and drained
- 2 cups Pepperidge Farm herb stuffing
- 1 cup finely chopped onion
- 6 eggs, lightly beaten
- ¾ cup melted butter
- ½ cup Parmesan cheese
- 1 tablespoon garlic salt
- ½ teaspoon crushed thyme
- ¼ teaspoon pepper

CRAB CASSEROLE

- 1 cup mayonnaise
- 2 teaspoons lemon juice
- 2 6½-ounce cans crab meat, drained and picked over
- 1 cup cubed Swiss cheese
- ⅓ cup green pepper, chopped
- ¼ cup onion, chopped
- 1 teaspoon salt

PALMER'S EDAM DIP

- Edam cheese, about 1¾ or 2 pounds
- 1 cup beer
- ¼ cup soft butter
- 1 teaspoon caraway seeds
- 1 teaspoon dry mustard
- ½ teaspoon celery salt

SHRIMP BALLS

1 pound shrimp, cooked and chopped
8 ounces cream cheese
1 small onion, minced
Dash Worcestershire sauce
Salt to taste
Minced parsley

Combine ingredients. Shape into small balls and roll in parsley. Serve at room temperature. May be served with the following cocktail dip.

yield: 40–45 small balls
DORIS LINDSLEY

COCKTAIL DIP FOR SHRIMP

1 garlic clove, crushed
2 tablespoons horseradish
1 tablespoon finely minced onion
2 tablespoons cream
1 teaspoon chopped chives
½ teaspoon dry mustard
1 cup Hellman's mayonnaise

Crush garlic in bowl and add remaining ingredients. Mix and chill for several hours. Serve with about 2 pounds cooked shrimp.

yield: 20 cocktail servings
ANN PECK

MENU II

RED CHICKEN WINGS

½ cup soy sauce
⅔ cup water
4 tablespoons sherry
6 tablespoons oyster sauce
4 slices ginger root
20 chicken wings, split

In pan bring first five ingredients to a boil. Add chicken wings. Simmer covered 30 minutes, uncover and simmer for 15 minutes, stirring occasionally. Serve hot or cold. Make at least one day ahead.

yield: 40 servings
LETHA W. REINHEIMER

MEXICAN LAYERED DIP

- 3 ripe avocados
- 2 tablespoons lemon juice
- ½ teaspoon salt
- ¼ teaspoon pepper
- 1 cup sour cream
- ½ cup mayonnaise
- 1 package taco seasoning mix
- 2 small cans bean dip
- 1 cup green onions, chopped
- 3 tomatoes, chopped
- 2 cans black olives, chopped
- 1 8-ounce package Cheddar cheese, shredded
- Large round tortilla chips

Peel, pit and mash avocados in a medium size bowl with lemon juice, salt and pepper. Combine sour cream, mayonnaise and taco seasoning in another bowl.

To assemble, spread bean dip on a large shallow platter; top with seasoned avocado mixture; layer with sour cream-taco mixture. Sprinkle with chopped onions, tomatoes and olives. Cover with shredded cheese. Serve chilled or at room temperature with round tortilla chips. Can make half of this recipe.

yield: 20 servings
JOANN DULWORTH

BAKED ARTICHOKE HEARTS

- 2 14-ounce cans artichoke hearts
- ¼ pound butter
- 4 ounces blue cheese

Pre-heat oven to 350°F. Quarter artichoke hearts. Place in oven-proof dish. Melt blue cheese and butter together. Pour over artichoke hearts and bake for 15 to 20 minutes. Serve hot with homemade melba toast or assorted crackers.

yield: 40 servings
NANCY KAUFMAN

CHEESE DREAMS

- ½ pound of butter
- ½ pound sharp Cheddar cheese
- ½ pound cream cheese
- 2 egg whites

Melt first three ingredients in double boiler. Pour slowly over 2 well beaten egg whites. Return to double boiler, dip 1 inch bread cubes in cheese mixture, coating well. Place cubes on cookie sheet and freeze.

When ready to serve, pre-heat oven to 450°F. and bake for 10 minutes.

yield: Varies, depends on type of bread used

Be sure to use a firm bread (French, Italian). Once frozen, the cubes can be put into plastic bags for future use. I have made these up to 6–8 weeks ahead.

DRU MILLER

CLAM BALLS

1	14-ounce can minced clams
8	ounces soda crackers
1	small onion, chopped
¼	cup green pepper, chopped
1	teaspoon Worcestershire sauce
1	tablespoon parsley flakes
1	garlic clove, minced
¼	teaspoon salt
¼	teaspoon pepper
¼	teaspoon paprika
½	cup butter, melted

Pre-heat oven to 325°F. Drain half liquid from can of clams and put remaining contents into bowl. Crush 4 ounces of soda crackers and add onion, pepper and seasonings. Add all to clams, add melted butter and mix thoroughly. If not thick enough to hold shape, use the other 4 ounces of crushed crackers. Shape into small balls. Bake for 15-20 minutes on ungreased cookie sheets. Can be frozen unbaked and used at a later date.

yield: 24 servings
LINDA SPROUL

HOT CRAB DIP

1	pound crabmeat
16	ounces cream cheese
2	tablespoons mayonnaise
2	teaspoons Worcestershire sauce
4	dashes Tabasco sauce
2	tablespoons lemon juice
	Garlic salt to taste

Pre-heat oven to 350°F. Drain and pick over crabmeat and combine well with the rest of the ingredients. Put in baking dish and bake for 30 minutes. This recipe can be used as an hors d'oeuvres with crackers or a main course item on a buffet.

yield: 2 dozen servings
RONALD WHITAKER

SAUSAGE AND BEEF APPETIZER

1	pound ground beef
½	pound hot sausage
½	pound mild sausage
1	pound Velveeta cheese, cut in cubes
1½	loaves Pepperridge Farm Party Rye Bread

Pre-heat oven to 325°F. Remove sausages from casing. Crumble, brown, and drain well. Brown and drain ground beef. Mix beef, sausages and melt with Velveeta cheese over low heat. Spoon onto Party Rye Bread and bake 5 to 7 minutes. Serve immediately.

Can be frozen before baking. If frozen bake at 350°F. for 10 minutes or until heated through. Easy to prepare and usually very popular with guests.

yield: 3 dozen servings
YVONNE CRONKEY

Combine all ingredients but coconut. Chill. Form into little balls; roll in grated coconut. Chill. Serve on toothpicks.

yield: 24 servings
JEAN GERRARD

CURRIED CHICKEN TIDBITS

- 1 8-ounce package cream cheese, softened
- 1 cup cooked chicken, finely chopped
- 1 cup blanched slivered almonds
- 2 tablespoons mayonnaise
- 1 tablespoon curry powder
- 1 tablespoon chopped chutney
- ½ teaspoon seasoned salt
  Grated coconut

Graduation Brunch

In 1844, a bell rang out across the Abington Hills for the very first time. Of finest bell metal, cast by L. Debozair in Philadelphia, it was purchased with the money raised at the Madison Academy Fair, held just for that purpose. This bell was hung in a tower which thrust resolutely into the heavens above the two-story frame building crowning the steep hill ninety feet above the intersection of Clinton Street and the Philadelphia and Great Bend Turnpike. From this tower a panorama spread outward to parts of Monroe, Pike, Wayne, Susquehanna, Wyoming and Luzerne Counties. And it was from those lands of scattered farms, sparse clusters of log cabins and simple frame houses that the scholars came to Madison Academy. This institution of higher learning offered young students instruction beyond the scope of the one-room schoolhouse in each village.

In 1836 the select Academy had opened in the home of Charles Bailey on the east side of the Turnpike, just opposite Church Street. Named to honor President James Madison who had died in June of that year, the academy classes were taught by young Horatio Nicholson from Wayne County who had graduated from Franklin Academy in Harford. So sound was this educational idea and so charismatic was this teacher, that by 1840 there were 60 pupils enrolled, and it was deemed appropriate to incorporate. This was done by the first Board of Trustees: Reverend John Miller, President, Benjamin F. Bailey, Dr. Andrew Bedford, Charles R. Gorman, Norval D. Green, Horatio Nicholson, Rodman Sisson, Thomas Smith and Lemuel Stone. By 1844 they raised $3,000 and built a white wooden school on an acre of land given by John Miller. At the same time, just west of the school, a house was built which was run by Esther L. Stone as a residence for those students whose homes were too far away for a daily journey.

Captain Samuel Tripp remembers, "It was

during the inclement season of the year, while active operations on the farm were suspended, that the Academy was in its glory. As soon as the crops were gathered in the fall, the farmers' boys and girls . . . who were desirous of fitting themselves for teachers or getting a higher education than could be obtained in the common schools, flocked to the Academy to drink of the Pierian spring. A large number of the country students hired rooms and boarded themselves, most of them going home for the weekend.''

Horatio Nicholson married Rhoda Stone, a pupil at the Academy, and left to read law in Wilkes-Barre where he was admitted to the Bar in 1841. Gilbert S. Bailey, one of his pupils, took over the teaching task until Harvey D. Walker was hired to lead the Academy in 1845. His regime included the golden years of the Academy which had 165 pupils in 1850. All who attended were governed by these "Rules and Regulations":

"Each applicant . . . shall have attained the age of fourteen years . . . shall pay $6.00 per quarter" and "will be expected . . . to pledge himself while a student:

1. To avoid all profane and impure language.
2. To avoid gambling, and playing of games of chance.
3. To avoid lounging at, and around taverns, groceries, stores, etc.
4. To drink no intoxicating liquors.
5. To maintain in all respects the character of an orderly student . . ."

Continuing, the rules set forth expectations for "regular and punctual attendance" at prayers and classes; for keeping in the neighborhood; and for keeping the Sabbath. Vandalism would be "charged to the author of the mischief, when known . . . or to the whole school." Students would not be excused to attend parties, circuses, cotillions or shows, such things "being regarded as foreign to the purposes of the school room."

"The discipline of the Academy is designed to be as nearly parental as possible. Where a kind appeal to the judgment and the heart are sufficient, further punishment and disgrace will be carefully avoided; but should this prove ineffective, such other means will be employed as may be necessary to prevent indolence and immorality, and to maintain good order." And, in this vein, Captain Samuel Tripp remembered a teacher who came to the Academy from Northern Vermont who was "long on discipline and short on those qualities that would endear her to those she instructed."

The Civil War, industrialization of the Lackawanna Valley, the decline of the turnpike due to the railroad; all of these elements contributed to the decline of Madison Academy which closed in 1868 in sad disrepair. A local subscription raised $1,000 for rehabilitation of the bell tower and the building, and the school reopened in 1870. By this time the Abington Baptist Association had founded Keystone Academy, chartered in 1868 in the village of Factoryville, along the new railroad line, and Madison Academy's resurrection was short lived. The last class, comprising nine girls, graduated in 1878.

But whether one graduates in a class of nine or of hundreds, it is a time of proud accomplishment and new beginnings; when the graduate becomes the cynosure of all eyes: brothers and sisters, aunts and uncles, grandparents and fond friends. And whether the celebration is with family or with fellow graduates, good food is the order of the day.

Graduation Brunch

FIRST VARIATION FOR 50
EGG SCRAMBLE FOR FIFTY
HAM AND CHICKEN LIVERS WITH GRAPES
SAUSAGE AND CHEESE STRATA
OVERNIGHT COFFEE CAKE
BRAN MUFFINS
CURRIED FRUIT COMPOTE

SECOND VARIATION FOR 6
SPINACH & EGG CASSEROLE
SWISS CHEESE SCRAMBLE
AUNT JO'S BISCUITS
BROWN BREAD
SLICED ORANGES WITH OLIVE OIL AND PEPPER

THIRD VARIATION FOR 6 TO 8
CRUSTLESS BRANDIED QUICHE
HAM LOAF
NEVER FAIL COFFEE CAKE
-OR-
KRUM KUCKEN
-OR-
COFFEE CAKE
SUMMER SALAD

FIRST VARIATION FOR 50

EGG SCRAMBLE FOR FIFTY

6	dozen eggs
2	quarts light cream
1	tablespoon salt
¾	pound of butter

Pre-heat oven to 350°F. Beat eggs slightly with a fork. Add cream and salt. Mix well. Melt butter in a 9" × 13" pan and add the egg mixture. Reduce heat to 300°F. and bake 20–30 minutes. The eggs will stand as long as necessary without separating. If sausage is to be served, eight pounds will be needed.

yield: 50 servings
CAROLYN PENCEK

HAM AND CHICKEN LIVERS WITH GRAPES

4	tablespoons butter or more
1	medium minced onion
1	cup chicken livers
	Flour
1	teaspoon dry sage
½	cup proscuitto *or* cubed ham
1	small bunch of green grapes, approximately 20
1	cup Marsala
8	slices cooked, dry, bacon, crumbled
1	tablespoon parsley
	Lemon slices
	Thinly sliced toast

Heat butter in skillet over medium heat. Sauté onion. Cut chicken livers in half - remove any fat, lightly flour and shake off excess. Add livers and sage to hot butter and onions. Cook 1 minute on each side. Stir in ham, grapes and marsala. Mix well but gently. Cook over medium heat for 2 minutes. Do not over-cook - liver will toughen. Add cooked, crisp bacon and parsley. Garnish with additional grapes and thin lemon slices. Serve with thin slices of toast.

yield: 4 servings

Simple, fast, and can be expanded at will, depending on the appetites of your brunch guests.

JANE BOVARD

SAUSAGE AND CHEESE STRATA

1½ pounds sausage
16 slices homemade-type bread, crust removed, cut into ½" cubes
1½ pounds monterey jack cheese, grated
8 large eggs beaten lightly
3 cups milk
1 teaspoon salt
   Pinch cayenne
2 tablespoons mustard
1 teaspoon Worcestershire

Brown sausage and drain. Divide bread and cheese into thirds. Put one-third of bread cubes on bottom of 4 quart casserole. Sprinkle with one-third cheese. Arrange ½ sausage on top. Repeat with ⅓ bread and ⅓ cheese and the rest of the sausage. Add remaining bread and cheese last. Combine eggs, milk, salt, cayenne, mustard and Worcestershire. Pour egg mixture over all. Cover and refrigerate overnight. Let stand at room temperature for 45 minutes before baking. Pre-heat oven to 350°F. Place in a water bath and bake 1 hour and fifteen minutes. Water should reach half-way up the side of casserole.

yield: 12 servings

For Graduation Brunch, make 2 casseroles.

BARBARA MACKINNON

OVERNIGHT COFFEE CAKE

Cake:
⅔ cup margarine or butter
1 cup sugar
½ cup brown sugar
2 eggs
2 cups flour
2 tablespoons powdered milk
1 teaspoon baking powder
1 teaspoon baking soda
½ teaspoon salt
1 teaspoon cinnamon
1 cup buttermilk

Topping:
½ cup brown sugar
½ cup chopped nuts
½ teaspoon nutmeg or cinnamon

Mix in order given, adding the cup of buttermilk last. Pour into a 9" × 13" greased pan. Put on topping. Cover and refrigerate overnight. Bake in a pre-heated 350° F. oven for 30–35 minutes.

yield: 12 servings

You'll need to make four of these cakes for the brunch.

CAROLYN PENCEK

BRAN MUFFINS

1	15-ounce box Raisin Bran
3	cups sugar
5	cups flour
5	teaspoons baking soda
2	teaspoons salt
1	cup oil
4	eggs
1	quart buttermilk

Optional:
2	teaspoons cinnamon
¾	teaspoon allspice
¾	teaspoon cloves
½	cup raisins

Pre-heat oven to 400°F. Mix dry ingredients. Combine liquids. Stir liquids into dry ingredients a little at a time until all is well mixed. Fill greased tins (or use muffin papers) ½ full. Bake for 20 minutes.

yield: 50–60 muffins

Will need a large bowl. Batter will keep, tightly covered, for 6 weeks in the refrigerator. Add the spices and/or raisins depending on your taste. Can freeze.

BETTY BROOKS

CURRIED FRUIT COMPOTE

3	large cans peaches
3	large cans pears
3	medium cans pineapple chunks
3	cups white raisins
2	cups brown sugar
9	teaspoons curry powder
1	cup butter, melted

Preheat oven to 325°F. Drain fruits. Blend sugar, curry and mix with butter. Place fruit in heatproof casserole. Pour butter mixture over top. Bake 1 hour. Refrigerate overnight.

yield: 24 servings

Can be made up to a week in advance. Double for graduation brunch or reduce if desired.

BARBARA MACKINNON

SECOND VARIATION FOR 6

SPINACH AND EGG CASSEROLE

2	10-ounce packages frozen chopped spinach
4	tablespoons butter
4	tablespoons flour
1½	cups milk
1	cup fine dry bread crumbs
2	hard cooked eggs, sliced
1	cup Cheddar cheese, grated
	Bread crumbs
½	cup cooked bacon, crumbled

Pre-heat oven to 350°F. Cook spinach according to package directions and drain. Melt butter, stir in flour. Add milk slowly, whisking all the time. This makes a cream sauce. Cook until smooth. Butter a one quart casserole dish. Layer spinach, sliced egg, bread crumbs, cheese and sauce. Top with a sprinkle of bread crumbs and crumbled bacon. Bake for 40–45 minutes.

yield: 6 servings

This is nice as a supper dish or great to do ahead for a breakfast or brunch.

DEANNA I. SMITH

SWISS CHEESE SCRAMBLE

8	slices bacon, cooked crisp, crumbled
2	cups soft bread cubes, no crusts
1¾	cups milk
8	eggs, slightly beaten
¾	teaspoon salt
⅛	teaspoon pepper
2	tablespoons butter or margarine
¼	teaspoon seasoned salt
½	pound Swiss cheese, shredded
2	tablespoons butter, melted
½	cup fine dry bread crumbs

Pre-heat oven to 400°F. Cook bacon; crumble, set aside. Combine bread cubes and milk; drain after five minutes, saving milk. Combine milk with eggs, salt and pepper. Melt butter in skillet. Cook egg-mixture until softly scrambled, not fully cooked. Remove from heat. Stir in bread cubes. Turn egg-bread mixture into 9-inch square or round shallow casserole that has been greased. Sprinkle with seasoned salt. Evenly cover with shredded cheese. Combine melted butter and dry bread crumbs, sprinkle over cheese. Top with bacon. Bake for 10-15 minutes until cheese melts in middle and bubbles on sides. Serve immediately.

yield: 6-8 servings

This can be made the day ahead and refrigerated. Increase baking time to approximately 30 minutes. Cook until cheese melts and bubbles. Doubles, triples well. Ideal for brunch.

MARTHA ADAMS

AUNT JO'S BISCUITS

½	cup sugar
3	tablespoons shortening
2	cups flour
2	teaspoons baking powder
1	egg
	Milk
1	teaspoon vanilla

Pre-heat oven to 375°F. Cream sugar and shortening until fluffy. Add vanilla. Break egg into liquid measuring cup. Mix with fork. Add milk until liquid equals 1 cup. Add flour and baking powder alternately with egg and milk. When all ingredients are thoroughly mixed, drop by tablespoon onto lightly greased cookie sheet. Bake for 20 minutes. Temperatures may vary according to individual ovens so watch carefully so that bottoms don't brown too quickly.

yield: 1 dozen

A delightful biscuit for tea or coffee. Raisins may be added or blueberries for variation. This is a recipe I've been enjoying since I was a little girl at my Aunt Jo's. She's known for her "goodies".

MADALINE LORI

SLICED ORANGES WITH OLIVE OIL AND PEPPER

6	navel or blood oranges
2-3	tablespoons olive oil
	Freshly ground pepper

Peel oranges, being careful to remove all of the white membrane. Slice one-quarter inch thick and arrange on a platter. Drizzle with olive oil, and grind pepper over the top.

yield: 6-8 servings
MARY ANN LA PORTA

BROWN BREAD

2	cups sour milk (sweet milk with 2 tablespoons vinegar)
1	teaspoon salt
½	cup sugar
½	cup molasses
2	cups Graham flour
1	cup white flour
2	teaspoons baking soda
	Milk

Pre-heat oven to 350°F. Combine above ingredients except baking soda. Mix well. Dissolve baking soda in small amount of milk and add to dough. Pour into greased 9" × 5" loaf pan and bake for one hour. Cool before slicing.

yield: 1 loaf

This is my grandmother's recipe.

PEG STROM

THIRD VARIATION FOR 6 TO 8

CRUSTLESS BRANDIED QUICHE

8	ounces Monterey Jack cheese, shredded, approximately 2 cups
2	tablespoons flour
3	eggs
1	cup plus 2 tablespoons skimmed milk
1	teaspoon seasoned salt
⅛	teaspoon Tabasco sauce
2	tablespoons brandy
¼	pound mushrooms, sliced
1	medium onion, chopped
2	tablespoons butter

Brush a 9" skillet lightly with oil. Set aside ½ cup cheese. Toss remaining cheese with flour and set aside. Beat eggs, milk, salt and Tabasco sauce with brandy. Stir in flour-coated cheese. Sauté mushrooms and onion in butter. Add sautéed vegetables to quiche batter. Pour into skillet and sprinkle remaining ½ cup cheese on top. Cover and cook 40 minutes on low heat until set.

yield: 8 servings
JANET HEALY

HAM LOAF

- 2 pounds ground ham
- 1½ pounds lean ground pork
- Pepper to taste
- 2 eggs, beaten
- 1 cup milk
- 1 cup cracker crumbs

Pre-heat oven to 325°F. Mix well and put into greased 9" × 5" loaf pan. Bake for one hour.

yield: 8 servings
IRENE REID

NEVER FAIL COFFEE CAKE

- 2 apples, peeled and sliced
- 15 maraschino cherries, sliced

Topping:
- 2 tablespoons melted butter
- ½ teaspoon cinnamon
- ¼ cup sugar

Batter:
- ½ cup sugar
- 1 tablespoon soft butter
- 1 egg
- ½ cup milk
- 1 cup flour
- 2 teaspoons baking powder

Pre-heat oven to 400°F. Grease 9-inch square pan. Prepare fruit. Make topping and set aside. In bowl, mix first three batter ingredients. Add and mix milk, flour and baking powder and mix well. Place batter in pan. Place fruit evenly over batter. Spoon topping over fruit. Bake for 15 minutes.

yield: 9 servings

This is very quick and easy. Can be made before breakfast and served right from the oven. The cherries are optional.

JULIA MUMFORD

KRUM KUCHEN (Crumb Cake)

- 4 cups sifted flour
- 2 cups sugar
- 4 teaspoons baking powder
- 1 teaspoon salt
- 1 cup butter
- 4 eggs, separated
- 1 cup milk

Topping:
- ¼ cup melted butter
- 2 teaspoons ground cinnamon

Pre-heat oven to 375°F. Sift the first four ingredients together. Cut in the butter with a pastry blender or two knives until pieces are the size of rice kernels. Measure one cup of the crumbs and set aside for topping. Beat the egg yolks until thick and lemon colored and add with milk to remaining crumb mixture; stir just until dry ingredients are moistened. Beat the egg whites until rounded peaks are formed. Fold into batter until blended. Turn into 2 well-greased (bottoms only) 9" × 9" × 2" pans and sprinkle top of each with one-half of the reserved crumbs. Bake for 20 to 25 minutes. After baking, sprinkle each cake with one-half of a butter-cinnamon mixture and remaining reserved crumbs.

yield: 18 servings

This recipe was one of my mother's, Mrs. George M. D. Lewis.

JOANNE LEWIS TODD

COFFEE CAKE

½	cup margarine
2	cups brown sugar
2	cups flour
1	egg
1	teaspoon baking soda
1	cup sour milk
	Nuts

Pre-heat oven to 350°F. Mix together until crumbly the margarine, brown sugar and flour. Set aside 1 cup. Add egg, soda and sour milk to the remainder. It will be lumpy after mixing. Place in greased 9" × 9" pan. Cover top with reserved mixture and broken nuts. Bake for 25 minutes.

yield: 8 servings
CAROLYN SANDHERS

SUMMER SALAD

2	bunches fresh spinach, washed and dried
1	pint fresh strawberries, washed, hulled and halved
½	cup sugar
2	tablespoons sesame seeds
1	tablespoon poppy seeds
1½	tablespoons minced onion
¼	teaspoon Worcestershire sauce
¼	teaspoon paprika
½	cup vegetable oil
¼	cup cider vinegar

Arrange spinach and strawberries attractively on individual serving plates. Place next 6 ingredients in blender. With blender running, add oil and vinegar in slow steady stream until thoroughly mixed and thickened. Drizzle over strawberries and spinach and serve immediately.

yield: 8 servings
THE SOJOURNER, NICHOLS VILLAGE

Summer

THE TOMATOES IN KARL NEU-ROTH'S PAINTING GROW FAT AND BRIGHT AMIDST A RIOT OF LEAF AND SHADE PATTERNS. To those who garden or who look forward to savoring the fruits of the garden, a tomato is the very essence of summer.

Summer is a plump and flavorful time: of strawberries, raspberries and sweet young lettuce. A time of bright, clear colors: of geraniums and daisies, tomatoes and pea vines, goldfinches and tanagers. A time of far-reaching sounds: of the Comm House bell striking the hour; the meadowlark exulting from the tree top; the after-supper games of kick-the-can or bloody-murder; the train coming around the mountain; all these sounds striking their familiar chords through the happily opened windows, curtains stirring in the evening breeze. And a time of evocative smells: of new-mown grass and tomato and marigold seedlings, of charcoal cookouts across

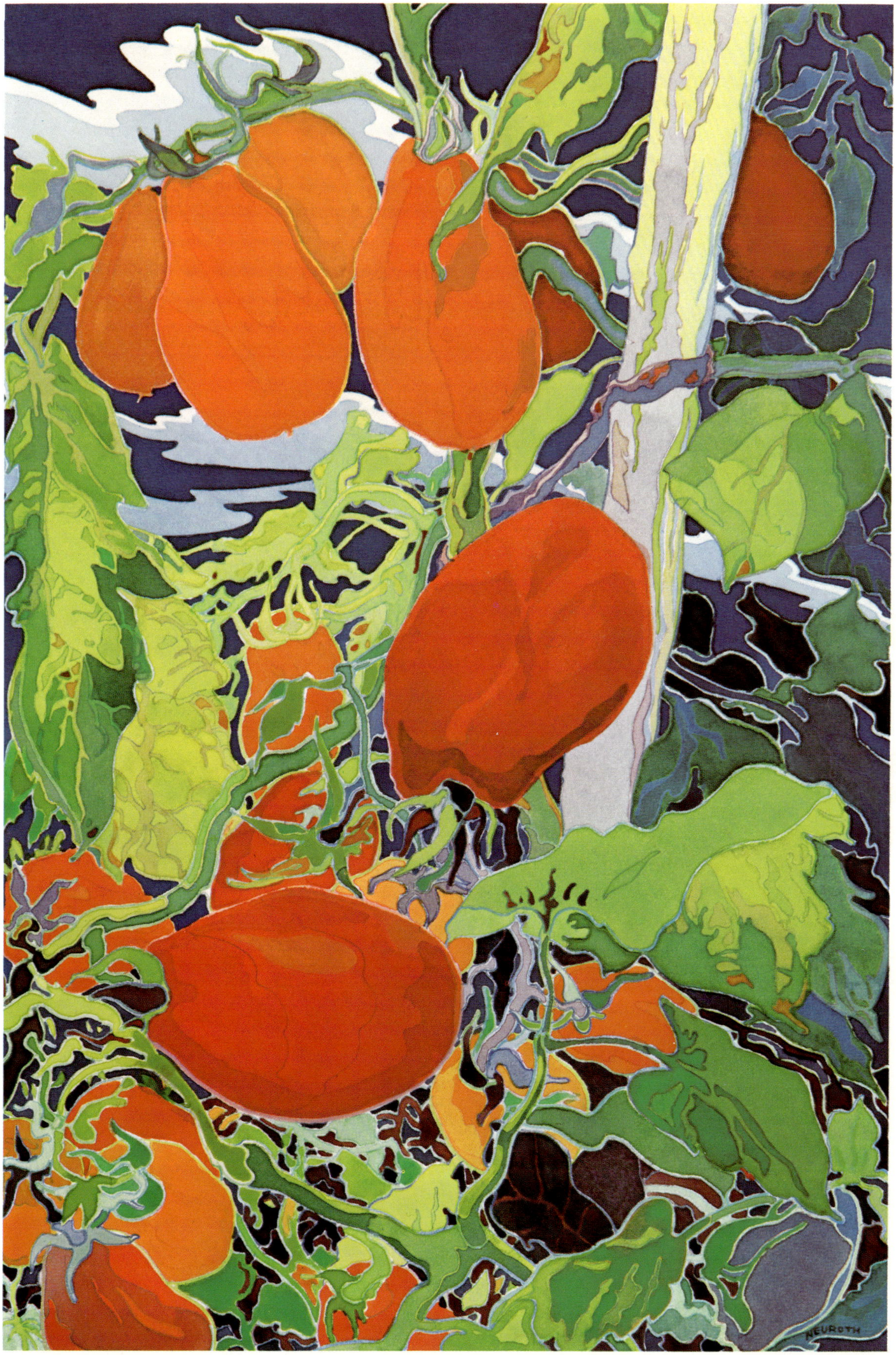
NEUROTH

the way; of roses heavy on the stem; of afternoon rain on hot pavements. A time of savoring sensations: of the cool tunnel of Carbondale Road or Glenburn Road, shaded by overarching sugar maples; of the welcome warmth of hot rocks after a cool swim; of the too-hot sidewalk on still tender bare feet; of the puffing arrival at Manning's for ice cream after a bike hike on roads of purple and red flecked pavement. It's a time of freedom from the tyranny of school schedules and bulky warm clothes.

The freedom of bare legs was not yet won for our nineteenth century Waverly women: The Reverend S.S. Kennedy, noted in his 1877 Scranton *Republican* newspaper column: "The fields and roads are alive with grasshoppers, affording rare enjoyment to chickens and turkeys, but giving great annoyance to pedestrian women, beneath whose flowing skirts they are caught in great numbers, soiling many a white dress, and filling many a fair country maiden with alarm and disturbing the devotions of many a grave matron on the Sabbath day. To such 'the grass hopper is a burden.'"

But the grasshoppers couldn't keep the farmers out of their fields, nor could the flying pests eat more than their share of the crops. In the summer of 1858 there were enough produce and livestock to show and plenty of people to attend the first fair of the newly organized Abington Agricultural Society. The fair was the culmination of the summer's efforts for farmers and their families. It provided a chance to show off and to admire, to learn and to teach, to compete and to relax.

Summer agricultural fairs were consistently successful and in 1895 the Maitland Fair and Driving Company organized a popular county-wide fair during Labor Day week. It dominated the hill overlooking Prickly Ash Flats (Wallsville) in what is now the high camping area at Lackawanna State Park. There were booths for displays and diversions. Horse fanciers and fancy horses came from far and near to race in spirited competitions. People coming by train from Scranton or Binghamton were met at the D.L.&W. station in Dalton and brought to the fairgrounds by horsedrawn hack. Large crowds of merrymakers attended and the fair enjoyed wide popularity for about a dozen years.

Then the Northern Electric Street Railroad started its regular hourly runs from Scranton to the Abingtons in 1907. The Glenburn platform, on the Waverly side of Glenburn Pond, provided very easy access to a new fairgrounds, built beside Ackerly Creek. By 1911, the Lackawanna County Fair and Grange Poultry Association, representing Newton and Ransom farmers like the Thompsons, LaCoes, Pallmans and Meyers, bought 14 acres for the fair grounds. The Fair Association built a grandstand large enough to seat over a thousand people watching the races on a well-laid-out track. There were two long stables and an exhibition building that were bustling all summer long. During the next twenty years, there was heavy attendance at the weekly races and lively participation in livestock and exhibit competition among area farmers and members of the local hunt. And then the Depression of the thirties brought bankruptcy to the Northern Electric and the fairs were no longer held. In the late thirties, medium size race cars used the track and the grandstands filled with avid, noisy fans once more. World War II cut off that form of entertainment. An annual summer horse show returned excitement to the post-war fairgrounds well into the fifties.

There is always a market for excitement. The Northern Electric Street Railroad had the vision to provide the end as well as the means when they opened a dazzling amusement park at their Clarks Summit stop. At the southwest corner of State and Grove Streets, passengers could disembark for a couple hours of fun on a rollercoaster that circled the perimeter; at the shooting gallery and ball rack, and several games of chance; or enjoy an ice cream at one of the shaded picnic tables and wait for the band to begin playing at the covered dance pavillion.

Today, the midways and the rides come to us via the Firemen's Carnivals. Games of chance, cotton candy and tummy-jolting rides tempt young and old to Dalton, Fleetville or Chinchilla for nights of excitement during the height of the summer.

The Waverly Community House has sponsored summer fairs of all sorts, over the years, featuring children's parades, jug bands, running races, pony rides, dunking tubs, mimes and pie eating contests. The summer is always punctuated by tennis tournaments for parent-child teams, juniors and seniors, round-robins, ladders and leagues. The hush in the bleachers at the Labor Day finals matches gives way to the Bull Roast in the side yard of the Methodist Church. And once again, we're eating for fun and profit!

Memorial Day Barbeque

The rifles fired a salute across the open fields to the south; the poignant notes of taps bugled into the morning air from the spruce grove over the rise. Paul Kendall placed a ceremonial wreath on the veterans' graves by the overlook every Memorial Day from 1918 to 1966. Girl Scouts and Boy Scouts, Brownies and Cub Scouts marched, fidgeted, attended and were dismissed. Memorial Day at Hickory Grove Cemetery has been observed with prayers, flags and flowers; another of the rituals which have the power to strike a chord that vibrates sympathetically to the human condition across time and space.

Abington Township was settled by many veterans of the Revolutionary War: William Clark served with distinction at Bunker Hill with his Connecticut companions; Jonathan Dean and Stephen Capwell served with the Rhode Island militia; Captain Robert Reynolds was under the command of General Nathaniel Green; his son, George Reynolds, enlisted in the Continental Army when he was seventeen years old; John Phillips was with the Continental Army in Vermont, then joined the company of Colonel George Dorrance in the Battle of Wyoming in 1778; William Stanton and Robert Freeland volunteered from Connecticut, Peter and Philip Calvin from Rhode Island; Ephraim Leach, from Connecticut, fought at the Battle of Monmouth.

These men of the Revolutionary Army recognized the value of preparedness and when they settled here they organized an Abington militia in the spring of 1801. On the green in front of the home of Deacon William Clark, eleven officers and privates came from as far away as twelve miles to train and be counted as ready to defend their homes and families in uncertain times.

The young American Republic went to war in 1812 and sent its armies into the field against Mexico in 1846. There were Abington men in their country's uniform each time, but these forays seemed distant from the agrarian tranquility of Abington.

The War Between the States was an upheaval felt close to home as almost 200 men from Abington went off to the War; Abington also sent men to the militia which rallied to defend Pennsylvania's southern frontier against the invasion of General Lee's army in 1863. At the Battle of Gettysburg, George O. Fell was one of the first Union soldiers to fall and is depicted on a memorial at the Battlefield. The George O. Fell GAR Post #307 was organized in Waverly in 1883 and held regular meetings until 1954.

Abington families have waved fearful farewells to their own, headed to the Spanish-American War, the First World War, the Second World War, the Korean War and the Vietnam War. They have welcomed them home to happy firesides or honored places among their forbears in our hillside cemeteries. Those who stayed behind did their share, as well.

Young girls learned to knit, making socks for "our boys" "over there" in World War I. Ladies sold World War II Liberty Bonds; Mrs. William Smith held up everyone she encountered in Waverly to buy a Liberty Bond with such success that she was awarded a medal for her efforts. School children took dimes and quarters to school to buy savings stamps to stick into little books until they totalled $18.75 and represented a $25 Bond "for the war effort." Aluminum foil was carefully peeled from gum wrappers and saved in large, light balls. Mothers saved kitchen grease and went to the grocery store with their "fat cans." And in September, 1942, a scrap drive piled ten tons of metal on the Community House lawn; bed springs, wash tubs, boilers and old tools joined a Model T; even the cannon from Hickory Grove Cemetery was sent from guarding the dead to make ammunition to defend the living.

Long skirts of early visitors rustled over the dusty pebbles of Cemetery Street from Academy Hill to Hickory Grove; cars drive through encircling stonewalls and along well-kept driveways; the honor brought to the village's dead on Memorial Day renews today's commitment to the freedom, equality, and justice for which they took up arms. And when ceremonies are over, we can cheer the beginning of summer with the season's first barbeque for the hungry celebrators.

Memorial Day Barbeque

GRILLED FLANK STEAK ORIENTALE
BRENNAN'S STUFFED BAKED POTATOES
BROILED TOMATOES WITH HORSERADISH
SPINACH PARMESAN
FRENCH SILK CHOCOLATE PIE
AMARETTO CHEESE CAKE

GRILLED FLANK STEAK ORIENTALE

- 2 cups soy sauce
- 2 cups olive oil
- 4 cloves garlic
- 4 teaspoons ground ginger
- 3 2 to 3-pound flank steaks

Combine the first four ingredients. Marinate steaks several hours, turning frequently so both sides are well treated to the flavors. Grill over charcoal or broil 4 to 5 minutes per side, basting with marinade.

yield: 12 servings

This recipe was presented at the first John Clancy cooking demonstration to benefit the Waverly Community House in September, 1960

JOHN CLANCY

BRENNAN'S STUFFED BAKED POTATOES

- 2 large Idaho potatoes
- 4 strips bacon, quartered
- ¼ cup chopped shallots or green onions
- ½ cup sour cream
- 2 tablespoons grated Parmesan cheese
- ½ teaspoon of salt
- ½ teaspoon black pepper

Pre-heat oven to 400°F. Scrub potatoes well, prick skins and bake for one hour. Grill bacon pieces until crisp. Drain off bacon fat except for 3 tablespoons. Add shallots and sauté slowly. Cut potatoes in half lengthwise and scoop out into a bowl, taking care to retain shells intact. Add bacon, shallots, sour cream, cheese, salt and pepper, mixing and mashing to blend thoroughly. Stuff mixture into potato skins. Bake 15 to 20 minutes at 350°F.

yield: 4 servings

This recipe can be multiplied easily. This recipe comes from "Brennan's" of New Orleans and Houston. It is one of our all-time favorite restaurants.

JAN KOCH

BROILED TOMATOES WITH HORSERADISH

Pre-heat oven to 450°F. Seed tomato shells, salt and turn upside down to drain for 10 minutes. Mix mayonnaise, horseradish and onion. Spoon into tomato shells. Bake for 10 minutes.

yield: 12 servings
JANICE PATTERSON

- 6 large tomatoes, halved
- Salt
- 1½ cups mayonnaise
- ¼ cup prepared horseradish or more to taste
- 1 small onion, minced very fine

SPINACH PARMESAN

Pre-heat oven to 350°F. Sauté onion and garlic in butter. Add spinach and sauté until all liquid has evaporated. Slowly add cream and milk, stirring until smooth. Add ½ cup cheese, bread crumbs and seasonings. Put into buttered casserole and top with remaining ½ cup Parmesan cheese. Bake for 30 minutes.

yield: 12 servings
PAT ATKINS

- 1 cup finely chopped onion
- 2 cloves garlic, minced
- ¼ cup butter
- 5 packages chopped spinach, thawed and squeezed dry
- 1 cup heavy cream
- 1 cup milk
- 1 cup Parmesan cheese
- ½ cup bread crumbs
- 1 teaspoon marjoram
- 1 teaspoon salt
- ¼ teaspoon pepper

FRENCH SILK CHOCOLATE PIE

Beat butter and sugar until fluffy, add chocolate and vanilla. Using mixer at medium speed, add eggs one at a time and beat thoroughly after each egg is added. Pour into shell. Let chill several hours. Top with whipped cream if desired.

yield: One 9" pie
TOM HEAFIELD-MORDAN

- 1 cup softened butter
- 1½ cups sugar
- 4 ounces unsweetened chocolate, melted and cooled slightly
- 1 teaspoon vanilla
- 4 eggs
- 1 baked 9" pie shell
- Whipped cream, optional

AMARETTO CHEESE CAKE

Pastry:
- 1½ cups flour
- 2½ tablespoons sugar
- ½ cup cold butter, cut in 8 pieces
- 2 egg yolks

Filling:
- 3 8-ounce packages cream cheese, softened
- 3 tablespoons flour
- ¾ cup sugar
- 6 eggs, separated
- ½ cup sour cream
- 1 cup light cream
- 2 ounces Amaretto di Saronno

Topping:
- 1 cup heavy cream, whipped
- 2 tablespoons powdered sugar
- 1 teaspoon almond extract
- Sliced almonds
- Nutmeg

Pastry: Pre-heat oven to 450°F. Mix flour and sugar, cut in butter until mixture resembles fine crumbs. Stir in egg yolks until mixture cleans sides of bowl. Flatten half of the dough and press in bottom of 10" spring form pan. Roll out other half into two rectangular pieces. Place around sides; patch holes. Refrigerate overnight. Line with aluminum foil and fill with dried beans. Bake 10 minutes. Remove foil, bake 5 minutes longer. Cool.

Filling: Reduce oven heat to 375°F. Beat cream cheese, flour and sugar. Add egg yolks, sour cream, light cream. Then add Amaretto. Beat egg whites until stiff. Fold thoroughly into creamed mixture. Place in pre-baked crust. Bake 1 hour. Chill at least six hours.

Top with whipped cream to which powdered sugar and almond extract have been added. Spread on cake. Sprinkle with sliced almonds and nutmeg.

yield: 12 servings

This pastry crust is very good, but may cause problems for some people. I have also used a graham cracker crust just on bottom of pan. The cheesecake itself is delicious.

YVONNE CRONKEY

Take-It-With-You Picnic

Arnold Foster was just a lad in 1881 when the band wagons started creaking past his farm house on Lily Lake Road. The bench seats sagged under the weight of whole families from Scranton, Providence and Hyde Park who were headed for an outing at the Corey place on Wall Lake, newly named the Lily Lake Hotel. The band wagons had lurched northward on the Turnpike, through the notch at Leggets Gap, past Chinchilla, Clarks Green and Waverly until Lily Lake Road crested the hill overlooking the northeast shore of Lily Lake. The path from the large frame building headed across the meadows, pastures and garden to the waters of the small lake. Excited children exploded into the freedom of the fields and woods, while grownups breathed deeply of the clean country air. The water beckoned. Fourteen rowboats nosed into the dock for the adventuresome, and a steam launch was provided for the last word in water excursions.

After the smoke and soot of the town, this was a treat for all, and the Lily Lake Hotel enjoyed many visitors. The hotel offered simple country fare and fun to the families of those who labored in the industries of the Lackawanna Valley. They came for weekends or for delicious chicken dinners, and returned to town refreshed.

Ten years later, Arnold Foster observed a new wagon on the road taken by the band wagons: the beer wagon began to make delivery runs to the hotel. Soon the family trade was replaced by men alone. Tired from a week in the mines, factories or railroads, the men relaxed on the shores of Lily Lake, but they did so with a beer and a rowdy release of energies. Fights followed, with carelessness in the boats and at the water's edge. The traffic once again told the tale to Arnold Foster as he watched another wagon pass his house. The Black Mariah came frequently to the hotel to provide the ill-fated visitor his last wagon ride. It doesn't take many visits of the undertaker's wagon to discourage a hotel keeper and advise his neighbors that the business is in its last days.

Lily Lake is quiet today, one among many places in the Abington hills just made for a peaceful outing. Many places invite the wanderer to stroll with an apple and book, to a bike hike or a spur of the moment picnic. The hills are full of sun-dappled glades and clear, loquacious brooks. Sunny hummocks hide beside supportive stone walls which tell of field-clearing labors from another year. Gather together the fixings for a picnic, plain or fancy, summon your companions, and go. Walkers have only to keep a sharp eye out for poison ivy, make sure the top of the drink jug is on tight and a wonderful outing is theirs for the taking. That's the best kind of take-out.

MARINATED BEEF SALAD
TORTELLINI SALAD
CRAB SALAD
RATATOUILLE
QUICHE IN PUFFED PASTRY
HERBED PITA TOASTS
CELESTIAL SQUARES
COCONUT FRUIT COCKTAIL CAKE

Take-it-with-you Picnic

MARINATED BEEF SALAD

2 pounds beef, sirloin, flank or round steak

Marinade:
- ¼ cup oil
- ½ cup wine vinegar
- ¼ cup soy sauce

Vegetables:
- 4 large boiling potatoes
- ½ cup green sweet pepper
- ½ cup diced red sweet pepper
- ⅓ cup chopped purple onion
- 2 scallions, thinly sliced
- ⅔ cup cooked green beans
- ⅔ cup garlic dressing
- ⅓ cup chopped Italian parsley
- Lettuce leaves
- Grated rind of one orange to garnish

Garlic Dressing:
- 1 egg yolk
- ⅓ cup red wine vinegar
- Salt and pepper to taste
- 1 tablespoon sugar
- 1 tablespoon chopped garlic
- 1 cup olive oil

Marinate beef in oil, vinegar and soy sauce for 3 hours. Drain and grill or broil until medium rare. Cool. Cut into thick julienne slices. Should be about 3-4 cups. Peel potatoes. Using a melon baller, scoop potatoes into small balls. Should be about 2 cups. Boil the potatoes in salted water until tender but not mushy. Drain. Combine potatoes, beef and remaining vegetables in a mixing bowl. Pour on garlic dressing and toss. Add parsley and toss again. Arrange on lettuce leaves and garnish with grated orange rind. Serve immediately.

Dressing: Combine yolk, vinegar, sugar, garlic, salt and pepper in blender. Blend briefly. Dribble in the olive oil with blender running. Taste and correct seasonings, if needed.

yield: 4-6 servings
JEAN COLOMBO

TORTELLINI SALAD

- 1 pound cheese-filled tortellini
- ¾ cup olive oil
- ½ pound prosciutto or smoked ham cut into ⅜ inch julienne strips
- ½ pound smoked turkey cut into ⅜ inch julienne strips
- 1 cup defrosted peas
- 2 medium carrots cut into 1½ inch by ⅛ inch julienne strips
- 1 large red bell pepper cut into 1½ inch by ⅛ inch julienne strips
- ½ cup finely chopped parsley
- 2 garlic cloves minced
- 1 head boston or leaf lettuce for garnish

Cook tortellini until just tender. Rinse under cold running water in colander. Let drain 15 minutes. Toss with ¼ cup oil. Cover and refrigerate. Add prosciutto, turkey, peas, carrots and red pepper to tortellini. Toss and refrigerate until 30 minutes before serving. Whisk parsley, garlic and ½ cup oil together for dressing. Pour over salad and toss well. Arrange lettuce around platter and fill center with tortellini salad.

yield: 6 servings

Homemade mayonnaise may be substituted for the oil dressing.

MARY LYNN MORGAN

CRAB SALAD

- 1 pound crab meat, picked over well
- 2 hard cooked eggs, chopped
- 2 stalks celery, sliced diagonally
- 1 sweet red pepper, julienned
- ⅓ cup chopped parsley
- ⅓ cup your favorite French or Italian dressing
- Salt and pepper to taste
- Fresh spinach leaves

Mix all ingredients together. Season to taste. Serve on a bed of fresh spinach leaves.

yield: 6 servings
MARGARETTA B. CHAMBERLIN

RATATOUILLE

- 1 small eggplant, diced
- 2 medium zucchini, diced
- 2 green peppers, chopped
- 2 onions, chopped
- 1 cup salad oil
- ¼ teaspoon thyme
- 2 bay leaves
- 3 cloves garlic, minced
- 4 tomatoes, quartered
- Salt and pepper
- 1 cup ripe olives, pitted
- ¼ cup olive oil
- 2 tablespoon parsley, chopped

Sauté eggplant, zucchini, green peppers and onions in salad oil, a few at a time. As the vegetables take on color drain and transfer them to a four quart casserole. Add thyme, bay leaves, garlic, tomatoes, salt and pepper. Cook in a slow oven, uncovered so that the liquid will evaporate, for 1 hour. Refrigerate overnight. When ready to serve, sprinkle the olives, olive oil and parsley on top.

YIELD: 6 to 8 servings
JOAN BELIN

QUICHE IN PUFFED PASTRY

- 1 box frozen puff pastry OR
- 2 packages frozen patty shells
- 1 cup grated Swiss cheese
- 2 tablespoons grated Parmesan cheese
- 2 tablespoons chopped parsley
- ¼ pound thinly sliced proscuitto, Kentucky or Virginia Ham
- 3 whole eggs
- 1 teaspoon garlic salt
- 1 teaspoon Accent
- 1 teaspoon liquid Maggi
- 1 drop Tabasco sauce
- 3 tablespoon heavy cream
- 1 egg plus 1 tablespoon of water for egg wash, if desired

Pre-heat oven to 400°F. Defrost pastry or patty shells. Take half the pastry or shells and roll out on a floured surface to a very thin crust. Keep remaining pastry or shells refrigerated until ready to roll out. Line the bottom of an 8" or 10" quiche pan. Then fill the crust with the cheeses, parsley and proscuitto or ham. In a separate bowl stir the remaining ingredients and pour over the filling in the crust. Roll out the second crust from remaining pastry or shells and place on top of the quiche. Trim and seal the edges. Make a few holes in the top crust. Brush with egg wash for a good brown color. Use left over trimming to make decoration for the top of pastry. Bake for 25–30 minutes or until pastry is brown and puffed. This makes a good luncheon or first course dish. Serve hot or cold. Great for picnics!

yield: 8 servings
MARY L. SCRANTON

HERBED PITA TOASTS

1	9-ounce package pita bread
½	cup butter
1	teaspoon Italian herbs
1	teaspoon dill
1	teaspoon savory

Pre-heat broiler. With scissors cut around pita breads and separate. Mix butter and herbs and spread very thinly on pita halves. Cut into quarters with scissors. Broil on middle shelf of oven until brown. Store in air tight container.

yield: 6 to 8 servings
MOLLIE WOEHLING

CELESTIAL SQUARES

2	ounces unsweetened chocolate
1	cup butter
2	cups brown sugar
1	teaspoon vanilla
½	teaspoon almond extract
3	eggs
½	teaspoon salt
2	cups flour
1½	cup chopped walnuts or pecans

Icing:
1	16-ounce package semi-sweet chocolate chips
5	cups confectioners' sugar
½	cup butter
⅓	cup heavy cream
1	teaspoon vanilla

Pre-heat oven to 350°F. Melt chocolate over hot water. Cream butter with brown sugar, vanilla and almond extract. Beat in eggs, one at a time, beating thoroughly after each addition. Sift flour and salt and blend into sugar mixture. Mix in nuts. Divide batter in half, and add the chocolate to half of the batter. Drop the batter alternately by spoonfuls into a greased 9" × 13" pan. Draw a knife through the batter to marblelize. Bake for 14–18 minutes. Cool.

Icing: Melt chocolate chips in double boiler. Beat sugar, butter, cream and vanilla together until smooth. Ice cooled cake. Drizzle melted chocolate over icing.

yield: 24 servings
ELLIE WARREN

COCONUT FRUIT COCKTAIL CAKE

1½ cups sugar
2 eggs
½ cup vegetable oil
2 cups flour
½ teaspoon salt
2 teaspoons baking soda
1 medium can fruit cocktail, with liquid
½ cup coconut

Topping:
½ cup margarine
¾ cups sugar
½ cup evaporated milk
1 teaspoon vanilla
½ cup chopped nuts
½ cup coconut

Pre-heat oven to 350°F. Beat sugar, eggs and oil together. Add flour, salt and soda, mix well. Fold in fruit cocktail and liquid. Pour into greased and floured 13½" × 7" × 2" pan. Sprinkle ½ cup coconut over batter. Bake for 45 minutes.

Topping: Combine margarine, sugar and milk and heat until margarine melts. Remove from heat. Add vanilla, nuts and ½ cup coconut. Spread over cake while still warm. Freezes well.

yield: 18 servings
DORA CIGARRAN

Fourth of July Salute

"We hold these truths to be self-evident, that all men are created equal, that they are endowed by their Creator with certain unalienable Rights, that among these are Life, Liberty and the pursuit of Happiness."

On July 4, 1776, the Continental Congress, meeting in Independence Hall in Philadelphia, adopted the final draft of the Declaration of Independence of the thirteen British colonies in North America from Great Britain. The ideas were not new, but were stated with such eloquence that they have stirred the hearts of men and women across this nation and the world from that day to this.

The anniversary of this momentous Declaration is celebrated with flying flags and bunting, ringing bells, and bursting firecrackers; and with picnics under dooryard elms, at parks, pavillions and village greens. To step out of a daily routine in order to design a celebration lends significance to the ideas and values that shaped the events being commemorated. It is in this way that we, in some small way, say that we still care, and renew our allegiance to first principles.

In different years, the Fourth of July has been celebrated in different ways. Several Abingtonians traveled to the Centennial Exposition in Philadelphia in the summer of 1876. In Abington Center in 1887 fireworks ignited the roofs of a barn behind the stores on Main Street. The village-threatening fire was put out promptly and the guilty boys were chastened. In other years there were strawberry socials in the Band Room. There were many band concerts on the back lawn of the Community House. But for many years, our most evocative testimonial to the Declaration of Independence was the community of blacks who lived on Carbondale Road.

Taking their lives in their hands, they had pursued happiness and liberty by escaping from slavery in the South. They had escaped with the help of sympathetic friends and strangers: abolitionists.

These blacks were among fifty thousand fugitives who were moved secretly along pre-arranged safe routes to freedom between 1830 and 1863. These routes were known as the Underground Railroad and Waverly was a regular station on the way to Canada, beyond the reach of the Fugitive Slave Law. The Abingtons had many citizens ready to offer assistance, food or hiding: the Baileys, Batchelors, Chases, Clarks, Colvins, Fells, Mumfords, Sissons and Tillinghasts.

So welcoming was the whole village, that many former slaves stayed to work for local farmers, and to buy and build houses in Abington Center. Lott Norris escaped from Maryland in the 1840's and made his way to Waverly. His master followed him, entitled by law to seize him if he could. But he was confronted by a group of Waverly farmers with pitchforks and spades who told him he had no claim on anyone in these parts and had better go back to Maryland. With that kind of reassurance and championship it is not surprising that there grew here the only sizeable black community between Wilkes-Barre and Montrose.

In 1850 Lott Norris built a salt box style house of recycled timbers on land purchased from John Stone on Carbondale Road. Four years later, he helped in the construction of the community's African Methodist Episcopal Church next door. The church was a cohesive force for the blacks who found steady and various employment at the nearby farms and many businesses. The census of 1860 counted forty-six blacks; eleven of them volunteered for the Union Army when President Lincoln called in 1862.

Few new black immigrants came to Waverly after the Civil War, but those who remained were the backbone of the labor force. For the haying in 1870, $2.00 per day and board were offered by farmers who "make no difference as to the color of the men they employ, but decide by the amount and quality of work performed," S.S. Kennedy wrote in his column in the Scranton *Republican*. The census of that year counted only 30 black residents. However, they were a respected part of the village life and, in 1897, John R. Johnson, the son of an ex-slave, was elected to the Waverly Borough Council and Grant Tillman, another black from the dwindling community, was High Constable.

The Reverend Charles Garner announced the Annual Camp Meeting of the Waverly A.M.E. Church for August 11, 1901. It was to be held, as always, in Fell's Grove on the eastern slope across

Main Street from Linair Farms. Everyone was invited and hacks were available to meet all trains. The usual popular caterer was to be on the grounds, and jubilee singing was a powerful attraction. Blacks from Scranton, Wilkes-Barre and Montrose joined nearby neighbors and the gathering was inspired, rousing, enthusiastic and renewing. It usually lasted a week and was a high point of the year.

By 1920 there were only six blacks left in Waverly and the little church was shuttered and sold in 1926. Changing living patterns had cut off the life blood of Waverly's black community. Village shops and factories had closed. Job opportunities elsewhere lured away the young and ambitious. While they lived in Waverly, references were made to "Darky Hill" or "Colored Town" and even, with Victorian sensibility, to "Waverly Sable." Styles of nomenclature change, economic imperatives dictate population shifts and thus Waverly has almost no racial diversity in the 1980's. But our egalitarian forefathers demonstrated the finest welcome to the blacks who came here in the nineteenth century. A practical, daily application of the principles of the Declaration of Independence made this a community of equals, enjoying life, liberty and the pursuit of happiness together. That is worth remembering and saluting with due honors on the Fourth of July.

Fourth of July Salute

GAZPACHO WITH CROUTONS
CHICKEN TONNATO
ZUCCHINI SOUFFLÉ
RICE SALAD
SWEDISH CREAM WITH RASPBERRIES
BLUEBERRY TARTS IN NUT CRUST

GAZPACHO WITH CROUTONS

Soup:
- 2 eggs, hard boiled and separated
- 2 tablespoons olive oil
- 1 garlic clove, crushed
- 1 dash Tabasco
- 1½ teaspoons Worcestershire sauce
- ½ teaspoon salt
- Freshly ground pepper
- Juice of one lemon
- 4 cups canned tomatoes, strained and chopped
- 1 green pepper, finely chopped
- 4 celery stalks, finely chopped
- 1 small cucumber, finely chopped
- 6 thin lemon slices

Croutons:
- 1 clove garlic, chopped
- ¼ cup butter
- 2 cups soft bread cubes
- 3 tablespoons freshly grated Parmesan cheese

In bottom of large bowl mash egg yolks and olive oil, blending to a smooth paste. Stir in garlic, seasonings and lemon juice. Add tomatoes, green pepper, celery and cucumber. Set to chill for at least 4 hours. When ready to serve, put into each soup bowl a slice of lemon and a share of the hard boiled egg whites cut into julienne strips. Add the soup, an ice cube and a sprinkling of hot croutons.

Croutons: Pre-heat oven to 325°F. Brown garlic in butter, then remove from frying pan. Turn bread crumbs into the butter, stirring constantly. Add cheese, Spread out on an ungreased cookie sheet, and bake for 15 minutes, turning occasionally. The only way one can botch this recipe is to get distracted while the croutons are in the oven.

yield: 8 servings
MARGERY BELIN CLARKE

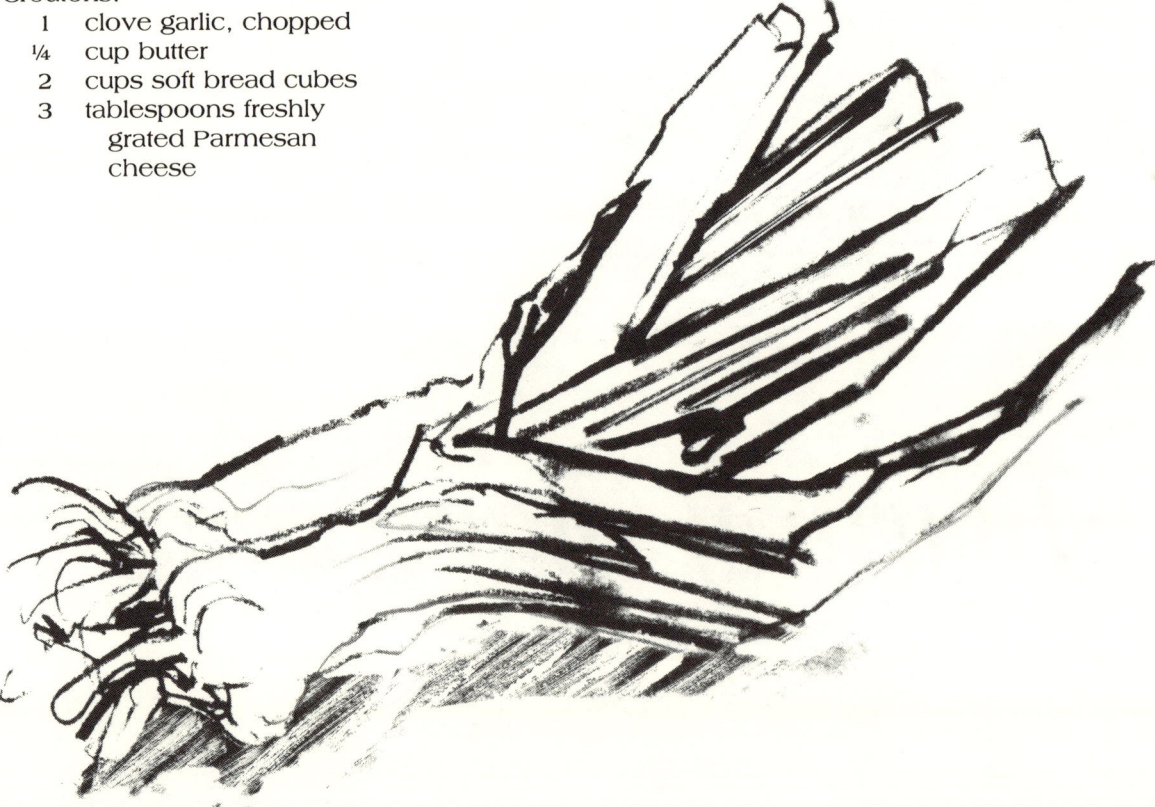

CHICKEN TONNATO

1	large onion, sliced
2	celery stalks, sliced
2	carrots, peeled and sliced
2	parsley sprigs
1	teaspoon salt
2	small bay leaves
2	cans chicken broth, undiluted
4	whole chicken breasts, split in half

Sauce:
1	cup mayonnaise
1	7-ounce can tuna, drained
2	anchovies, chopped
½	cup finely chopped celery
½	teaspoon salt
	Dash black pepper
1	tablespoon lemon juice
	Capers for garnish

Chicken: In 6 quart kettle combine onion, celery, carrots, parsley, salt, bay leaves, and chicken broth. Add 1 cup water and chicken breasts. Simmer covered 15 minutes or just until tender. Let chicken cool in broth. When cool, remove from broth, discard skin, bone and trim edges. Place in serving dish.

Sauce: Combine all ingredients in food processor or blender. Blend until smooth. Pour sauce over chicken, garnish with capers, chill until ready to serve.

yield: 8 servings
DORA CIGARRAN

ZUCCHINI SOUFFLÉ

2½	pounds small zucchini
⅓	cup flour
4	eggs, large
1	cup heavy cream
1	cup Swiss cheese, grated
1½	teaspoon salt
½	teaspoon white ground pepper
	Sprinkle of nutmeg

Pre-heat oven to 350°F. Wash zucchini and cut into chunks. Steam until crisp-tender. Drain thoroughly and cool. Using metal blade in food processor, add zucchini and flour. Process until blended. Add eggs, one at a time, and then remaining ingredients. Pour into buttered 2-quart casserole, and add sprinkle of nutmeg on top. Place casserole in shallow pan and pour in boiling water to a depth half-way up side of casserole. Bake 45 minutes. Soufflé is done when knife inserted in center comes out clean. Remove from oven and let rest 10 minutes before serving.

yield: 6 servings
ROSEMARY TRANE

RICE SALAD

- 2 cups cooked rice
- 4 tablespoons wine vinegar
- 12 tablespoons olive oil
- Salt and pepper to taste
- 1 cup cooked peas
- ¼ cup chopped green pepper
- ¼ cup chopped red pepper
- ½ cup chopped parsley
- ¼ cup chopped chives
- ¼ cup chopped cucumber
- ½ cup chopped scallions
- ¼ cup chopped pimento
- 3 tablespoons capers

Mix rice with vinegar, oil, salt and pepper while still warm. Cool. Mix in remaining ingredients, tossing. Refrigerate. Serve in a bowl of greens decorated with sliced hard cooked eggs, sliced olives, or other garnishes of your choice. Vary the amount of vegetables and herbs, according to your preference.

yield: 8 servings
JEAN C. MORI

SWEDISH CREAM

- 2½ cups heavy cream
- 1 cup sugar
- 2 envelopes gelatin
- 2 cups sour cream
- 1 teaspoon vanilla
- 2 packages frozen raspberries

Mix heavy cream, sugar and gelatin. Heat gently until gelatin dissolves. Cool on back of stove until slightly thickened. Fold in sour cream and vanilla. Chill at least four hours. Top with raspberries or other optional fruit toppings.

Heat all fruits, adding sugar to taste. Liquor optional. Cool before topping the Swedish cream.

Suggested topping variations:

Pears, rum, ground cloves
Apples, applejack, cinnamon
Bananas and rum
Mandarin oranges, orange liquor
Strawberries, Kirsch or Curacao
Cherries, Kirsch
Peaches, bourbon or brandy
Apricots, Kirsch, Cognac or brandy
Blueberries, lime rind and bourbon
Italian plums, lemon rind
Fresh kiwi, blueberries, raspberries

yield: 8 servings
JANE BOVARD

BLUEBERRY TARTS IN NUT CRUST

Nut Crust:
- ½ pound and 2 tablespoons butter, softened
- 10 ounces finely chopped almonds
- ⅓ cup sugar
- 1 egg
- 1 tablespoon grated lemon rind
- 1 teaspoon vanilla

Creme Patissiere:
- 2 cups milk
- 6 egg yolks
- 3¼ cups sugar
- Grated rind of 1 lemon
- ⅓ cup all purpose flour
- ⅛ teaspoon salt
- 1 teaspoon vanilla

Glaze:
- 1 6-ounce jar apricot jam
- 1 tablespoon gelatin
- ¼ cup Grand Marnier

Filling:
- 1 quart blueberries

Pre-heat oven to 350°F. Crust: Beat softened butter. Add rest of ingredients and beat well. Press mixture into two 9" tart pans or twelve 3" tartlet pans. Bake for about 20 minutes or until golden.

Creme Patissiere: Scald milk in saucepan. In a medium, heavy saucepan beat egg yolks, sugar and lemon rind until thick and lemon colored. Add flour and salt and blend only. Gradually add scalded milk to egg yolk mixture and cook over low heat, whisking constantly until mixture boils, then cook for 2 minutes more. Remove from heat and add vanilla. Strain. Cool, stirring occasionally, or put wax paper directly on creme patissiere to prevent a skin from forming.

Glaze: Heat jam in saucepan. Soften gelatin in Grand Mariner. Add softened gelatin to hot jam and stir over medium heat until dissolved. Strain.

To assemble blueberry tart, spread approximately 1 cup creme patissiere on 9 inch tart. Chill slightly. Arrange 1 quart blueberries, washed and dried, on creme patissiere. Glaze.

Note: Freeze remaining creme patissiere, or if using for 3 inch tartlets use approximately 3 tablespoons per tartlet.

You can substitute small red seedless grapes, kiwi, strawberries or raspberries to vary this dessert. When using strawberries or raspberries substitute ¼ cup Chambord or raspberry brandy for Grand Marnier.

yield: Two 9" tarts or twelve 3" tarts
PAT ATKINS

Intimate Summer Dinner

"Many strangers from abroad are spending the summer here . . . and the demand for boarding places is increasing . . . There are persons from Scranton, Wilkes-Barre, Philadelphia, New York, Brooklyn, Newark, and other places. They seem to enjoy the bracing air, variegated scenery and generous diet peculiar to these Abington hills and houses." Rev. S.S. Kennedy wrote this in his column for the Scranton paper in 1877 as George R. Fuller was building a summer house for his family from a design published in Godey's Lady Book. With towers, porches, and walls of double brick it is still a distinguished sentinel looking across to Bald Mountain from the road to Glenburn.

Scranton was becoming the anthracite capital of the world. The booming mine industry created breakers, powder mills, railroads, car shops, congestion, smoke, soot, and noise. Waverly residents noted that "Scranton is a loud city, when the wind is right we can hear the steam gong." Those who could afford it, began to look for a more healthful environment for their families.

In 1890, Scranton industrialist Henry Belin, Jr. persuaded the widow of Dr. Van Sickle to sell "Glenverly," the house which had hosted many early summer boarders. This gracious white brick home with its broad porticos and generous windows is raised on a terrace above beautiful stone walls and a stately border of sugar maples. It was built in 1850 by Horatio Nicholson when he left his law practice in Wilkes-Barre and returned to Waverly to be closer to his responsibilities as attorney for the new Leggets Gap Railroad.

In 1907, local farmers advertised for summer board by day, week or season, with garage, stables and "all water accommodations within the house, including shower bath." Visitors came to board and stayed to build. The pleasures of summering in Waverly brought the Linens and Blairs to build Linair Farm. The Simpsons, Watkins, Jermyns, Fullers,

Belins, Langstaffs, Woolworths, and many more, each built a gracious summer "cottage." By 1925 most of the Abington hills were crowned with summer homes and laced with carriage drives and formal gardens.

As the summer afternoon shadows lengthened, the steam whistle signaled the arrival of the 5 o'clock "Banker's Special." Puffing around Glenburn ice pond from Scranton and Clarks Summit, it stopped at Glenburn's Abington Station. The stage to Waverly was there to meet it, driven in successive years by Edwin Bliss, Thomas Kennedy and Henry Cole. The stage met the 8:00 A.M. and the 5:00 P.M. trains. It carried the mail as well as passengers between the station and the Hotel on the southwest corner of Main Street and Clinton Street. Private buggies met Scranton's returning bankers, brokers and manufacturers; and if George Stevenson had gone to Scranton that day, his saddle horse would have come over, unattended, from his barn in Waverly to meet him, and carry him home.

Children played ball on wide lawns; tennis and croquet raised wonderful competitive furors. Greenhouses and gardens generated spirited races for the first green peas, the first red tomato and the first ear of corn. Paul Belin even built a 10 foot wall on the north side of his garden by the creamery to achieve an advantage in this race. The Fullers brought a tea house from the World's Fair to adorn their lawn and built a house for the trophies of an African safari. Swimming pools were set in terraced landscapes and children encouraged to stretch their limbs. There was even a private golfcourse laid out for Thomas Watkins. Others made use of the Waverly Country Club whose fairways and porches welcomed members from 1912 on. Carriage rides pleasantly transported ladies in embroidered afternoon frocks to tea with a neighbor.

These elegant ways were continued into later generations and generously shared with others in the community. There were invitations to use the swimming pools and tennis courts during designated hours. Wonderful dinner parties, formal dances with Myer Davis' orchestra, party weekends of legendary hospitality made Waverly remembered beyond the boundaries of the state.

The rusticators came to Waverly as their counterparts went to Newport and Bar Harbor: to get away from the heat and congestion. But they also came *to* something as well: clean air, pure water and an environment conducive to the growth of healthy children. By 1900, Waverly had faded as a trading center. The buildings on Main Street stood in need of paint and commerce. But it was the center of a population of farmers who had a long tradition of creating and supporting institutions which nourish human social need. These solid values were part of the texture of life that attracted the summer visitors to become year 'round residents when modern transportation afforded that option. Summer continues to offer all the Abington residents a spacious and elegant outdoors, wonderfully suited to gracious dining with fine foods for favored friends.

Intimate Summer Dinner

ASPARAGUS SOUP
STUFFED VEAL ROLL WITH FRESH TOMATO SAUCE
CARROTS IN LEMON SAUCE
GRATED ZUCCHINI IN CREAM
PAVLOVA

ASPARAGUS SOUP

2	pounds asparagus
4	tablespoons butter
1	cup chopped onions
3	tablespoons flour
6	cups chicken broth
1	egg yolk, optional
¾	cup light cream
	Salt and freshly ground pepper
2	tablespoons butter, optional

Cut off the top 2 inches of the asparagus. Blanch these tips for 2-3 minutes. Drain and set aside.

Trim the ends of the remaining asparagus and chop the stalks into ½ inch pieces. Melt 4 tablespoons of the butter in a 3-4 quart saucepan. Add the leeks or onions and cook slowly until wilted but not browned, about 8 minutes. Stir in the raw asparagus and cook, covered, for 5 minutes. Uncover, stir in the flour, and cook for 2-3 minutes. Add the broth, bring to a boil, reduce the heat, and simmer, partially covered, for 30 minutes, stirring occasionally.

When the soup has cooked, pureé the mixture and put it through a food mill to remove fibers. The texture should be very fine. Beat the egg yolk, if you wish to use it, and cream in a bowl and slowly whisk into it ½ cup of the hot soup. Whisk mixture back into the hot soup. Add a garnish of the chopped asparagus tips and reheat without boiling. If desired, add 2 tablespoons butter as a final enrichment. Season to taste. Omit butter enrichment if serving chilled.

yield: 4-6 servings

Spring arrives late in our garden, so the first true promise of the season - asparagus tips peeking through the soil - is cause for great celebration in our family. Waiting to harvest the first picking requires great patience and restraint, but once the bed reaches top production we enjoy asparagus almost every day for six weeks. At the peak of the summer season, when you can bear not to eat it whole, this is a delightful soup that captures the marvelous fresh-from-the-garden flavor of this special vegetable. And, you can freeze it so you can enjoy it anytime.

SUSAN BELIN

Intimate Summer Dinner

ASPARAGUS SOUP

STUFFED VEAL ROLL WITH FRESH TOMATO SAUCE

CARROTS IN LEMON SAUCE

GRATED ZUCCHINI IN CREAM

PAVLOVA

ASPARAGUS SOUP

- 2 pounds asparagus
- 4 tablespoons butter
- 1 cup chopped onions
- 3 tablespoons flour
- 6 cups chicken broth
- 1 egg yolk, optional
- ¾ cup light cream
- Salt and freshly ground pepper
- 2 tablespoons butter, optional

Cut off the top 2 inches of the asparagus. Blanch these tips for 2-3 minutes. Drain and set aside.

Trim the ends of the remaining asparagus and chop the stalks into ½ inch pieces. Melt 4 tablespoons of the butter in a 3-4 quart saucepan. Add the leeks or onions and cook slowly until wilted but not browned, about 8 minutes. Stir in the raw asparagus and cook, covered, for 5 minutes. Uncover, stir in the flour, and cook for 2-3 minutes. Add the broth, bring to a boil, reduce the heat, and simmer, partially covered, for 30 minutes, stirring occasionally.

When the soup has cooked, pureé the mixture and put it through a food mill to remove fibers. The texture should be very fine. Beat the egg yolk, if you wish to use it, and cream in a bowl and slowly whisk into it ½ cup of the hot soup. Whisk mixture back into the hot soup. Add a garnish of the chopped asparagus tips and reheat without boiling. If desired, add 2 tablespoons butter as a final enrichment. Season to taste. Omit butter enrichment if serving chilled.

yield: 4-6 servings

Spring arrives late in our garden, so the first true promise of the season - asparagus tips peeking through the soil - is cause for great celebration in our family. Waiting to harvest the first picking requires great patience and restraint, but once the bed reaches top production we enjoy asparagus almost every day for six weeks. At the peak of the summer season, when you can bear not to eat it whole, this is a delightful soup that captures the marvelous fresh-from-the-garden flavor of this special vegetable. And, you can freeze it so you can enjoy it anytime.

SUSAN BELIN

STUFFED VEAL ROLL WITH FRESH TOMATO SAUCE

3	whole ¼" slices cut from center of leg of veal, approximately 10" × 3" each
½	pound each, salami, mortadella and prosciutto, sliced paper thin
2	garlic cloves, minced
¼	cup fine dry bread crumbs
¼	cup finely chopped parsley
½	teaspoon basil
3	tablespoons olive oil
	Salt and pepper
5–6	hard boiled eggs
5–6	slices of bacon, blanched for three minutes in boiling water, pat dry

Sauce:
10	ripe tomatoes, peeled, seeded, chopped
¼	cup butter
½	cup dry vermouth
2	tablespoons finely chopped parsley
1	tablespoon finely chopped onion
1	tablespoon chopped celery leaves
½	teaspoon basil
	Salt and pepper

Pre-heat oven to 350°F. Pound the veal slices until they are 1/16 inch thick. Arrange them on wax paper overlapping to form one large piece. Pound seams to seal. Over the veal make rows of overlapping slices of the salami, mortadella and prosciutto.

Rub the garlic into the bread crumbs until absorbed and sprinkle over meat. Sprinkle with parsley and basil. Sprinkle the crumb mixture with 3 tablespoons of olive oil and salt and pepper to taste. Put a row of hard boiled eggs along center of meat. Using the wax paper to help, roll the veal tightly. Be careful to keep the eggs in center while rolling. Tie the veal securely in several places. Arrange bacon on top. Place in baking pan large enough to hold roll and sauce.

Sauce: Cook tomatoes and butter, stirring until tomatoes are reduced to a purée. Add the rest of the ingredients and cook for 10 minutes. Season to taste.

Pour tomato sauce over veal. Bake for 1 hour, basting with sauce occasionally. Transfer veal to a heated platter. Remove bacon and string. Pour sauce over roll and garnish with parsley.

yield: 6 servings
PAT ATKINS

CARROTS IN LEMON SAUCE

1	pound carrots
3	tablespoons butter
1	tablespoon flour
1	tablespoon sugar
	Rind of one lemon, grated
½	cup lemon juice

Cook carrots until tender but firm enough to slice in narrow even julienne strips. Place in even rows in dish and keep warm on hot tray. Melt butter, stir in flour, sugar and grated lemon rind. Add lemon juice. Stir and cook until thickened. Pour hot sauce over carrots. Can be made day before and re-heated in a 350°F. oven for 15 minutes.

yield: 6 servings
DORA CIGARRAN

GRATED ZUCCHINI IN CREAM

- 2½ pounds small zucchini
- 2 teaspoons salt
- 3 tablespoons butter
- ¼ cup minced shallots
- 1 cup heavy cream
- Salt
- Pepper

Grate zucchini and put in colander. Toss with salt and drain for up to one-half hour. Squeeze by handfuls to dry. Saute shallots in butter, add zucchini and turn and stir for 2 to 3 minutes. Add cream slowly while stirring until zucchini has absorbed it all. Add salt and pepper to taste.

yield: 6 servings
PATTI SCHRECKENGAUST

PAVLOVA

- 4 egg whites, at room temperature
- ½ teaspoon salt
- 1 cup sugar
- 2 teaspoons cornstarch
- 2 teaspoons vinegar
- 3-4 cups sliced fresh fruit: bananas, pineapple, apple, kiwi fruit, Mandarin oranges, strawberries or papaya
- 1 cup heavy cream, whipped

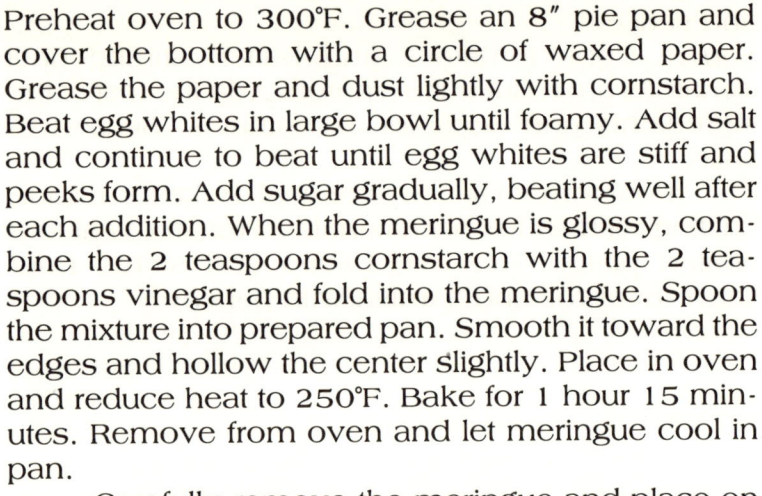

Preheat oven to 300°F. Grease an 8" pie pan and cover the bottom with a circle of waxed paper. Grease the paper and dust lightly with cornstarch. Beat egg whites in large bowl until foamy. Add salt and continue to beat until egg whites are stiff and peeks form. Add sugar gradually, beating well after each addition. When the meringue is glossy, combine the 2 teaspoons cornstarch with the 2 teaspoons vinegar and fold into the meringue. Spoon the mixture into prepared pan. Smooth it toward the edges and hollow the center slightly. Place in oven and reduce heat to 250°F. Bake for 1 hour 15 minutes. Remove from oven and let meringue cool in pan.

Carefully remove the meringue and place on serving plate. Drain fruit and place in meringue. Cover with whipped cream. Garnish with fruit slices. Serve immediately.

yield: 6 servings

Pavlova is probably the most well-known Australian dessert. Named after the Russian ballerina Pavlova, it should be crisp and very lightly tinted on the surface, yet remain soft and the consistency of marshmallow in the center. Like its namesake, it should be light as a feather.

HELEN HYDE

CORNFLAKE DROPS

1 cup peanut butter
2 12-ounce packages butterscotch chips
6 cups cornflakes

Melt peanut butter and chips in a double boiler. Put cornflakes in a bowl and pour melted ingredients over them and combine well. Drop cookies by the spoonful onto wax paper and leave until set.

Variation: If you prefer carmel chips, substitute them for one of the packages of butterscotch chips.

yield: 4 dozen

Cornflake drops were one of the first cookies I made as a child. They have always been very popular in our family, so a few years ago Ron and I started serving them at the Waverly Club. We have had so many compliments on them and so many requests for the recipe that I felt this one would be good to include in the Waverly Book.

SHARON WHITAKER

GREAT CHICKEN

2 8-ounce bottles Russian Salad Dressing
2 cups orange marmalade
2 envelopes dried onion soup mix
2 3-pound chickens, cut and skinned

Pre-heat oven to 350°F. Combine first three ingredients in a large bowl. Mix well. Add chicken, turn to coat. Cover and marinate overnight. Place in baking dish. Cover with sauce. Bake for one hour, or until chicken is tender. Baste 2 or 3 times during baking. Very simple recipe.

yield: 8 servings

If there are dieters in the family, low calorie dressing and marmalade can be substituted, and it is just as good.

BARBARA SCHEUER

CHOCOLATE PEANUT BUTTER PIE

Crust:
- 6 ounces chocolate chips
- 1 cup peanuts, chopped
- 1 tablespoon Crisco

Filling:
- 8 ounces cream cheese
- 1 cup powdered sugar
- ½ cup peanut butter
- ½ cup milk
- 8 ounces Cool Whip or heavy cream, whipped

Crust: Melt chocolate in double boiler. Add nuts and Crisco. Spread in pie plate lined with tin foil. Freeze for 15 minutes. Unmold and peel off foil. Return chocolate crust to pie plate.

Filling: Beat cream cheese and sugar; add peanut butter and milk. Fold in Cool Whip or whipped cream. Freeze. It will last one month in freezer if well covered. Defrost 20 minutes before cutting.

yield: 8 servings
LETHA REINHEIMER

CHICKEN AND GREEN BEAN CASSEROLE

- 2 packages frozen french cut green beans
- 8 boneless breasts of chicken: 4 whole breasts, split
- 1 can cream of chicken soup
- 1 can cream of celery soup
- 1 package onion soup mix
- 16 ounces sour cream
- 1 package stuffing
- ¼ cup butter

Pre-heat oven to 325°F. Thaw beans and place in large baking dish. Add layer of chicken. Mix soups and sour cream together and spread over chicken. Sauté stuffing in butter and sprinkle over top. Cover with foil and bake for 45 minutes. Remove foil and bake 15 minutes longer.

yield: 6-8 servings
ANN CHAMBERLIN

CHEESE BUTTERED CORN

- 2 packages frozen corn
- 15 ounce jar cheese spread with bacon
- ½ cup butter, softened
- ¼ teaspoon onion salt

Pre-heat oven to 350°F. Defrost corn. Beat cheese spread, butter and onion salt together until fluffy. Put corn in baking dish and spread cheese-butter mixture on top. Bake for 15 minutes, or until thoroughly heated.

yield: 6-8 servings
LAURA FRIEDER

MINUTE STEAKS PARMESAN

- 1 egg
- 1 tablespoon water
- Dash pepper
- ¼ cup finely crushed saltine crackers, 6 or 7 crackers
- ¼ cup Parmesan cheese, grated
- 2 tablespoons cooking oil
- 6 beef cube steaks, about 4 ounces each
- 1 8-ounce jar pizza sauce

Beat together egg, water and pepper. Combine cracker crumbs and half of the cheese. Dip steaks in egg mixture, then in crumbs. In a skillet, brown the steaks in the hot oil: electric skillet at 350° F. Drain off fat. Pour in pizza sauce. Cover; reduce heat to 220 °F. Simmer 20 minutes, adding a little water if necessary, to keep the sauce from sticking. Sprinkle with remaining cheese.

yield: 6 servings
CAROL COMSTOCK

NOODLE PUDDING

- 1 pound Pennsylvania Dutch noodles, broad
- 1 pound package cottage cheese
- 1 pint sour cream
- 5 eggs, separated
- 3 tablespoons sugar
- ½ pound butter, melted
- Frosted corn flake crumbs

Pre-heat oven to 350° F. Boil noodles in salted water until tender, about 10 minutes. Drain. Put cottage cheese, sour cream, egg yolks and sugar into blender and blend thoroughly. Melt butter in pot in which you cooked noodles, Add drained noodles and mix. Add blender mixture. In another bowl beat egg whites until they peak. Fold into noodle mixture. Put in ungreased 13" × 11" pyrex pan or into several smaller loaf pans. Sprinkle with frosted corn flakes on top. Bake for 1 hour, or until brown.

yield: 12 servings
ROSELLE FINE

BROCCOLI SALAD

- 2 bunches broocoli
- 8 slices bacon, cooked, drained and crumbled
- ½ cup raisins
- ½ cup chopped sweet Bermuda onion

Dressing:
- 1 cup mayonnaise
- 2 tablespoons sugar
- 2 tablespoons wine vinegar

Use only tender tips of broccoli. You should have about 4 cups. Fix salad a day ahead without dressing. Mix dressing ingredients well. Toss salad with dressing right before serving (1-2 hours). Looks attractive in crystal serving dish.

yield: 8 servings
PAULINE FOLEY

OVEN BEEF BARBECUE

1	2½-3 pound chuck roast
	Salt and pepper
1	large onion, chopped
½	cup celery, diced
2	tablespoons brown sugar
4	tablespoons lemon juice
1	cup catsup
3	tablespoons Worchestershire sauce
1	teaspoon chili powder
1½	cups water
	Hamburger rolls

Pre-heat oven to 350°F. Put raw beef in roaster pan. Salt and pepper the meat to taste. Place the onion and celery on top of the meat. Combine the remaining ingredients and pour them over the meat. Cover and cook for approximately two hours, or until the meat shreds easily. Remove the meat from the roaster and remove the fat and bone. Shred the meat with two forks while hot. Return the shredded meat to the sauce and cool. Serve on hamburger rolls. Freezes well. Should be made a day ahead.

yield: 15-20 sandwiches
MARY ANNE FRIEDMAN

PEANUT SALAD

4	cups cabbage, finely chopped
4	medium apples, coarsely chopped
	Enough mayonnaise to hold it all together
½	cup peanuts, chopped

Mix cabbage and apples. Add enough mayonnaise to moisten. Arrange on salad plates and sprinkle the top with peanuts.

yield: 12 servings
CAROLYN SANDHERR

PISTACHIO DESSERT

1	cup flour
¼	pound margarine, softened
½	cup almonds, ground
8	ounces cream cheese
1	cup powdered sugar
2	cups Cool Whip, large size
2	small packages instant pistachio pudding
	Almonds for garnish

Pre-heat oven to 350°F. Grease a 13" × 9" × 2" pan. Combine flour, margarine and nuts and pat in pan. Bake for 15 minutes. Cool. Cream the cream cheese with powdered sugar. Add one cup Cool Whip, mix well and spread very carefully on baked crust. Mix pistachio puddings as directed and pour over cheese mixture. Cover with remaining Cool Whip. Sprinkle almonds on top.

yield: 12-15 servings
SHIRLEY KETCHUM

III
CHICKEN AND GREEN BEAN CASSEROLE
CHEESE BUTTERED CORN
CORNFLAKE DROPS

IV
GREAT CHICKEN
STUFFED BAKED POTATOES
BROCCOLI CASSEROLE
FLUFFY PEANUT BUTTER PIE

V
BARBEQUED CHICKEN LEGS
ROMANOFF POTATOES
GLZED BABY CARROTS
RIGHT NOW STRAWBERRY ICE CREAM

VI
POOR MAN'S CORDON BLEU
STRING BEAN CASSEROLE
HERSHEY BAR PIE

VII
CREOLE CHICKEN
AVOCADO SALAD WITH BLUE CHEESE & BACON
PEACH TORTE

Kids in the Kitchen

I
OVEN BEEF BARBECUE
PEANUT SALAD
PISTACHIO DESSERT

II
MINUTE STEAKS PARMESAN
NOODLE PUDDING
BROCCOLI SALAD
CHOCOLATE PEANUT BUTTER PIE

fitted with seats and rubber side curtains. Ed's son Roger had long been driving the students from North Abington and he proudly took the controls of the new vehicle. The descendants of that first bus turn the parking lots yellow at the consolidated schools which sprawl over the Abington hills. This is an area which still cares about education. Much has changed, but much has stayed the same.

The end of the year at Waverly School was marked by Field Day. Divided into White and Blue teams, the children poured onto the grassy playing fields. The day was rich with cheers and dirty knees, tousled hair and rosy cheeks. Everyone was drawn into the excitement as teachers became referees and starters. Races, jumps, relays, throws and games were capped off with a total participation tug-of-war. What a grand way to say "good by, school" and "hello, summer!"

And in the long days of summer, Waverly children gather at the wading pool and the jungle gym, the square dances and the youth center, the tennis court and the swimming pool or pond. The woods and fields invite explorers and bike hikes lure a small crowd of pedalers. Girl Scouts flock to Camp Archbald and Boy Scouts canoe down the Susquehanna. Rain? Put up the umbrella and play in the puddles; get out the Monopoly game; or invade the kitchen to concoct a treat. There is always something within the ability of any child who wants to make something in the kitchen, even if it's only spreading peanut butter on a plateful of crackers. And the satisfaction of sharing that treat is too good to pass up. The gratification the cook experiences is just as real as that of the eater, so open the door and let's have the kids in the kitchen.

STUFFED BAKED POTATOES

8	baking potatoes
8	strips bacon, crumbled
1½	sticks butter or margarine
¼	cup hot milk
¼	cup chives and/or
¼	cup chopped sauteed onions
8	tablespoons sour cream
4	tablespoons grated cheese
4	slices American or Swiss cheese chopped or grated
1¼	teaspoon salt
½	teaspoon pepper

Pre-heat oven to 400°F. Bake potatoes 1 hour and 15 minutes or until very soft. While potatoes are baking, cook and drain bacon. Crumble coarsely. Slowly warm butter and milk together until butter melts.

While potatoes are hot, cut tops off and scoop out and reserve pulp, leaving potato shells whole.

Place potato pulp and all other ingredients in mixing bowl. Mash, or if using a mixer, put on medium speed, until cheese is melted and well incorporated. Consistency can be adjusted with more sour cream, if necessary to reach the consistency of stiff mashed potatoes. Pile mixture back in shells. Bake 20-25 minutes in a 350°F oven and serve.

yield: 8 servings
MARWORTH

BROCCOLI CASSEROLE

3	packages frozen chopped broccoli
2	cans cream of mushroom soup
6	ounces Cheddar cheese, grated
½	cup grape nuts
½	can onion rings, crumbled

Pre-heat oven to 350°F. Cook broccoli according to package directions. Drain, place in a 2 quart buttered baking dish. Mix soup and cheese together and pour over broccoli. Place grape nuts and onion rings on top. Bake covered for 30 minutes. Take cover off and bake 15 minutes more.

yield: 10 servings

This can be frozen before it is baked. This is a very easy recipe, but is just delicious and looks very pretty.

LINDA SUGERMAN

FLUFFY PEANUT BUTTER PIE

- 1 8-ounce package cream cheese
- ½ cup peanut butter
- 1 cup confectioners' sugar
- ½ cup milk
- 1 9-ounce carton Cool Whip
- 1 10-inch graham cracker pie crust
- ¼ cup peanuts, chopped
- 1 cup whipped cream, optional

Using an electric mixer, whip cream cheese until fluffy. Beat in peanut butter and sugar. Add milk and blend. Fold Cool Whip into mixture. Scrape into pie crust. Sprinkle top with nuts. Freeze until firm. Take out of freezer at least an hour before serving and put in refrigerator. You can top with whipped cream, if desired.

yield: One 10" pie
PAULA STAVISKY

BARBECUED CHICKEN LEGS

- 1 pound chicken legs, 8 to 10
-    Salt
-    Pepper, freshly ground
- ¼ cup margarine, softened
- 2 tablespoons light brown sugar
- 1 tablespoon catsup
- 1 tablespoon prepared dark mustard
- 1 tablespoon Worcestershire sauce

Pre-heat oven to 400°F. Arrange chicken legs in baking dish; season with salt and pepper. Blend together margarine, brown sugar, catsup, mustard and Worcestershire sauce. Spread ⅓ mixture on chicken. Bake 20 minutes. Turn chicken and spread ⅓ mixture on the chicken again. Bake 20 minutes longer. Turn chicken and spread with remaining mixture. Bake 20 minutes longer or until chicken is tender. You can remove the chicken legs from baking dish and decorate the end of each leg with a paper frill before serving.

yield: 4–6 servings
MARY JOY HAVEY

ROMANOFF POTATOES

- 6 cups medium potatoes, peeled and quartered
- 1 cup cottage cheese
- 1 cup sour cream
- ¼ teaspoon paprika
- ¼ teasoon garlic salt
- 2 tablespoons chopped onions
- 1 cup yellow cheese, grated

Pre-heat oven to 350°. Cook potatoes until done and mash them in a large bowl. Add the rest of the ingredients to the potatoes and mix. Place mixture in a large buttered casserole (2½ to 3 quarts) and top with the cheese. Bake for 40 to 45 minutes or until it is bubbly and looks done.

yield: 4 to 6 servings
ELLIE MESSNER

GLAZED BABY CARROTS

3 dozen baby carrots
3 tablespoons butter, softened
2 tablespoons sugar
1½ tablespoons water
Salt and pepper to taste

Scrape carrots. Combine all ingredients in a skillet, cover and bring to a boil. Reduce heat to low and simmer 10 minutes or until carrots are crisp-tender. Uncover and cook over medium heat until liquid evaporates and carrots are glazed.

yield: 6 servings
SALLY MARQUARDT

RIGHT NOW STRAWBERRY ICE CREAM

1 pint frozen whole strawberries
1 cup milk; skim, low-fat, whole or half-n-half
2 tablespoons sugar, more or less to taste

Place all together in food processor, with knife blade, or in a blender. Process until strawberries are cut up and mixture is frozen. Eat right away; it will be soft and cannot be frozen to eat later.

yield: 4 to 6 servings
ABBY WARMAN

POOR MAN'S CORDON BLEU

2 cups cooked chicken or turkey, cubed
1 cup ham, cubed
1 cup American or Cheddar cheese, cubed
1½ cans cream of mushroom soup
Seasoned bread crumbs

Pre-heat oven to 350°F. Combine first three ingredients in buttered casserole. Spoon soup over mixture; sprinkle with seasoned bread crumbs. Cover and bake for 35 minutes. Uncover and bake ten minutes longer. This recipe can also be used in the Microwave.

yield: 4 to 5 servings
DRU MILLER

STRING BEAN CASSEROLE

2 packages french styled green beans, cooked and drained
1 can cream of mushroom soup
1 can french fried onion rings

Pre-heat oven to 350°F. Mix mushroom soup with green beans. Pour into buttered casserole. Bake 20 minutes; cover with onion rings. Bake 10 minutes longer.

yield: 6 servings
TERI STAHLLER

HERSHEY BAR PIE

- 1 4-ounce Hershey bar with almonds OR 5 small bars
- 20 Large marshmallows
- ⅓ cup milk
- ½ pint heavy cream, whipped
- 1 graham cracker pie crust, baked and ready for filling

Heat chocolate bars, marshmallows and milk in a double boiler. Stir until ingredients melt and are well blended. Cool. Fold in whipped cream. Pour into baked pie shell. Cover with cellophane wrap and chill for twenty-four hours.

yield: 8 to 10 servings

My mother-in-law, Alice Koch, gave me this recipe when I married Von. It's cherished because it was her family's favorite pie.

JAN KOCH

CREOLE CHICKEN

- 1 whole chicken, including giblets, cut into serving pieces
- ⅓ cup flour
- 1½ teaspoons salt
- 1 teaspoon paprika
- ¼ teaspoon poultry seasoning
- ⅛ teaspoon pepper
- ¼ cup butter, melted

Creole Sauce:
- 1 cup uncooked rice
- ½ cup onion, chopped
- ½ cup green pepper, chopped
- 3 cups chicken broth, made from giblets and neck
- 2 large tomatoes, cut into wedges

Pre-heat oven to 400°F. Dredge chicken pieces in flour, salt, paprika, poultry seasoning and pepper. Melt butter in a 9" × 12" × 2" pan and place dredged chicken in it. Bake for at least 25 minutes. Remove chicken, set aside. Place the rice in the pan, add chopped onion and pepper. Place browned chicken on top, add the 3 cups of chicken broth. Place tomato wedges on top of chicken. Bake for 45 minutes, uncovered.

yield: 6 servings

I heard this recipe given on television years ago. It is delicious. Men love it, and so do I. Whole Italian pear shaped tomatoes, canned, may be used instead of fresh tomatoes. Instead of chopping the green peppers, you may slice them and place on top of rice and onions.

RUTH RICHARDS

AVOCADO SALAD WITH BLUE CHEESE AND BACON

½ head each, Boston, Romaine, Chicory
2 avocados peeled and sliced
½ pint cherry tomatoes

Spiced Clear Dressing:
½ cup grapefruit juice
¼ cup honey
2 tablespoons wine vinegar
½ teaspoon onion salt
¼ teaspoon cardamon

Garnish:
3 slices bacon, crisp and crumbled
¼ cup crumbled Blue Cheese or Roquefort

Arrange the lettuce on individual salad plates and place avocado slices and cherry tomatoes decoratively on top. Mix all dressing ingredients together in glass jar and shake well. Pour over salads and top with crumbled bacon and cheese.

yield: 6 servings

This was one of my mother's favorite recipes.

JOANNE LEWIS TODD

PEACH TORTE

4 egg whites
1 cup sugar
¼ teaspoon cream of tartar
½ teaspoon vanilla
17 Ritz crackers, crushed
½ cup nut meats, chopped

Filling:
Vanilla ice cream
Sliced fresh peaches, sweetened

Pre-heat oven to 350°F. Beat first four ingredients together until stiff but not dry. Fold in crackers and nuts. Put into greased 9" pie plate. Bake about 1 hour. When cool and ready to serve, fill with vanilla ice cream and garnish with sliced sweetened peaches.

yield: 6 to 8 servings
DITTY QUIGG

Fall

MOTHER NATURE DONS HER TAFFETA PETTICOATS OF DRY LEAVES AND EVERY STEP IS ACCOMPANIED BY A TELLTALE RUSTLE. Fall is a noisy season, and the clear air carries the sounds across russet hillsides: cheers from hockey fields, football stadiums, soccer games and playgrounds at recess; wild geese overhead; clouds of starlings skirling in practice formations for their trek south; blue jays arguing over a plump sunflower; squirrels scolding intruders into their acorn and nut territories.

Colors run riot. Orange flares across the bough of the sugar maples, the pumpkin field and the wings of the monarch butterfly, leaving our milkweed for the tropical winter of Central America. Crimson bursts in dogwood, sumac and climbing woodbine; and in shiny apples, bowing branches to the ground and filling Northup's cider mill with that most delicious of all drinks. Rust lingers on the oaks, and larches flash yellow across the darkening hillside. Gold and yellow

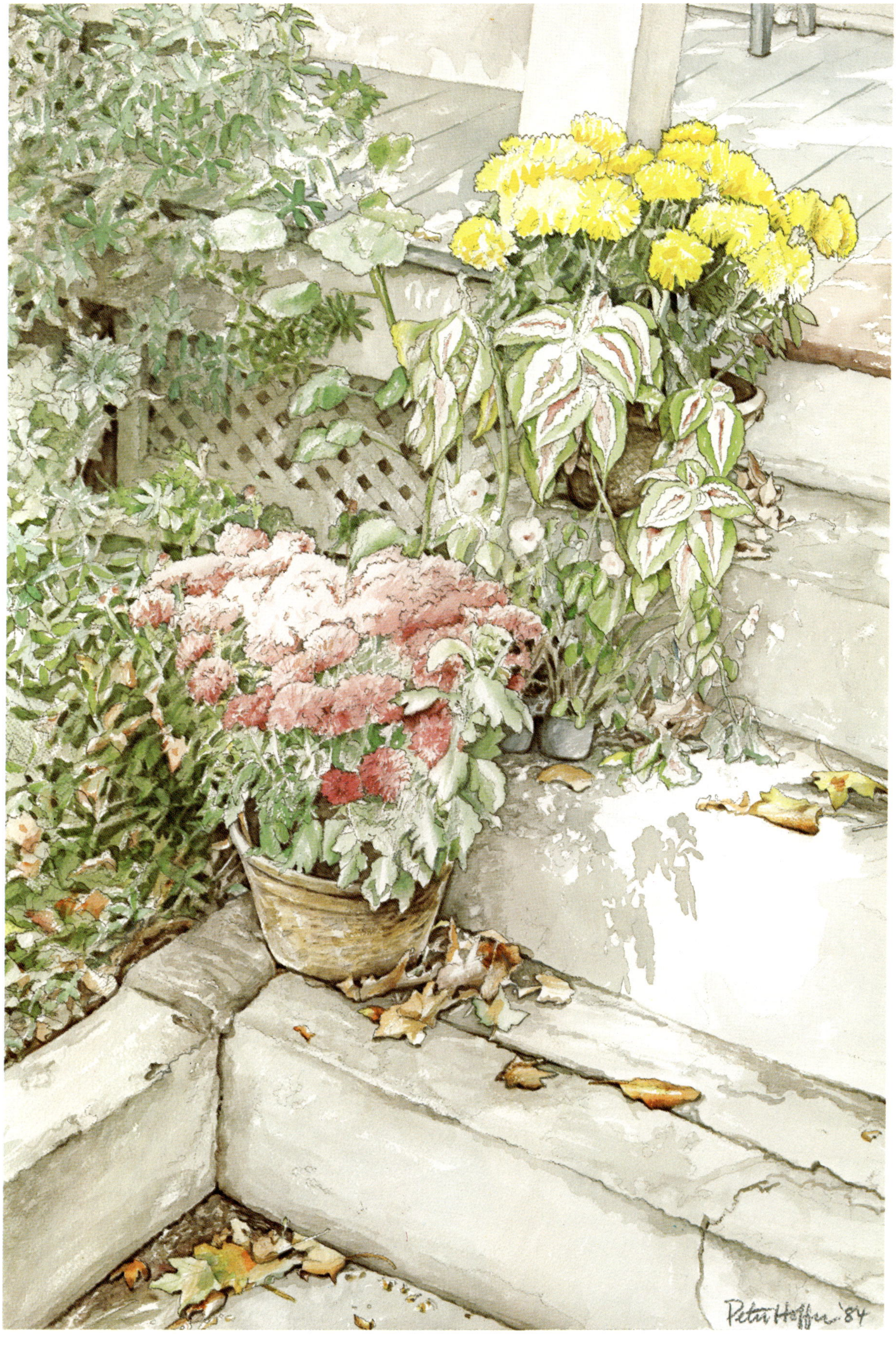
Peter Hoffer '84

dress the poplars and birches, paint the western sky with sunset light and radiate from the ripe harvest moon hanging heavily in the evening blue.

The Halloween party at the Comm entices hundreds of children and whole families into costumes; choirs, highland clans, jack frost and helpers, mummies, pumpkins, cigarette boxes, clowns, ballerinas, hobos, Martians and ghosts parade around and around. The judges ponder diligently to discern the prettiest, the funniest, the scariest, the most original, from the wonderful chaos. Everyone bobs for apples, races to eat along the string to the doughnut, listens eagerly to a fortune-telling crone, and braves the walk through the haunted house. UNICEF money is turned in at the door and a movie rewards the efforts of neighborhood canvassers.

Halloween tricks are timeless: doorbell ringing, window soaping, a rope across the road, or porch furniture hauled up the flagpole. However, one memorable Halloween feat was accomplished by a group of boys who lassoed and towed the last operating outhouse in town from its convenient backyard to an adjacent field; there were those who claimed that the owner was caught inside and inadvertently made the trip as well.

Fall drops the beechnut, walnut, hickory and horse chestnut to the ground and the prickly husks yield their treasures of sweetness and beauty. There is nothing as smooth and shiny as a horse chestnut, fresh out of its jacket. A pocketful never looks as beautiful when reviewed later. The nut is of no practical use, now or later, but to hold in hand that soft and satiny, gloriously brown, waxy smooth, friendly globe is one of fall's high moments.

Autumn leaves dance through the air, scurry across roads, play tag over lawns, eddy around steps, crowd against hedges, drift into ditches, mulch gardens, snuggle up against foundations, get raked together to stuff a jack-o'-lantern mannikin, pile high for jumping in, burn acridly under tall sentinels of grey smoke, or get bundled ignominiously into plastic bags to slump at the curb on the way to the dump. The last bright exuberances of faltering flower beds darken, dry and settle to the earth like a blanket for the long sleep ahead. People pull back from the yard, to the porch, to the sunny window. Peter Hoffer's painting has brought the chrysanthemum garden to the doorstep. It speaks of gathering in and seeking shelter, house, village, community.

Mother Nature's smile is fading; the friendly rustle sounds a warning of harshness to come. The rhythms of life suggest the circling of a dog before settling down to sleep. We check the storm windows and clean out the rain gutters, put the garden to bed and bring in the hammock and picnic table. A couple of inspection circuits and the welcoming lights inside pull us into the cozy home that has been worked into readiness for winter.

Antiques Show Luncheon

The annual Waverly Antiques Show generates a hospitality committee of the whole community. Since 1943 it has provided a focus of interest and a source of support for the Community House. Hundreds of workers come together to make arrangements for exhibitors; to provide flowers, desserts and hospitality; to gather "almost antiques" and generally grease the wheels. Friends come from near and far to revel in the gleaming surfaces and carefully crafted lines that conjure up anecdotes, traditions and appreciation for our heritage.

A century earlier, there were browsers and buyers on the same grounds. But then, the main street was known as the Philadelphia and Great Bend Turnpike and the block where the Community House now stands was lined with tightly spaced frame buildings. These housed stores and hotels. Between 1840 and 1880 this was the growing trading center for a prosperous farming community. S.S. Kennedy wrote a column from Waverly for the Scranton *Republican* in which he noted: "We are a busy, industrious community, and have but few loafers who sit at the hotel door, or in front of the stores, to make remarks upon men and women as they go by."

And when a Waverly housewife walked "uptown" in the 1870's to buy buttons for the shirt she was making, she could walk dry shod on sidewalks quarried from "the Hollow" below the Methodist Church. She could buy school shoes for the children and have her own shoes mended by Mr. Mahoney while she took the boys for a haircut. Mrs. Sherman and Mrs. Singer had a dressmaking establishment where she could peruse magazines for the latest fashions. Even in 1879 there was a thrifty practicality among village women whose grandmothers, a half century earlier, used the maxim, observed by Elder Miller in his journal: "Cut your coat according to your cloth. It was seldom that a dress sleeve was seen larger than the arm for which it was made." But, thrifty or not, a lady did not leave home without a hat. For this she could have the assistance of Miss Gorman and Mrs. Stone, both milliners, who could work wonders with a wisp of veil, a sweep of feathers or a silken bloom to set off a happy smile and tame a tumble of curls into decent propriety.

E. H. Bailey cleaned and repaired watches or sold you a new one when the time came. He also displayed fine watch chains and fobs, a golden locket, a cameo brooch, or a pair of combs to catch the eye of a shopper. Though she paused to look, the practical housewife made her way to one of several general stores. She could choose among Bailey's, Bliss's, Green's, Shaw's or White's. If she were shopping for a new tin measure, she would seek out Mrs. E.M. Cowles' store, full of stoves and tinware.

Among an Abington population of almost 3,000 there were 77 farmers and their families who lived in Waverly and regularly traded in the village. They provided plenty of business for the blacksmiths, Calkins, Perry, Whaling and White. S.S. Kennedy noted in his column: "A Waverly blacksmith has been heard to say that Parker's Hill has been worth hundreds of dollars to him for the extra horse-shoeing and repairing which it brought to his shop. In winter, portions of this Hill are usually glazed with ice, rendering the frequent shoeing of teams necessary."

And if the shaft of the wagon broke, Grey or Rice, carriage makers, fashioned the needed repairs. Harness makers, T.C. Kennedy and J.T. Mead, were ready to mend the heaviest working farm gear or the fine leather used to drive Mrs. Nicholson's dainty, parasol-topped grey phaeton. The leather for these was probably from Charles Tinkham's tannery on Ackerly Creek below Hickory Grove Cemetery.

Farmers for miles around sought out the Foundry in the Bedford barn in the Alley behind Main Street. There, Gilbert Sherman invented and manufactured the Waverly Hiller and the Waverly Plow. Sherman was also available as a carpenter, with Mr. Winchell, for projects beyond the ability of the farmer or householder. The lumber for these projects could be prepared at the sawmills operated by Mr. Spencer and Mr. Hallstead. And bricks were made at the brick works on the Sherman farm along the flats on Carbondale Road. This was the source of the bricks used to build Horatio Nicholson's big house on the Glenburn Road, and the store on the northwest corner of Main and Clinton Streets.

Waverly's three physicians, Dr. Grattan, Dr.

Miles, and Dr. Van Sickle, made long, difficult trips to visit patients, carrying many pills and potions from the drugstore of Bedford & Sons. When all else failed, Mr. Mershon was called in. Mr. Mershon showed handsome furniture in his shop; the coffins for his undertaking business were discreetly kept in the back room. And, making the rounds at twilight every day, George Perry lighted the gas lamps that illuminated the village streets after dark.

The items that we now treasure as antiques were the homely articles of everyday life in the Abingtons of the 19th century. In their utility and beauty they speak to us of time-honored traditions, as times change and populations shift. The thousands of visitors to the Annual Waverly Antiques Show attest to the power of this message. Borrowers and buyers alike enjoy the charm of the village and the efforts of the committees; pausing under the striped awning on the side lawn, they refresh themselves with a delicious luncheon.

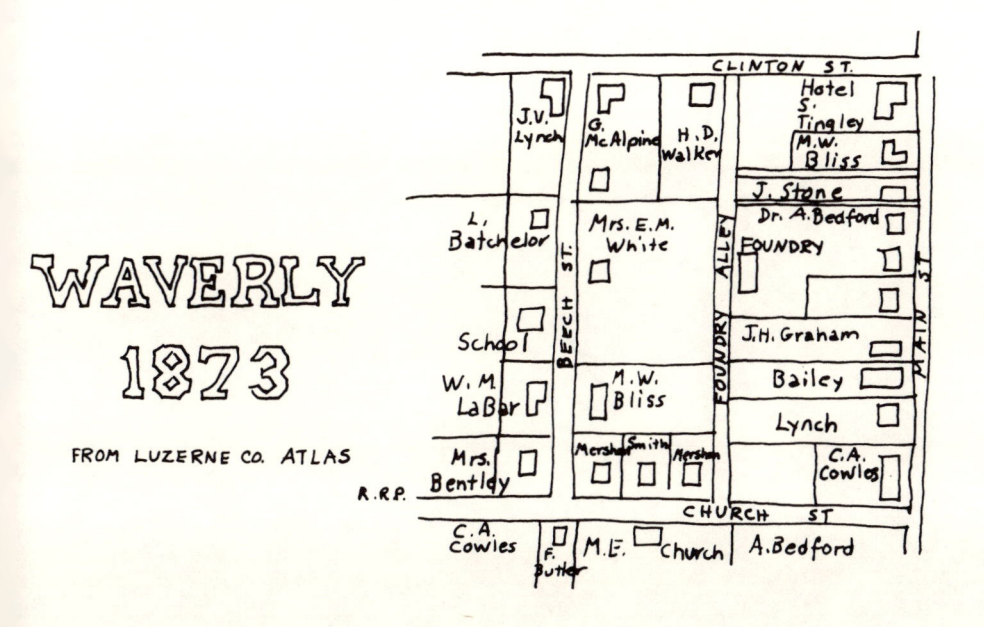

WAVERLY 1873

FROM LUZERNE CO. ATLAS

Antiques Show Luncheon

1974 ANTIQUES SHOW LUNCHEON
CHICKEN CREPES WITH CURRY SAUCE
OR
HAM AND CHEESE CREPES WITH MORNAY SAUCE
TOMATO ASPIC WITH GREEN MAYONNAISE
SUMMER FRUIT COMPOTE
EASY CHEESY LEMON BARS
CHEWY COOKIE BARS

1984 ANTIQUES SHOW LUNCHEON
CURRIED CREAM OF PEA SOUP
COLD POACHED BREAST OF CHICKEN WITH
PEPPERCORN SAUCE
MARINATED BROCCOLI AND CARROTS
APRICOT CREAM

1974 ANTIQUES SHOW LUNCHEON
Kathleen C. Graff, Susan S. Belin, Chairmen

BASIC CREPE RECIPE

- 4 eggs
- 2 cups milk
- ½ teaspoon salt
- 2 cups flour
- 4 tablespoons melted butter

Mix all ingredients in blender or food processor. Cover and refrigerate at least 2 hours. Cook in 7" crepe pans.

yield: Twenty-four 7" crepes

BASIC SAUCES

The curry and mornay sauces are each derived from the basic Bechamel or Velouté sauce, which is quickly made:
- 3 tablespoons butter
- 3 tablespoons flour
- 2 cups hot liquid: milk for Mornay sauce *or* chicken stock for Curry sauce
- Salt and Pepper to taste
- 1 cup combined Swiss and Parmesan cheese, grated, for Mornay sauce *or*
- 1 tablespoon curry powder for Curry sauce

Melt butter in heavy bottom sauce pan. Blend in flour and cook slowly, stirring constantly for 2 minutes. Add liquid, stirring vigorously with wire whisk. Bring to boil and simmer for 1 minute. Add salt and pepper to taste, and then the cheese or curry.

yield: 2 cups Mornay sauce
2 cups Curry sauce

BASIC FILLINGS

For Chicken Crepes:
- 2 tablespoons butter
- ¼ cup shallots or onions, minced
- 2 tablespoons flour
- ½ cup hot milk
- ½ cup hot chicken stock
- ¼ cup dry white wine
- ¼ teaspoon dried tarragon
- 2 egg yolks, lightly beaten
- 2 cups diced, cooked chicken
- Salt and Pepper to taste

Melt butter in saucepan, add shallots or onions and cook, stirring for 2 minutes. Add flour and stir to blend. Add hot milk and stock, stirring vigorously with wire whisk. Add wine, tarragon and bring to boil. Boil 1 minute. Beat ¼ cup hot sauce into yolks and then stir yolk mixture into sauce. Heat for 1 minute but do not boil. Add chicken and salt and pepper.

yield: Filling for 12 crepes

Pre-heat oven to 375°F. Assemble crepes with fillings and arrange in separate buttered baking dishes large enough to accommodate the crepes. Cover with appropriate sauce. Bake for 30 minutes or until thoroughly heated.

yield: Filling for 12 crepes

For Ham Crepes:
- 12 slices baked ham, trimmed to fit crepe
- 12 slices Swiss cheese, trimmed to fit crepe
- Mustard to taste

FRESH TOMATO ASPIC

- 4 pounds very fresh, ripe tomatoes, chopped
- 2 envelopes gelatin
- ¼ cup minced onion
- ½ cup minced celery
- Salt and Pepper
- 1 teaspoon sugar, optional
- 2 tablespoons lemon juice, optional
- 2 tablespoons fresh basil, minced

Simmer tomatoes with 1½ cups water over medium heat, stirring often for 15 minutes. Meanwhile, dissolve gelatin in ½ cup cold water. Put cooked tomatoes through food mill or strainer, then return pureé to the pan. Add onion, celery, salt to taste (it will need quite a lot - up to 2 teaspoons), pepper and sugar and lemon juice if desired. Cook 15 minutes, stirring. Remove from heat. Add basil and the gelatin, stirring until thoroughly dissolved. Turn into 2-quart ring mold and chill until firm.

yield: 12 servings

GREEN MAYONNAISE

- ¾ cup chopped fresh greens-watercress or spinach leaves
- ¼ cup chopped fresh herbs: parsley, basil, tarragon *or*
- 1 tablespoon dried herbs
- 1 egg
- 1 egg yolk
- 1 cup olive or vegetable oil
- 2 tablespoons vinegar or lemon juice
- Salt and pepper to taste

Blanch greens for 1 minute in boiling water. Drain and pat dry. Place greens, herbs, egg and egg yolk in blender or food processor. Blend until pureed. Add ¼ cup of the oil in slow stream, then add vinegar or lemon juice and finally the remaining ¾ cup oil. Add salt, pepper to taste. If too thick, blend in small amount boiling water.

yield: 1¾ cups

SUMMER FRUIT COMPOTE

Combine your choice of fresh, end-of-the summer fruits to make six to eight cups. Toss well. Cover and refrigerate at least two hours to blend flavors and allow fruit juices to flow. Suggested fruits - fresh from the garden or local fruit stands: blueberries, raspberries, red and green seedless grapes; chopped apples, peaches, pears (tossed with lemon juice to prevent discoloring); sliced plums, (use several different varieties); Canteloupe or watermelon (chopped or cut into balls).

Add ¼ cup orange liquor if desired. Serve in large glass bowl.

yield: 12 servings

EASY CHEESY LEMON BARS

- 1 package lemon cake mix
- ¼ pound butter, melted
- 3 eggs
- 1 package lemon frosting mix
- 1 8-ounce package cream cheese, softened

Pre-heat oven to 350°F. Combine cake mix, butter and 1 slightly beaten egg. Mix with fork until moist. Pat into 9" × 13" pan, greased on bottom only. Blend frosting mix with cream cheese. Reserve ½ cup of this mixture. Add 2 eggs to the larger portion of the frosting mixture and beat 3 to 5 minutes. Spread over cake mixture in pan. Bake 30 to 35 minutes. Cool. Spread with reserved ½ cup frosting mixture.

yield: 36 bars

CHEWY COOKIE BARS

- 1½ sticks butter, softened
- 2 cups brown sugar, firmly packed
- 2 eggs
- 1 cup flour
- ½ teaspoon baking powder
- 1 cup walnuts, coarsely chopped

Pre-heat oven to 325°F. Cream butter and sugar. Add eggs, beating well. Add flour, baking powder and nuts. Spread in greased 9" × 13" pan. Bake 30 to 35 minutes.

yield: 36 bars

1984 ANTIQUES SHOW LUNCHEON
Kathy Cesare, Mary Lynn Morgan, Chairmen

CURRIED CREAM OF PEA SOUP

Add vegetables to one cup of stock. Bring to a boil, then simmer for 15 minutes. Process in blender or food processor in two batches. Stir in curry powder and another cup of stock and cream. Add salt to taste. May be served hot or cold.

yield: 4 cups

- 1 cup frozen peas
- 1 medium onion, sliced
- 1 small carrot, sliced
- 1 stalk celery with leaves, sliced
- 1 medium potato, peeled and sliced
- 1 clove garlic
- 1 teaspoon curry powder
- 2 cups chicken broth
- 1 cup heavy cream
- Salt to taste

COLD POACHED BREAST OF CHICKEN WITH GREEN PEPPERCORN SAUCE

Poach chicken breasts by simmering in chicken stock for 15 minutes. Let cool in stock. When cool, skin and bone the breasts. Wrap well and refrigerate until ready to use.

Sauce: Place mustard, wine, sugar, salt, pepper and egg yolks in top of double boiler. Cook over hot, not boiling water, stirring constantly until thickened, about 5 minutes. Remove from heat and add peppercorns and butter. Whip cream until stiff and fold into mustard mixture. Cover and chill at least 8 hours. Sauce will keep about a week in the refrigerator.

Arrange chicken decoratively on serving platter. Mask breasts with sauce and decorate with parsley or watercress.

yield: 1½ cups

Chicken:
- 4 whole chicken breasts, split
- 2 cups chicken stock, or enough to cover breasts

Sauce:
- 2 tablespoons Dijon mustard
- 2 tablespoons white wine
- 2 teaspoons sugar
- ½ teaspoon salt
- ¼ teaspoon white pepper
- 2 egg yolks
- 2 tablespoons green peppercorns, rinsed and drained
- 1 tablespoon butter
- ½ cup heavy cream

Garnish:
Chopped parsley or fresh watercress

MARINATED BROCCOLI AND CARROTS

Vegetables:
- 3 cups broccoli, cut into flowerets
- 3 cups carrots, sliced

Marinade:
- ½ cup salad oil
- ½ cup olive oil
- 1½ cups red wine vinegar
- ¼ cup sugar
- ¾ teaspoon black pepper
- 1½ teaspoons basil
- 2 teaspoons garlic salt

Bring marinade ingredients to a boil and pour over prepared vegetables. Refrigerate for 48 hours and turn occasionally.

yield: 12 servings

APRICOT CREAM

- 1 6-ounce can frozen lemonade
- ½ gallon vanilla ice cream
- 1 10-ounce jar apricot preserves

Partially thaw lemonade and soften ice cream. Mix all ingredients together. Return to container and place in freezer.

yield: 16 servings

Harvest Supper

There is a reassuring quality about the landscape associated with the family farm. The plowed field and the mowed, the ripening grain, the hillside orchard and stone-walled pasture contrast and complement each other in harmonious patterns. The whole vista suggests a patchwork quilt, thriftily crafted and thrown lovingly over the earth by someone who cares. And there must be a subconscious understanding that this land feeds our bodies which makes its emotional message so benign. It is not spectacular, imposing, breathtaking or awesome. But it is a place that men and women can call home, where there is promise of shelter, nourishment and comfort in exchange for effort.

John Miller's journal, in 1843, describes this Abington countryside: "It is situated upon the waters of the South Branch of the Tunkhannock and of the Lackawanna Creeks. There are several places where these waters have their heads only a few rods from each other, the waters of the Tunkhannock running northerly, and the others southerly, which enter the Susquehanna River some 20 miles apart. The town is rather hilly, well-watered, of a good soil, timber generally called beech and maple, but consisting of a great variety of other kinds of wood, very beneficial and useful for the farmer and mechanic. It is fine grazing country and produces fine crops of grain, when properly cultivated. It is high land and very healthy."

For the first settlers, farming was not a choice. It was an activity required for survival, for basic food and clothing. When the Abington woods were cleared, white clover sprang up spontaneously and flourished. This created good pasturage for the family cow and sheep essential for dairy products and wool. Plowed acreage yielded wheat, oats, corn and hay for man and beast. Flax was widely grown and spun into linen thread, woven and sewn to make "tow britches," the durable and omnipresent ancestor of blue jeans.

In 1805 there were more than twenty homesteads in Abington, but only two yoke of oxen and one span of horses to assist in the heavy labor of farming. In that year, Jeremiah Clark and his new wife, Sophie Hall, harvested 100 bushels of wheat from 4 bushels of wheat planted, and they raised the first real barn in the township in which to store it.

By 1830, wild land in Abington was selling for $3-$5 per acre; it was becoming a prosperous farming region. The Yankee farmers produced plenty for their own families with sufficient for market: market in Wilkes-Barre, twenty miles to the south through the dark wilderness; in Philadelphia and New York City, after the turnpike was built in 1821; and in Scranton, as that town emerged and grew after 1840.

The earliest settlers struggled through the forest along narrow and difficult walking paths; perhaps a traveller was accompanied by a horse with a pack or a drag. They carried little baggage. But almost no one came without a bucket for collecting sap, and a syrup kettle in which to boil down the sweetly flavored juice of the sugar maple tree. One of the first tasks attended by Robert Reynolds, William Wall, Ezra Dean and Job Tripp upon their arrival in the Abington wilderness in February of 1797 was that of tapping the many maple trees and concentrating the sap into syrup by long boiling.

Current residents of the area pursue the same process and are also rewarded with elegant amber deliciousness. It takes forty gallons of maple sap and many hours of hot fire, boiling and steam to produce one gallon of maple syrup. For this operation, our forbears built a sugar shack operation in the woods. If today's neighbor boils it down on his suburban kitchen stove, he's asking for trouble as well as syrup. He may be dismayed to discover his water-logged ceiling on the floor among his gleaming jars of syrup.

The Abington dairies produced good quality milk, cream, butter and cheese for the city folk as well as country folk. And Abington's farmers were in the forefront of improving their herds. In 1857 they formed the Abington Agricultural Society led by the Millers who had imported Holstein-Friesians from Holland. These fine cows were the foundation of herds across northern Pennsylvania and Southern New York. In 1925 the Arthur Miller farm had the oldest Holstein herd in the state, all direct descendants of the original Dutch stock. It was recognized as a great influence on the breed in America. The white and black Holsteins are valued today for the high volume of low butter-fat milk they produce and have almost totally replaced the once familiar Guernsey and Jersey cows.

Delivery trucks fanned out from the Abington dairies: Decker Farm Dairy, Linair Farms, Manning's, and Parker's Oldfield Farms. The clattering glass bottles of milk and cream were delivered to homes and school lunch cafeterias until the 1960's. In the following years, local dairy farms have dwindled down to a precious few. Cream is no longer free to rise to the top of the bottle. Pastures are filling with alder and wild roses, or the houses of new generations of milk drinkers and ice cream lickers.

Today, the neighbor's dog may trample the petunias or his cat may lurk under the bird feeder. In 1870, it was more likely to be his cow that caused a problem. The Waverly Column in the Scranton *Republican* reported, "Farmers for miles around are tormented all summer by a drove of street cows from the village . . . And some farmers are indignant because their cattle and horses have been shut up in our village pound and a fine demanded before they could be recovered. Alleged boys have gone out to the suburbs to drive cows into the village to shut them up to obtain a small fee." The village pound was a fenced-in area on Foundry Alley, and fees were established by town council: "$1.00 fine for horse, mare or mule, $.30 for cattle or cow, $.20 for swine, sheep or goats and $.10 for each goose."

Although dogs did not make the list of problem creatures ransomed by the pound, in 1893 they made the news. An uncontrolled pack of dogs chased and mutilated dozens of sheep from local flocks. And these were business flocks like that of Farmer Clark who butchered 1,600 head of sheep in the winter of 1897 and sold them in the boom town of Scranton. Losses and hard work continue to be hallmarks of farm life.

Wheat, rye, corn and oats were staple crops for home and market. The harvest and threshing involved only simple machines and employed many laborers for miles around. Good workers were appreciated. Though William Shannon had lost one arm, in September of 1893, he threshed out 76½ bushels of oats in one hour, with one arm and a one-horse machine. It seems a prodigious feat of lifting for two arms!

These grain harvests caused mills to be built wherever a run of water was sufficient to drive a water wheel to turn a stone. The first was Slocum's and Abbot's mill at the confluence of the Lackawanna River and Roaring Brook. Abington grain growers soon had Dean's mill, down stream from Dalton, States' mill along the creek in Wallsville and another at the end of Baylor's Lake. Ackerly Creek was dammed to create Glenburn Pond in 1848, and George Humphrey built a huge mill with four courses of millstones. By 1864, C.C. Cowles had built in Waverly a coal-fired steam-driven mill for grinding grain or sawing lumber. The miller no longer needed a stream for power.

The hillsides sloping upward from the township streams were natural locations for orchards. Fruit and nut trees bloomed riotously each spring and bore generously each fall. As the farms prospered and the markets became more sophisticated, fancier varieties were selected for planting. Waverly orchards, like Parker's, and Stevenson's, grew a reputation and loyal consumers as well as plump fruits.

Over the hill and closer to the dooryard was the hen-house. It too changed in nature. Chickens were part of the early settlers' basic household equipment, like a pump, a churn, a spinning wheel and a cow. Even after the village grew up and houses were close together, most housewives stepped across the backyard to collect the daily eggs. Roosters competed to salute the dawn across village and farms. And some of the farms, like George Stevenson's searched out fancy poultry, exotic birds, for their collections. Peacocks, guinea fowl, pheasant, grouse and decorative ducks brought glamour to the roost and the community that could afford such luxuries.

When Paul Belin dedicated the Community House in 1921, it was to the farming community he addressed his remarks. It was their values he evoked and their organizations he invited to the new rooms. We are all enriched by the lives of these farmers of the Abington Hills although few farms are still operating. Their efforts have created the landscapes against which we instinctively measure all others. Their husbandry built healthy individuals, and their cooperative work and vision nurtured strong families and supportive institutions. Their lives and work are our heritage, and our lives and work are supported by that foundation.

Harvest is a time of Thanksgiving. For the nourishment of food, family and friends lavished upon us here in Waverly, may we be truly grateful.

Harvest Supper

CORN, RED PEPPER AND LEEK SOUP
GRILLED LEG OF LAMB
BROCCOLI AND CHEESE PIE IN PHYLLO PASTRY
BAKED ZUCCHINI
TOMATOES PROVENÇALE
APPLE CAKE
WHITE CLOUD CHEESECAKE WITH PEACHES

CORN, RED PEPPER AND LEEK SOUP

5	ears of corn
2	tablespoons unsalted butter
3	tablespoons oil
3	leeks, cleaned and coarsely chopped
1	large red bell pepper, seeded and coarsely chopped
1½	quarts chicken stock
½	cup whipping cream
½	teaspoon salt
¼	teaspoon coarsely cracked white pepper
	Pinch of cayenne pepper
2	tablespoons chopped parsley

Scrape kernels off corncobs with sharp knife. Reserve ¼ cup for garnish. Heat butter and oil in large saucepan. Add leeks and sauté over medium heat, stirring occasionally until soft, about 5 minutes. Add red pepper and continue sautéing until soft, about 5 minutes. Add corn and cook 3 minutes. Add chicken stock and bring to boil. Reduce heat and simmer slowly, uncovered for 30 minutes. Pour into blender or food processor and process for 1 minute. Put through food mill. If this step is eliminated texture will be coarser. Return to saucepan. Add cream, salt, pepper and cayenne. Reheat over low heat. Taste for seasoning. Immerse reserved corn in boiling water for 2 minutes. Drain. Pour soup into bowls. Garnish with corn and parsley. May be prepared ahead up to three days. Keep in refrigerator. When reheating, taste for seasoning.

yield: 8 servings

After ten years away, living in California, I still think fondly of our years in Waverly. We have remained in touch with friends there and have kept up with most of the news. I still believe it was a wonderful place to bring up children. I remember well the first cooking demonstrations done by John Clancy and have renewed acquaintance with him when he does classes here in the Bay area. Our fondest regards to all who remember us and best wishes to the Waverly Community House in its 65th year.

ZELDA BERGMAN

GRILLED LEG OF LAMB

1	teaspoon marjoram
1	teaspoon thyme
½	teaspoon caraway seeds
¼	cup chopped parsley
1	large onion chopped
1	clove garlic, minced
½	cup olive oil
½	cup lemon juice
2	slices lean bacon, cut into 1" slices
1	leg of lamb, boned and butterflied

Combine first eight ingredients and marinate bacon pieces in the mixture for ½ hour. Remove any fat from the lamb. Make as many gashes in both sides of lamb as you have pieces of bacon and insert bacon into gashes. Place lamb flat in a flat pan, pour marinade over it and cover it tightly. Marinate in refrigerator 24 hours, turning occasionally. Cook over charcoal for 10-15 minutes per side depending on desired doneness and thickness of meat. Coals should be hot but subsided, as oil in marinade will drip and cause flaming. Have pitcher of water handy to douse any flames.

yield: 8-16 depending on weight of lamb and appetites.

Origin unknown, but a family summer favorite for years. Delicious second time around if any is left over.

MARGARETTA CLARKE CHESSLER

BROCCOLI AND CHEESE PIE IN PHYLLO PASTRY

- 8 phyllo pastry leaves
- 2 pounds fresh broccoli, or 3 packages frozen
- ¼ cup butter
- ½ cup finely chopped onion
- 3 eggs
- ½ pound feta cheese, crumbled
- ¼ cup chopped parsley
- 2 tablespoons dill
- ½ teaspoon salt
- Dash pepper
- ½ cup butter, melted

Pre-heat oven to 350°F. Remove phyllo pastry from freezer to thaw. Coarsely chop broccoli, stems and flowerets. Add to large skillet with ½ cup boiling water. Cook, covered, 5 minutes. Drain well. In ¼ cup butter sauté onion about 3 minutes, add broccoli, and sauté 1 minute stirring. Remove from heat. In large bowl beat eggs, add cheese, parsley, dill, salt, pepper and broccoli. Mix well.

Line inside of 9 inch springform pan with 6 phyllo leaves, overlapping edges; brush each leaf with melted butter. Pour filling into prepared pan. Fold overhanging edges of pastry leaves over top of filling. With scissors cut four 9" circles from remaining phyllo leaves, using 9" cake pan for guide. Brush each circle with melted butter and layer one over the other on top of pie. With scissors, cut through leaves to make eight sections. Pour remaining melted butter on top. Place springform pan on jelly roll pan, to catch drippings. Bake 40–45 minutes or until crust is golden brown. Remove to rack; cool 10 minutes.

To serve: remove side of pan; with sharp knife cut into wedges. Can serve up to 16 if you cut more sections with scissors before cooking.

yield: 8 servings
KATHY CESARE

BAKED ZUCCHINI

- 6 cups thinly sliced unpared zucchini
- Salt
- 2 slightly beaten egg yolks
- 1 cup sour cream
- 2 tablespoons flour
- 2 stiffly beaten egg whites
- 1½ cups shredded sharp Cheddar natural cheese
- 6 slices crisply cooked bacon, crumbled
- ½ cup fine dry bread crumbs
- 1 tablespoon butter, melted

Pre-heat oven to 350°F. Simmer squash until just tender, drain, sprinkle with salt. Combine egg yolks, sour cream and flour. Fold in egg whites. Place half of zucchini in 12 × 7½ × 2 inch baking dish; top with half of egg mixture, half the cheese, and all the bacon. Repeat layers of zucchini, egg mixture, and cheese. Stir crumbs in melted butter and sprinkle over all. Bake for 20–25 minutes.

yield: 8 servings
MARY GRAHAM

TOMATOES PROVENÇALE

4	tomatoes, halved
¾	cup butter
¾	cup bread crumbs
1	large clove garlic, chopped
3	tablespoons chopped parsley
1	teaspoon Italian seasoning
	Salt and Pepper
	Parmesan cheese

Pre-heat oven to 350°F. Cream butter. Add bread crumbs, garlic, parsley, Italian seasoning, and salt and pepper to taste. Mix thoroughly and spread on tomatoes. Top with Parmesan cheese. Bake for 15 minutes. Run under broiler briefly to brown.

yield: 8 servings
MOLLIE WOEHLING

APPLE CAKE

3¼	cups flour
2	tablespoons baking soda
1½	teaspoons salt
½	teaspoon nutmeg
½	teaspoon cinnamon
3	large eggs
2½	cups sugar
¾	cup margarine, softened
5	cups chopped apples
1½	cups chopped walnuts, optional

Pre-heat oven to 350°F. Sift flour, baking soda, salt and spices. Beat the eggs, then add the sugar and margarine until well mixed. Gradually add the dry ingredients, mixing well between additions. Add the apples and nuts and mix by hand. Grease and flour a 10" tube pan. Place the batter evenly in the pan. Bake for 1 hour 15 minutes or until done. Let cake sit upright in pan 15-20 minutes before removing. Freezes well.

yield: 8-10 servings
MARY ANN FRIEDMAN

WHITE CLOUD CHEESECAKE WITH PEACHES

Crust:
- 1½ cups flour
- ¼ cup sugar
- Dash of salt
- ½ cup butter or margarine
- 1 egg yolk
- 1–2 tablespoons water

Filling:
- 2 cups cottage cheese
- 2 eggs, separated
- ¾ cup confectioners' sugar
- 2 tablespoons cornstarch
- 1 teaspoon grated lemon rind
- 1 teaspoon grated orange rind
- 1 teaspoon vanilla extract
- 1½ cups fresh peaches, peeled and sliced
- 1 tablespoon sugar

Pre-heat oven to 375°F. Prepare crust and fit into a 9" tart pan or springform pan, allowing 1½" of pastry to cover the sides of the pan. Prebake the crust for 15 minutes. Reduce oven temperature to 325°F. In a food processor or blender, mix the cottage cheese, egg yolks, ½ cup confectioners' sugar, cornstarch, lemon and orange rinds, and vanilla. Beat the egg whites until stiff peaks form. Beat in the remaining ¼ cup confectioners' sugar. Fold the egg whites into the cheese mixture. Arrange the sliced peaches on the bottom of the tart and sprinkle with 1 tablespoon granulated sugar. Spoon the cheesecake mixture on top of the peaches. Bake for 40 minutes. Cool the cake before serving.

yield: 8–10 servings
SIGRUN BERTHOLD

Waverly Women's Club Luncheons

"Will the meeting please come to order." Chairmen come and presidents go, but the urge to organize lingers on in the sociable nature of each man and woman. Pleasures may be intensified with sharing, skills improved by teaching, and good works made possible through the cooperation of many hands. In the 1800's, barns were raised, corn was husked, and coverlets were quilted, with sociable dividends augmenting the practical results. Today, the industrial revolution has given us mechanical assistants, and a money economy has allowed us to delegate unappealing tasks. We have been given time and energy for commitments and cooperation of a different sort amid the natural needs for interconnectedness.

In Abington Center of 1847 the International Order of Odd Fellows held regular meetings. In 1856 the Masons organized Waverly Lodge #301 and met in the large room above Bliss's store on Main Street. This group was very active and drew from a wide area this side of Leggets Gap. As the population grew, new lodges were organized by former members of the Waverly Lodge. By 1894 the original lodge had lost strength and numbers, and it was relocated in Clarks Summit. Forty members formed the Waverly Chapter of the International Order of Good Templars in 1866. This temperance organization attracted many prominent citizens of both sexes to its membership. They published two monthly papers, "Waverly Magazine" and "Ladies Templar." This effort must have exhausted them, for their charter was surrendered in 1880. By this time, the village had a flourishing chapter of the Patriotic Order of the Sons of America. Among other activites, it lent its support to a rousing production of "Ten Nights in a Barroom" with local talent and an enthusiastic audience at the Rink. In 1883, Waverly's Civil War hero, George Fell, was honored by his fellow veterans, when they included his name in the title of their newly formed Grand Army of the Republic Post #307. This organization evolved into the Veterans of Foreign Wars and moved to Clarks Summit as that town became the population center of the Abingtons.

By 1908, Waverly was a shadow of its earlier busy trading self and Methodist Minister Dr. L.C. Floyd felt that a social club would be a good idea for the ladies of his church. He must have been right, for a week after the opening meeting, the by-laws and constitution had been prepared, presented and adopted. The Women's Social Club was organized with three objects: Social, Benevolent and Intellectual. In 1915 the club joined the National Federation of Women's Clubs, and by 1930 the twice monthly teas were attended by thirty or more members. Although the meetings were informal (neither hats nor gloves were worn), the group had grown too large for all the homes but those of Mrs. Knapp and Mrs. Smith. So they decided to meet at the Community House once a month, and for lunch instead of tea, so as not to interfere with dinner at home.

The membership has continued to grow, to the limit of seventy imposed by the size of the scout room and adjacent kitchen; and then to one hundred allowed by the new kitchen near the gymnasium. The luncheons are lively and the programs widely varied, meeting the social and the intellectual objectives. The benevolent aspect has changed the most dramatically since the early days. From the beginning, donations were made to worthwhile causes such as the Community Chest, the Red Cross, Student Aid or local School Prizes. Then, in 1922, they gave the year-old Waverly Community House a contribution of ten dollars. Over the following years, the White Elephant Booth at the Annual Fair made a presentable profit. In 1950, it was transformed into a year-round Attic Shop. With outgrown clothing to sell or buy, it is run by committed club members, and furnished a whopping $10,000 donation to the Community House for the year 1984.

Back in 1912, the Waverly Baptist Church sponsored the King's Daughters whose activities were directed toward ministering to home-bound friends and raising money to support a home for the aged. They met regularly to quilt their own projects or commissioned works, and the results were wonderful to behold. Forty or fifty ladies produced a steady flow of beautifully stitched coverlets. But the membership dwindled and in 1980 they set aside needles and thread, and an era ended.

Coming together in 1956 and 1957, several

women who had recently moved to Waverly felt the need for a way to meet new friends and channel their abundant energies. The Waverly Women's Club couldn't squeeze any more members into their scout room luncheons, so a new club was formed under the aegis of the Community House. Marge Black won the contest to name the young organization "The Comm-Unity Club." Under the initial leadership of Betty Hopkins, Dona Shuptar, Zelda Bergman and Helen Hyde, the Club attracted many young women from all over the Abingtons to their lively evening meetings. They sponsored very successful craft bazaars and completely captivated many imaginations with a fashion show featuring wedding gowns from the past one hundred years. The funds raised benefit the Waverly Community House and other charities, and the young women lend their enthusiasms to the Waverly Library and other worthy enterprises.

    Organizations come and go as the needs of a population change, but one enduring feature of our social enterprise is the opportunity we seize to eat together. It is an ancient demonstration of trust and generosity, and it still contributes more than calories to those who share. So feed your spirits while you feed your bodies with some of these familiar favorites.

Waverly Women's Club Luncheons

ANNUAL JUNE PICNIC
CHICKEN CECI
FRUIT AND NUT BREAD
LEMON SQUARES

SEPTEMBER SEASON-OPENER
DIG DEEP SALAD
JORDAN MARSH BLUEBERRY MUFFINS
FROSTY MANDARIN DESSERT MOLD

CHRISTMAS LUNCHEON
PARTY SANDWICH
CRANBERRY-RASPBERRY MOLD
MERRY CHERRY CHEESECAKE BARS

ANNUAL JUNE PICNIC

CHICKEN CECI

12	ribs celery and leaves, diced
3	large red onions, diced
6	1-pound cans chick peas, drained and rinsed
1	pound baked ham, diced
2	sticks pepperoni, skinned and diced
25	whole cooked chicken breasts, boned, skinned and cut into bite-size pieces
2	cups salad oil
12	tablespoons vinegar
3	teaspoons Italian seasoning
	Salt and Pepper

In large bowl mix celery, onion, chick peas, ham, pepperoni and chicken. In another bowl blend oil, vinegar, Italian seasoning, salt and pepper. Pour over chicken mixture. Toss well and refrigerate overnight. Serve cold, surrounded by lettuce and garnished with quartered tomatoes and sliced cucumbers.

yield: 50 servings

FRUIT AND NUT BREAD

5	cups flour
4½	cups sugar
¾	teaspoon baking powder
3	teaspoons soda
2¼	teaspoons salt
3	teaspoons ground cloves
3	teaspoons cinnamon
1½	teaspoons nutmeg
1½	cups vegetable oil
1½	cups water
3	cups canned pumpkin or applesauce or mashed bananas
6	eggs
1½	cups coarsely chopped nuts

Pre-heat oven to 325°F. In large bowl, mix together the first 8 ingredients. Stir in oil, water, and pumpkin, applesauce or mashed bananas. Beat eggs lightly and stir into mixture; add nuts. Grease five 8" × 4" loaf pans. Fill each loaf pan two-thirds full of batter. Bake 1½ hours.

yield: Five 8" × 4" loaves

LEMON SQUARES

1	cup butter
2	cups flour
½	cup powdered sugar
¼	teaspoon salt
4	eggs
2	cups sugar
4	tablespoons flour
5	tablespoons lemon juice
	Grated rind of 1 lemon
	Powdered sugar

350°F. Blend first 4 ingredients and [press into] 3" pan. Bake 15 minutes. Do not [cool] 5 minutes. Beat together the remaining [ingredie]nts and pour over pastry. Bake for [... Re]move from oven and while warm, [sprinkle with p]owdered sugar. When cool, cut into [squares].

yield: 24 squares

SEPTEMBER SEASON OPENER

DIG DEEP SALAD

In a large glass salad bowl, layer first six ingredients in order given. Cover with mixture of well blended mayonnaise and sour cream. Sprinkle cheese over mayonnaise. Cover and refrigerate overnight. Remove from refrigerator half-hour before serving. Garnish with tomatoes and bacon. "Dig deep" to serve.

yield: 12 servings

1	10-ounce package fresh spinach
6	hard boiled eggs, sliced
1	pound thickly sliced imported ham, cut into finger-size pieces
1	head iceberg lettuce, shredded
2	pounds zucchini, sliced
2	Bermuda onions, thinly sliced
3	cups mayonnaise
1	cup sour cream
½	pound Swiss cheese, shredded
3	fresh tomatoes, sliced
½	pound bacon, cooked and crumbled

JORDAN MARSH BLUEBERRY MUFFINS

- ½ cup butter
- 1¼ cups sugar
- 2 eggs
- 2 cups flour
- 2 teaspoons baking powder
- ½ teaspoon salt
- ½ cup milk
- 1 pint blueberries
- 1 teaspoon vanilla
- 2 teaspoons sugar

Pre-heat oven to 375°F. Cream sugar and butter until fluffy. Add eggs one at a time beating after each addition. Sift dry ingredients and add to the sugar mixture, alternating with the milk. Mash ½ cup of the blueberries and add these along with the vanilla to the batter. Stir the remaining whole berries into the batter. Fill paper lined muffin tins ⅔rds full, sprinkle the tops with sugar. Bake for 25 to 30 minutes or until golden brown. Cool in the pan 30 minutes.

yield: 18–24 muffins

This recipe is from the Jordan Marsh Company of Boston and has long been a club favorite. The muffins are more like cupcakes than muffins as they are cake-like and fine textured.

FROSTY MANDARIN DESSERT MOLD

- 6 3-ounce packages orange gelatin
- 6 cups boiling water
- 3 cans mandarin oranges
- 3 pints orange sherbet

Dissolve gelatin in boiling water. Drain oranges and reserve juice. Add water to juice to make 3 cups. Add to gelatin. Chill until slightly thickened. Fold in sherbet and oranges. Pour into 4½ quart mold or individual serving dishes. Chill until firm.

yield: 24 servings

CHRISTMAS LUNCHEON

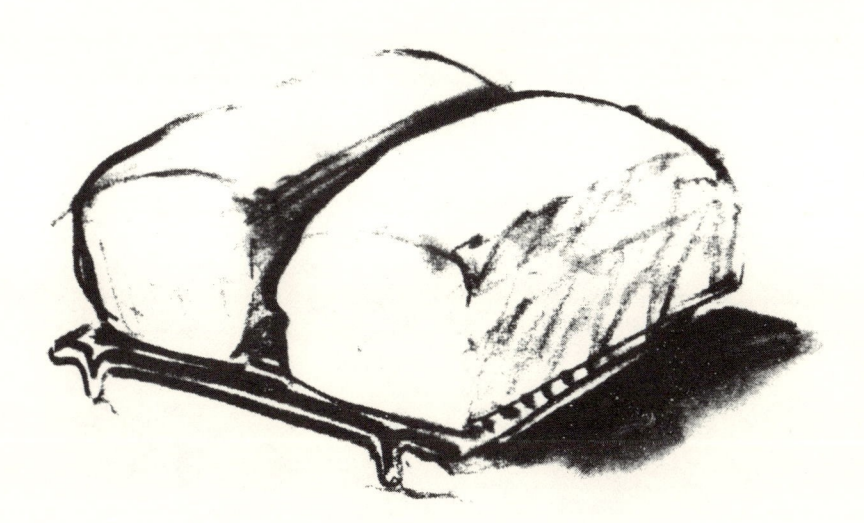

PARTY SANDWICH

Mix first six ingredients together, blending well. Place six slices of bread in a 9" x 14" pan. Top with ½ of the above mixture. Cover with the other six slices of bread and top with remainder of the mix. Blend sauce ingredients and pour the sauce over all. Top with grated cheese. Refrigerate overnight. Bake at 325°F. for about 1 hour. To serve, cut into individual squares and garnish with chopped parsley.

yield: 12 servings

- 3 cups cooked chicken breast, cut into bite size pieces
- ⅓ cup onion, chopped
- 2 hard-boiled eggs, chopped
- ⅓ cup green olives, chopped
- 1 cup mushrooms, chopped
- ½ cup Hellman's mayonnaise
- 12 slices bread, trimmed and buttered both sides
- 1½ cups Cheddar cheese, grated

Sauce:
- 1 cup sour cream
- 1 can cream of chicken soup, warmed first, undilluted

Garnish:
  Chopped parsley

CRANBERRY-RASPBERRY MOLD

Dissolve gelatin in boiling water. Add frozen raspberries. Stir until melted. Add rest of ingredients and mix well. Pour into 6-quart mold and refrigerate until set. Unmold onto serving platter.

yield: 12 servings

- 1 6-ounce package raspberry gelatin
- 1 3-ounce package lemon gelatin
- 2 cups boiling water
- 1 10-ounce package frozen raspberries
- 1 14-ounce jar cranberry-orange relish
- 1 1-pound 4-ounces can crushed pineapple

MERRY CHERRY CHEESECAKE BARS

Crust:
- ⅓ cup cold butter
- ⅓ cup firmly packed brown sugar
- 1 cup all purpose flour

Filling:
- 1 8-ounce package cream cheese, softened
- ¼ cup sugar
- 1 egg
- 1 tablespoon lemon juice
- ¼ cup each chopped glazed red and green cherries

Pre-heat oven to 350°F. In a one-quart mixer bowl, cut butter in chunks. Add brown sugar and flour, mix at low speed. Beat at medium speed, scraping sides of bowl, one minute. Reserve ½ cup crumb mixture for topping. Press remaining mixture into greased 8" square pan. Bake for 10-12 minutes. Beat cream cheese, sugar, egg and lemon juice until fluffy. Stir in chopped cherries. Spread filling over crust. Sprinkle with reserved crumb mixture. Continue baking 18-20 minutes or until filling is set. Cool and store in refrigerator.

yield: 36 bars

Dutch Treat Supper for Election Night

A voting booth has magical powers. When the curtain is closed, a citizen becomes a participant in one of civilization's greatest political experiments. The ankles that show beneath that green curtain belong to the free, fortunate and franchised. It is a privilege to take our children inside and show them how the magic works—translating a conviction into a vote.

In 1808, 48 residents (nearly 100% of the total male adult population) of Abington walked through the thick woods to the house of Robert Stone on the site of the Glen Oak Country Club. There were no roads for the Reynolds, Walls and Deans to travel down from the Factoryville area; the Phillips and Leaches from Chinchilla; the Baileys, Capwells and Halls from Dalton and Glenburn. Here they joined the Parkers, Clarks, Millers, Stones, Smiths, Tripps, Briggs, Lewins, Gardners, and Shermans from what is now Waverly, Fleetville and Scott. Some walked as far as twelve miles to cast a hard-earned and treasured vote. They reported thirty-six votes in that Presidential election for Federalist Charles C. Pinckney of South Carolina and twelve for Democrat James Madison of Virginia.

Many issues and many votes have been pondered and counted in the ensuing years in a community which continues to be predominantly conservative. The citizens were involved and they participated. When slavery and abolition were at issue in the middle years of the nineteenth century, union and secession were hotly argued. Pulpit, barbershops, and hotels along the Turnpike vibrated with debate. The center of Copperhead sentiment, sympathetic to the South and states' rights, was the store at Wallsville corners. In July, 1863, the *New York Daily News* and the papers of all the counties of Northeastern Pennsylvania published a resolution composed by Thomas Smith, Waverly lawyer, with Alvah Van Fleet, Uriah Gritman, Theron Finn and other Copperheads from Benton and Newton. This resolution was long and stated their outrage: ". . . if secession is treason in Jeff Davis, the records show that President Lincoln preached in Congress in 1848 what Jeff Davis is practicing in 1862 . . . Abraham Lincoln . . . is guilty of treason and . . . ought to be impeached . . ."

In rebuttal, a contingent from Waverly, Dalton and Glenburn met at the Glenburn Hotel overlooking the pond and waterfall, and passed a resolution that they were dedicated to saving the Union and would fight to the finish to do so. One night soon after, a liberty pole on the green near Glenburn Manor House was burned by the Copperheads. Though the ideals were passionately held, most action was orderly and the Abington voters favored Lincoln and, later, delivered a 200 vote majority for Ulysses S. Grant as Reconstruction President.

A century later, one of the most exciting events in local political life was the Presidential candidacy of an Abington friend and neighbor, Governor Bill Scranton. His integrity, commitment and warmth rallied the community behind him and renewed faith that "the process" could produce good men for hard times. Though his 1964 bid for the Presidency failed, he is a man who would serve the U.N., consult with the nation's and the world's leaders and still come back home and take out the garbage.

Alexis deToqueville observed that America is not a young nation but an ancient one. Come to this continent from very old civilizations, the people brought their beliefs and philosophies. But with a significant difference: they lived their beliefs here and put into practice in their daily lives what Europeans theorized and debated. This practice made Americans a political population long before the people of Old World nations had achieved the opportunity to participate in government.

We continue to vote our minds and mind our votes; and when all that democracy whets our appetites, we join our fellow citizens for a little non-partisan dining.

Dutch Treat Supper for Election Night

TOFU LASAGNE

MONTEZUMA PIE

SHRIMP ROCKEFELLER

BEANS BOURGUIGNON

CHICKEN WITH LEMON, ARTICHOKES AND OLIVES

SPINACH SALAD
LAYERED GARDEN SALAD
VEGETABLE AND PASTA SALAD
ROLLS
BROWN BREAD
SPOON BREAD
NATURAL APPLE CRISP
CARROT CAKE
LEMON MERINGUE PIE
CHOCOLATE BOURBON CAKE
PUMPKIN BARS

TOFU LASAGNA

¼	cup butter or margarine
½	pound fresh sliced mushrooms or small can drained mushrooms, pieces & stems can be used
3	cloves garlic, minced
½	teaspoon salt
⅛	teaspoon pepper
3	cups bottled spaghetti sauce
½	cup raw wheat germ
1	cup mashed tofu
¼	cup Parmesan cheese
½	pound shredded mozzarella cheese
¼	cup parsley, chopped
1	8-ounce package lasagna noodles, cooked

Pre-heat oven to 350°F. Melt butter; sauté mushrooms, garlic, salt and pepper. Cook 5 minutes. Add sauce and wheat germ. Heat thoroughly and keep warm. Combine mashed tofu and Parmesan cheese in small bowl. Set aside. Combine mozzarella cheese and parsley in another bowl. Place 1/3 of cooked noodles in baking dish 11¾" × 7½". Spread ½ of the tofu mixture on top; pour ⅓ of sauce over tofu and top with ⅓ of mozzarella. Repeat this layering and then make final layer of lasagna, sauce and mozzarella. Bake about 45 minutes. Let stand 10–15 minutes before cutting.

yield: 6 servings

You'll never miss the meat in this super supper recipe. Wheat germ and mushrooms make it extra special. You can find tofu in grocer's vegetable section or a health food store.

DOROTHY NOSAL

MONTEZUMA PIE

1½	pounds ground beef, browned
2	tablespoons oil
2	onions, chopped
1	clove garlic, minced
2	28-ounce cans tomatoes
	Salt and pepper to taste
2	4-ounce cans chopped mild green chiles
	oil for frying tortillas
12	corn tortillas
8	cups grated Montery Jack cheese (2 pounds)
2	cups sour cream

Pre-heat over to 350°F. Sauté onion and garlic in 2 tablespoons oil until transparent. Add tomatoes, salt and pepper and simmer for 10 minutes. Stir in chiles. Pour about ½ inch oil into small skillet and heat over medium heat. Dip each tortilla into hot oil just to soften, about 5 seconds. Remove from oil and drain on paper towels. In two 2½ quart casserole dishes, make layers of tortillas, sauce, beef, and grated cheese. Repeat layers, ending with cheese. Baked uncovered for 30 minutes. Top with sour cream just before serving.

yield: 8 servings
ANN CHAMBERLIN

SHRIMP ROCKEFELLER

- ½ pound spinach, washed and well drained then dried in a towel
- 6 little green onions
- ½ head lettuce (makes 2 cups chopped)
- 1½ stalks celery
- 1 clove garlic
- ½ cup parsley
- ½ cup butter
- 1 tablespoon Worcestershire sauce
- 2 teaspoons anchovy paste
- 1½ teaspoons salt
- ⅛ teaspoon Tabasco sauce
- ½ cup bread crumbs
- 2 pounds cooked shrimp

Sauce:
- 3 tablespoons butter
- 3 tablespoons flour
- 1½ cups milk
- ¼ teaspoon Worcestershire sauce
- 3 tablespoons grated Parmesan cheese
- ¾ teaspoon salt
- ⅛ teaspoon pepper

Topping:
- ½ cup buttered cracker crumbs

Pre-heat over to 350°F. Chop all vegetables very fine. Heat together butter, Worcestershire sauce, anchovy paste, salt and Tabasco sauce. Add chopped greens to the seasoned mixture and simmer 10 minutes. Add ½ cup bread crumbs. Spread the greens over the bottom of shallow baking dish or 6 scallop shells. Cover with 2 pounds of cooked shrimp. Pour sauce over shrimp. Sprinkle with buttered cracker crumbs. Bake 20 minutes until sauce bubbles up and top browns. Serve very hot.

Sauce: Melt butter in saucepan. Stir in flour until smooth. Gradually add milk. Stir over low heat until thickened. Add seasonings and cheese.

yield: 6 servings
MARG AYDELOTT

BEANS BOURGUIGNON

8	medium onions
4	tablespoons butter or margarine
2	cups claret or dry red wine
6	cups cooked red kidney beans: 30-ounce cans
2	teaspoons Worcestershire sauce
¼	cup red wine
2	tablespoons butter
½	cup fresh chives, parsley, and/or chervil or combination of all, chopped

Slice onions thinly. Sauté in butter until transparent. Simmer with wine until it is reduced to half. Cook beans and onions together for 15 minutes, until the sauce thickens. Just before serving add Worcestershire sauce, wine, butter. Garnish with fresh chopped herbs. May be kept warm on top of stove or in a warm 200°F. oven for an hour or more.

yield: 6 servings
ROSAMOND PECK

CHICKEN WITH LEMONS, ARTICHOKES AND OLIVES

2	2½ to 3 pound chickens, quartered
½	cup vegetable or olive oil
6	cloves garlic, peeled and crushed
3	cups chopped onion
4	ripe tomatoes quartered; can be peeled or cut smaller
¾	cup chicken broth
	Pinch of salt
1	teaspoon freshly ground pepper
2	teaspoons ground ginger
1	teaspoon turmeric
½	teaspoon coriander, ground
2	teaspoons parsley, fresh if possible
2	cups salad olives, cut in small pieces
1	8½-ounce can artichoke hearts quartered
1	lemon cut into small pieces

Pre-heat oven to 325°F. Wash the chicken. Brown chicken in hot oil and add garlic and onion and stir fry for 3-4 minutes. Cook over medium heat, turning pieces for 5-8 minutes. Add tomatoes and reduce pan juices. Remove chicken pieces to a casserole large enough to hold all the pieces easily. Add chicken broth to juices in pan. When thick add all the seasonings and blend well for several minutes. Spread juices over chicken and place, covered, in oven for about an hour. Test to see if chicken is done. Add olives, artichoke hearts and lemon pieces and return to oven for 15 minutes.

This recipe can be adjusted for more or less individuals to be served. It can be held in a low oven for another 15-30 minutes and any leftovers are delicious the next day. If you prefer wine or half and half, to chicken broth, either works very well.

yield: 8 servings
FODDY VIPOND

SPINACH SALAD

Salad:
- 1 package fresh spinach
- 1 can bean sprouts, drained
- 1 can water chestnuts, sliced
- 2-4 hard boiled eggs, sliced
- ½ pound bacon, fried and crumbled
- ½ cup mushrooms, sliced

Dressing:
- 1 cup oil
- ¾ cups sugar
- ¼ cup white wine vinegar
- 1 tablespoon Worcestershire sauce
- 1 medium onion, chopped

Mix dressing ingredients in blender 24 hours before using. Clean and remove large stems from spinach. Drain, dry, and chill to crisp. Toss spinach lightly with remaining ingredients and add dressing. Toss again.

yield: 8 servings
PAULA LOWE

LAYERED GARDEN SALAD

- 1 head iceberg lettuce
- 1 package frozen peas, cooked
- 1 small red onion, chopped
- 3 hard boiled eggs, sliced
- 6-8 slices bacon, cooked and crumbled
- ¾ cup grated Cheddar cheese
- Mayonnaise
- 2 tomatoes, sliced

Layer the above ingredients in a glass bowl or rectangular glass dish, beginning with lettuce, then peas, onions, eggs, bacon, cheese. Spread with mayonnaise, like a frosting, and top with tomato slices. Refrigerate, covered, overnight. Do not toss.

yield: 6 servings
JUDY DIXON

VEGETABLE AND PASTA SALAD

6-8	ripe tomatoes, peeled, seeded, coarsely chopped
½	pound mozzarella cheese, coarsely shredded
1	jar marinated artichoke hearts, marinade reserved
5	tablespoons olive oil
2	cloves garlic, minced
1	tablespoon minced fresh parsley
	Salt and pepper to taste
1	pound pasta: spirelli are best

Combine all ingredients except pasta and let the sauce stand at least one hour. Cook pasta in salted water until done. Drain. Combine with sauce immediately and toss until cheese melts. Serve immediately. You may add some of the reserved marinade for flavor and seasonings. This salad is great when served immediately after preparing but is equally as good when served chilled after being refrigerated.

yield: 6 servings
LESLEE J. DOHERTY

ROLLS

1½	cups milk
½	cup sugar
¾	cups shortening
4	tablespoons yeast
½	cup tepid water
1	egg, beaten
½	teaspoon salt
6	cups flour

Combine milk, sugar and shortening in a saucepan. Heat over low heat until shortening melts. Shake yeast on top of tepid water. Pour milk mixture into a mixer and mix until milk cools to about 120 degrees. Add yeast, eggs and flour to milk all at once and mix with a dough hook. Dough is mixed enough when it comes away from the sides. You may have to use a little more flour. Set on a floured surface and let rise until it has doubled. Pre-heat oven to 425°F. Roll dough into small balls and put on greased pans an inch apart. Let rise 15 to 20 minutes before baking. Bake for 10 minutes.

yield: 54 rolls
RON WHITAKER

BROWN BREAD

½	cup molasses
1½	cups sour milk
½	cup sugar
½	teaspoon salt
1	teaspoon baking soda
3	cups whole wheat flour

Pre-heat oven to 350°F. Put liquids, sugar, salt and soda in bowl. Add flour and mix well. Bake in greased 9" × 5" × 3" loaf pan for one hour. Cool before slicing.

yield: One 9" × 5" loaf
MARGARET HULL

SPOON BREAD

- 2 cups scalded milk
- ½ cup cornmeal
- ½ teaspoon baking powder
- 1 teaspoon salt
- 3 eggs, separated
- 2 tablespoons oil

Pre-heat oven to 375°F. In double boiler, stir cornmeal gradually into milk and cook until consistency of mush. Add baking powder, salt and egg yolks. Fold in stiffly beaten egg whites. Pour into hot, greased baking dish, 1 quart or larger. Bake for 30 minutes.

yield: 6 servings
LAURA PECK

NATURAL APPLE CRISP

- 6 large apples, peeled and sliced
- ¼ cup apple juice
- 1 cup rolled oats, uncooked
- ⅓ cup wholewheat flour
- ½ cup corn oil
- ⅛ cup water
- 1 teaspoon cinnamon

Pre-heat oven to 350°F. Prepare apples and layer in buttered loaf pan, and then pour apple juice over apples. Mix remaining ingredients together and spread over apples. Bake for 30 minutes. May be served warm or cold.

yield: 6 servings
CORAL AND LT. GOVERNOR BILL SCRANTON

CARROT CAKE

- 4 eggs
- 1½ cups oil
- 2 cups sugar
- 3 cups shredded carrots
- 2 cups flour
- 2 teaspoons cinnamon
- 1 teaspoon baking soda
- 1 teaspoon salt
- Dash each of nutmeg and cloves

Pre-heat oven to 350°F. Beat eggs slightly and blend in all other ingredients. Bake for 45 minutes in two 9" round pans, or for 60 minutes in a 9" × 13" pan. Cool before frosting and then refrigerate. Freezes well. Can be done ahead.

yield: 12 servings
IRENE REID

Frosting:
- 8 ounces cream cheese
- ¼ pound butter
- 1 box confectioners' sugar
- 2 teaspoons vanilla
- 2 cups chopped nuts, optional

LEMON MERINGUE PIE

Crust:
- 1 cup flour
- ½ teaspoon salt
- ⅓ cup shortening
- 2-3 tablespoons water

Lemon Filling:
- 7 tablespoons cornstarch
- 1½ cups sugar
- ½ teaspoon salt
- 2 cups boiling water
- 3 egg yolks
- ¼ cup lemon juice
- 2 tablespoons butter
- 1 tablespoon grated lemon rind

Meringue:
- 3 egg whites
- 6 tablespoons sugar

Crust: Pre-heat oven to 450°F. Sift together flour and salt. Cut in shortening. Add 2 to 3 tablespoons water until dough is moist. Roll out to about ⅛" thickness. Put in 9" pie plate and prick bottom and sides. Bake for 12 to 15 minutes. Cool completely.

Filling: Combine cornstarch, sugar and salt. Add 2 cups boiling water and cook until thick and transparent, stirring constantly. Add 3 egg yolks, slightly beaten, into which a little of the hot mixture has been added. Cook 2 minutes longer, stirring constantly. Blend in lemon juice, butter and lemon rind. Cool and turn into the pie shell.

Meringue: Pre-heat oven to 350°F. Beat egg whites until they form mounds, and add sugar, one tablespoon at a time. Spread over pie filling evenly. Bake 10 minutes or until golden brown.

yield: 8 servings
ELLIE HYDE

CHOCOLATE BOURBON CAKE

- 2 cups butter
- 1 cup sugar
- 1 cup powdered sugar
- 12 eggs, separated
- 4 ounces unsweetened chocolate, melted
- 1 teaspoon vanilla
- 1 cup chopped pecans
- 12 double lady fingers
- 4 dozen macaroons, broken and soaked in ½ cup bourbon
- 1½ cups heavy cream, whipped

Cream butter and sugars until light and fluffy. Beat egg yolks until light and blend into butter mixture. Beat in chocolate; add vanilla and pecans. Beat egg whites stiff but not dry. Fold into chocolate mixture. Line a 10" springform pan around sides with split lady fingers. Alternate layers of soaked macaroons and chocolate mixture over lady fingers. Chill overnight. Remove sides of springform pan and cover top with whipped cream. If frozen, add whipped cream after defrosting. Can be done ahead. Can be frozen (without whipped cream on top). Takes 30 minutes to prepare plus chilling time.

yield: 16-18 servings
IRENE REID

PUMPKIN BARS

- 4 eggs
- 1 2/3 cups granulated sugar
- 1 cup oil
- 1 16-ounce can or 1 1/3 cups pumpkin
- 2 cups flour
- 2 teaspoons baking powder
- 2 teaspoons ground cinnamon
- 1 teaspoon salt
- 1 teaspoon baking soda

Topping:
- 1 3-ounce package cream cheese, softened
- 1/2 cup butter
- 1 teaspoon vanilla
- 2 cups confectioners' sugar

Pre-heat oven to 350°F. Mix eggs, granulated sugar, oil and pumpkin in blender. Set aside. Mix together flour, baking powder, cinnamon, salt and baking soda and add to pumpkin mixture. Spread into 15" × 10" × 1" pan and bake for 25 to 30 minutes or spread in 13" × 9" × 2" pan and bake for 50 minutes. Cool.

Topping: Cream together cream cheese and butter. Stir in vanilla. Add sugar a little at a time. Beat well. Spread over cooled bars.

yield: 3 or 4 dozen pieces

When the leaves begin to fall it is a reminder to us to ascend to the attic and get down our pumpkin man. He is then stuffed with dry leaves that have fallen from the beautiful huge maples that reside at the back of the Waverly Community House.

Ever since my children were small, the pumpkin man stands on our porch and we wait with great anticipation for the Waverly Elementary School to have their annual Halloween Parade.

Such an array of hobgoblins, fairies and the latest movie characters appear walking around the Comm. The children are so eager to say hello to people in the crowd they know.

We live near a wonderful structure known as, "The Comm".

JEANNE BROWNING

WAVERLY 1873

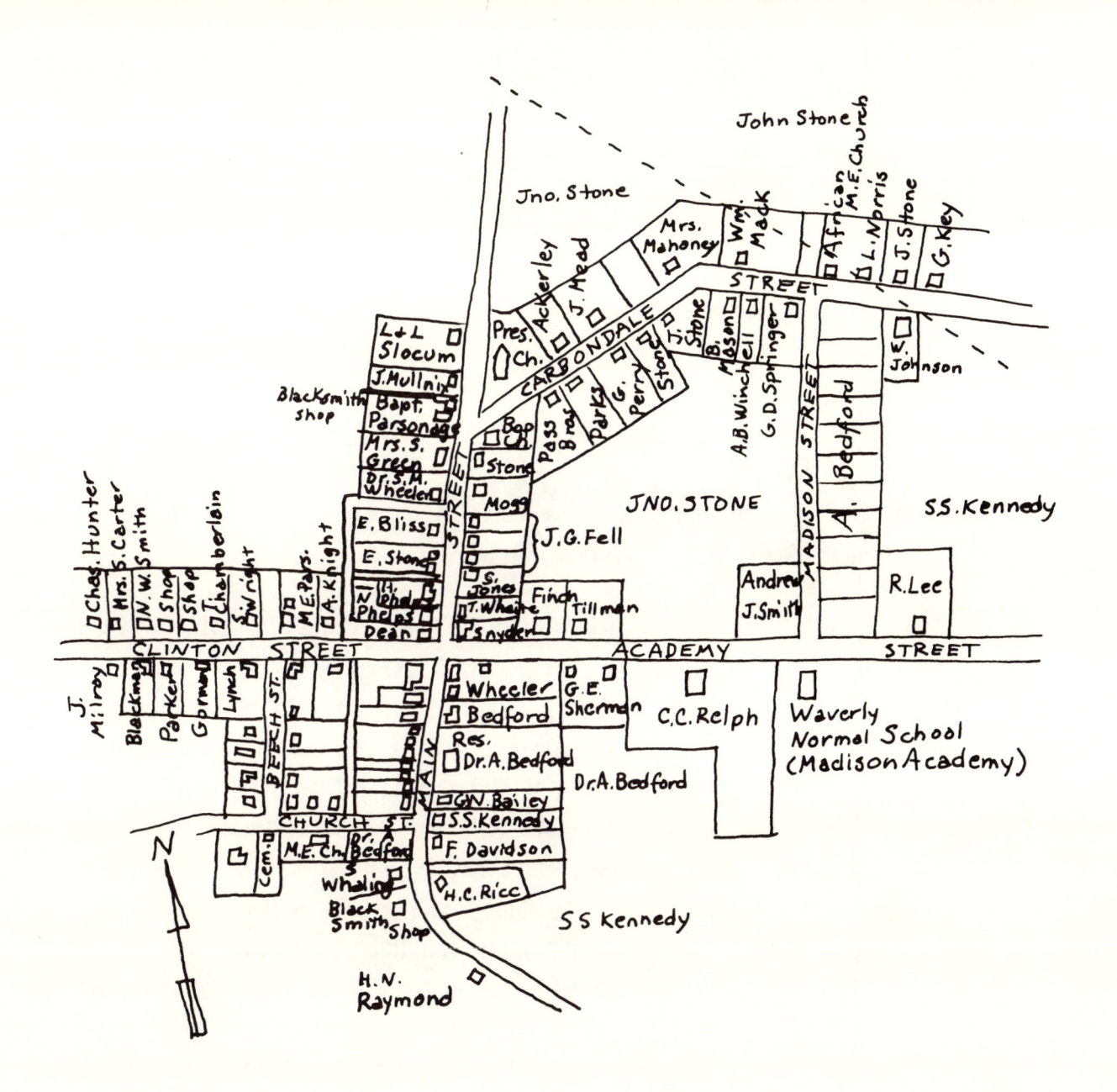

Winter

IN WINTER, THE ABINGTON HILLS ARE REMARKABLY PURPLE. And when the late afternoon sun brightens the snow, the buds and branches glow with the health of hidden life. It's good to be alive and aware of these beauties, and to be heading for hot soup. Ed Parkinson's painting says all these things with breathtaking precision.

These beautiful woods are home to many creatures. Alert and cautious, camouflaged and elusive, they are rarely encountered. Winter is the time hunters seek them out. The camaraderie developed by tracking, stalking and waiting, creates a uniquely exhilirating mystique for the hunters who participate. The deer which browse on foundation plantings and lettuce all the rest of the year, magically know when to evaporate from woods and field. The rabbits who thrive on petunias learn to step lively, ahead of the baying hounds. Grouse and pheasant in the cornfield are startled into throb-

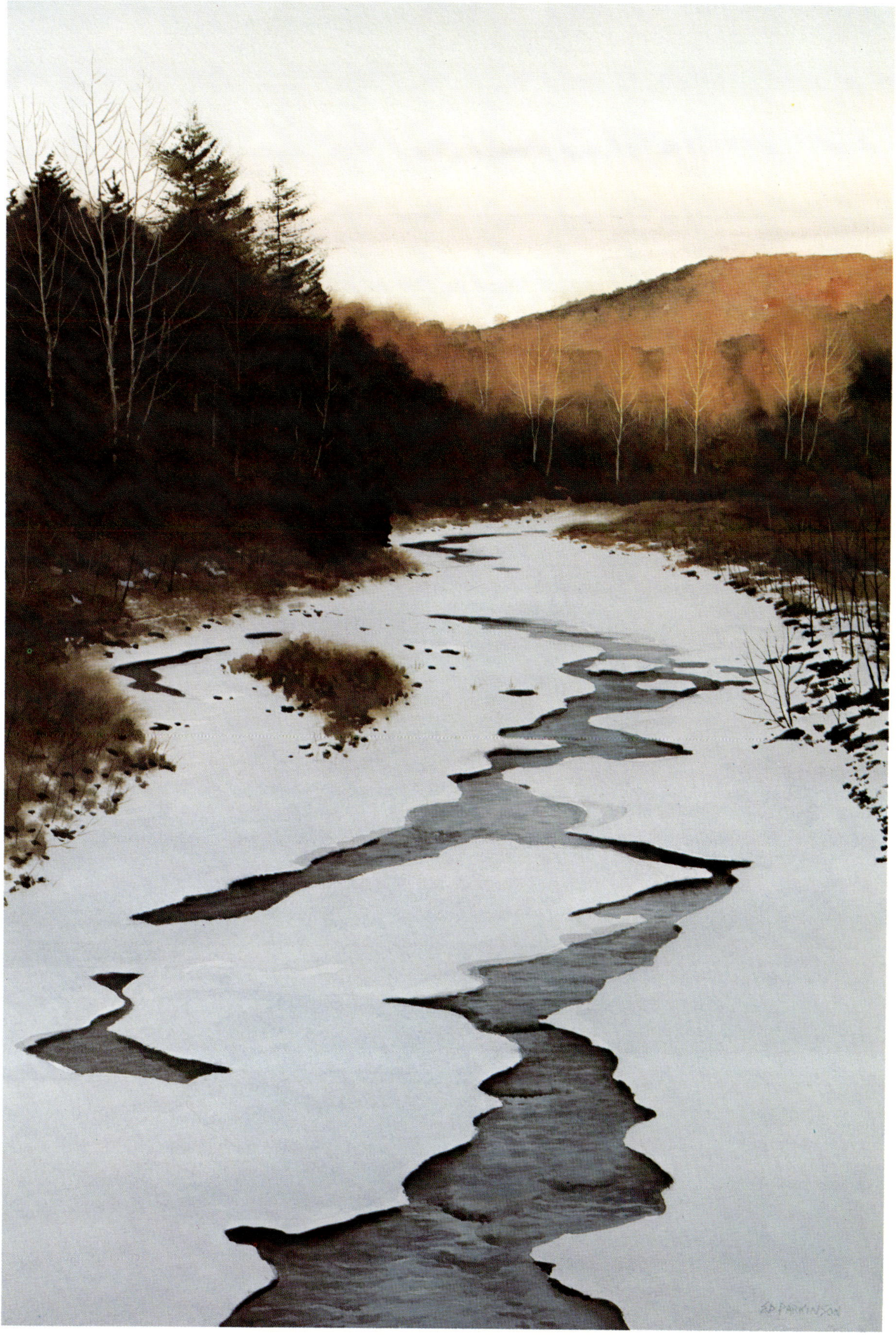
ED PARKINSON

bing flight by dogs and firearms. A caucus of crows disperses when it sees the first glint of a gun. Foxes and coons are hunted at night by excited long-legged dogs and stumbling, eager men. And not too far away, black bears can be shot before they settle down for their long winter's nap.

Of all these creatures, only the deer herd boasts greater numbers today than it did in colonial days, attributable to the close management of the Pennsylvania Game Commission. Although no Indians lived here, this area was designated as hunting territory by the Iroquois councils. The earliest white visitors to the Abingtons probably came to trap beaver in the many clear streams and willow-edged ponds, to sell the pelts for the omnipresent beaver hat. The deer, rabbits and birds that the early settlers killed were needed additions to their garden produce for the health and growth of the families scattered sparsely through the "howling wilderness."

Jonathan Hall left his home in Glenburn, near what is now Waterford Road, and walked through the woods to visit his sister Polly Miller, who lived with her husband John on the hill below the present Hickory Grove Cemetery. When Jonathan reached what is now the Community House square, he was startled by a bear which he promptly shot and killed. He barely had time to reload before a second bear was upon him and his accurate shooting not only saved his life, but provided hearty feasting for many families of Abington.

In these early years of the 1800's even ordinary daily tasks were fraught with peril. The nearest mill was on Roaring Brook, all the way down at Slocum Hollow in the Lackawanna Valley. Our forebears had to carry their corn, wheat and oats to be ground into meal and flour. In 1799 Ephraim Leach settled in the flat land along Legget's Creek in what is now Chinchilla. He remembered, "Many a time, in passing through the notch with my little grist upon my shoulders, have I kept the wolves at bay with a long club which I kept swinging vigorously as they came growling around me, and to my faithful club, often bitten and broken, have I been indebted for my life." And on another occasion, he kept the wolves at bay by thrumming on a saw blade which he was carrying through the dark woods path.

Even without woods, winter is a dark time of year. We no longer face serious threats from wild animals or starvation and cold. But, in the midst of our comforts, modern man faces isolation and loneliness. With all of our technical know-how, we often don't know how to care for each other in matters that cannot be seen, measured or bought. And it is too important to leave it to others, to the experts, the specialists. As Saint-Exupery's fox told the Little Prince, "It is only with the heart that one can see rightly; what is essential is invisible to the eye."

Our own hearts can see rightly, even on dark and dreary days; guided by the invisible, we can bring a ray of sunshine into another life and our own. No wonder that winter is the season of two great festivals of light, Christmas and Channukah. Everything needs light to grow, inside and out. And it is a joy to celebrate.

The beauties of our countryside are also worthy of celebration. The first lines of Jay Parini's poem, "Ice Fishing," sets a familiar scene:

> The snow ticks off my cheeks, I raise my eyes,
> and flakes like houseflies buzz against my gaze.
> The ice squeaks underfoot as I go out
> to fish on Hatchet Pond through frozen gauze.
>
> The day whites out whichever way I look.
> Big hemlocks ring the pond, their branches light
> as dove wings, dropping feathers to the ground . . .

Skiing or sledding, skating or gathering greens for Christmas, ice fishing or hunting or just sitting on a stump to watch the crows or the snow fly; any activity which lures us out into the cold fresh air is something to be glad about. And, as the December night falls like a cold ax, a warm home to return to is cause to be gladder still.

Grandma's Kitchen

Grandma's kitchen evokes the thrift of an economy that saw a very close connection between the efforts of the farmer in the field and those of the cook in the kitchen and pantry. What you grew and preserved was what you and yours ate.

In 1801 Stephen Parker came to Abington with his two sons and cleared land, planted wheat and potatoes, and built a log cabin. After the harvest, the cabin was filled with the grain and potatoes, and they returned to Connecticut to spend the winter preparing for the move to this new home on Parker Hill. In the spring, he and his family left their Connecticut home and journeyed in a one-ox cart, loaded with trunks and a few pieces of furniture and high hopes. Imagine their feelings when they opened the cabin to find rodents had eaten all the riches of last fall's harvest, and they were without food or seed! The Clarks, neighbors up the hill, helped them out with grain and seed potatoes for the spring planting.

The nearest market was Wilkes-Barre, twenty-five miles through the dark forest. If kitchen, cellar or barn didn't have it, a family went without or turned to a neighbor. When Polly Hall Miller needed a quart of molasses, she received some from a nearby household; in payment, she borrowed a spinning wheel and spun two skeins of linen thread from the flax her husband John had grown.

The pioneers of Abington provided the markets in Wilkes-Barre, Scranton, New York or Philadelphia with quantities of good quality maple sugar, butter, cheese, wool, domestic flannels and linens, oats, horses, cattle and sheep. In 1830, John Miller, Stephen Parker and John Stone built the first store on the northwest corner of the intersection of the Turnpike and the path to Bailey's Hollow, present-day Main and Clinton Streets. For the next fifty years Waverly continued to grow as the trading center of a productive farming community. What is now the Community House Square was a commercial center with hotel, drug store, harness shop, hardware store, barbershop, dressmaker and milliner and general store. Route 407 was the Philadelphia and Great Bend Turnpike, full of traffic, to and from markets, near and far. There were several stores to augment supplies of the Victorian pantries in the village. The countryside was full of grazing livestock and fields of grain, ample barns of hay, and cool spring houses for milk. Cellars housed root vegetables, barrels of flour and shelves of preserves. Grandma's kitchens produced butter from the churn, candles from the mold, sauerkraut from the crock, jelly from the bag, jams from the kettle, and bread, warm and aromatic, from the oven.

Present day Waverly kitchens are just as full of good smells as today's cooks prepare treats to be sold at the traditional annual Grandma's Kitchen sale at the Community House.

Grandma's Kitchen

CRUMB CAKE

HELEN GURLEY BROWNIES

MOIST AND DELICIOUS CHOCOLATE CAKE

PEANUT BUTTER COOKIES

ORANGE POUR CAKE

CHOCOLATE CHIP RICE KRISPIE COOKIES

WELSH COOKIES
CHRISTMAS GINGERBREAD MEN
ZUCCHINI MUFFINS
BROWN BREAD
STREUDEL
PEANUT BRITTLE
TERRIBLE TRUFFLES
SUGARED WALNUTS
NEVER FAIL PEANUT BUTTER FUDGE
ZUCCHINI PICKLES
PICKLED PEPPERS
SPICED CRAB APPLES
JALAPEÑO JELLY

CRUMB CAKE

1½	cup light brown sugar
2	cups sifted flour
½	cup shortening
1	egg
1	cup buttermilk
1	teaspoon baking soda
1	teaspoon cinnamon
½	teaspoon nutmeg
½	teaspoon salt
1	teaspoon vanilla

Pre-heat oven to 350°F. Combine brown sugar, flour and shortening to make crumbs. Reserve ½ cup crumbs. Add rest of ingredients to remaining crumbs. Mix together just until blended, not smooth. Pour into a 9" cake or pie pan, ungreased. Put reserved crumbs on top and bake for 45 minutes.

yield: 10–13 servings

Gail Bower got this recipe from a Pennsylvania Dutch college friend. Gail sent her son Eric to visit one crisp fall Saturday morning, along with warm crumb cake in hand. The aroma is marvelous, but only a hint of the wonderful taste.

MARY JOY HAVEY

HELEN GURLEY BROWNIES

4	ounces unsweetened chocolate, broken into bits
¼	pound unsalted butter
2	cups sugar
4	eggs, beaten
¼	teaspoon salt
1	teaspoon vanilla extract
1	cup sifted all-purpose flour
1	cup coarsely chopped walnuts

Pre-heat oven to 325°F. Grease and flour a 9" square baking pan. In a double boiler, melt chocolate with butter over hot, not simmering water until smooth. Cool. In a large bowl combine sugar, eggs, and salt and beat until light and smooth. Stir the chocolate-butter mixture into the eggs and sugar. Add the vanilla and beat until smooth. Add the flour, stirring just enough to make mixture smooth again. Gently fold in nuts. Pour into prepared pan. Bake for 30 minutes.

yield: 12 to 15
PAT ATKINS

MOIST AND DELICIOUS CHOCOLATE CAKE

- 4 squares chocolate
- ½ cup butter: do not use margarine
- 1 cup boiling water
- 2 cups sugar
- 3 eggs, well beaten
- ½ cup milk
- 2 cups all purpose flour
- ¾ teaspoon salt
- 1¼ teaspoon baking soda
- 1 tablespoon vanilla

Pre-heat oven to 325°F. Melt chocolate and butter with boiling water in large sauce pan over low heat. Mix until smooth and remove from heat. Stir in sugar. Beat eggs together with milk and mix into chocolate mixture with wire whisk. Stir in flour, salt and soda until well combined. Stir in vanilla last. Pour into well-greased 9" × 13" pan. Bake for 45 minutes. Cool in pan.

yield: 9" × 13" cake

This cake is our family's favorite. We like it best un-iced, served topped with ice cream. This recipe came from Dona Shuptar, former resident of Waverly, now living in Korea. Quick and easily made right in the saucepan used for melting chocolate. It takes 1½ times the recipe if you want to make a double 9" layer cake.

MARTHA ADAMS

PEANUT BUTTER COOKIES

- 1 cup shortening: ½ cup margarine; ½ cup crisco
- 1 cup granulated sugar
- 1 cup brown sugar
- 2 eggs, beaten
- 1 cup smooth-style peanut butter
- 1 teaspoon vanilla
- 3 cups sifted all purpose flour
- 2 teaspoons baking soda
- ¼ teaspoon salt

Preheat oven to 350°F. Cream shortening well with sugars. Add eggs and beat until light. Add peanut butter and vanilla and beat well. Add dry ingredients slowly - mixture becomes thick. Place heaping teaspoon of cookie dough on ungreased cookie sheet. With a fork press down dough in a criss-cross fashion. Bake approximately ten minutes until lightly browned. Freeze well.

yield: 4 dozen
BARBARA VON STORCH

ORANGE POUR CAKE

- ½ cup butter
- 2 cups flour
- 2 eggs
- 1 cup sugar
- 1 teaspoon baking soda
- 1 tablespoon grated orange zest
- ¾ cup sour cream
- ½ cup chopped nuts, optional

Topping:
- ½ cup sugar
- ¼ cup orange juice
- 1 tablespoon grated orange zest

Pre-heat oven to 375°F. Cream butter with 2 teaspoons flour. Beat eggs, add sugar and beat until combined. Mix well with butter mixture. Sift remaining flour with baking soda. Add slowly to egg mixture, blending well. Add orange zest, sour cream and nuts. Pour into buttered 9" × 4" loaf pan or 3-4 cup mold. Bake for 50 minutes. Prepare topping by blending all ingredients together. Remove cake from oven and while hot, pour topping over cake. Un-mold when completely cool.

yield: 1 loaf
KATHLEEN C. GRAFF

CHOCOLATE CHIP-RICE KRISPIE COOKIES

- 1 cup margarine
- 1 cup brown sugar
- 1 cup white sugar
- 1 egg
- 1 cup Rice Krispies
- 1 cup oatmeal
- 1 cup oil
- 1 teaspoon salt
- 1 teaspoon soda
- 1 teaspoon vanilla
- 3½ cup flour
- 1 large package mini-chocolate chips
- ½ cup nut meats

Pre-heat oven to 375°F. Cream butter and sugars. Add remaining ingredients. Drop by the spoonful onto ungreased cookie sheet. Bake until brown.

yield: 4 dozen
JOANNE DULWORTH

WELSH COOKIES

- 1 cup butter
- 1 cup lard
- 2 cups sugar
- ½ cup milk
- 3 eggs
- 4 cups flour
- 1 teaspoon salt
- 1 teaspoon soda
- 1 teaspoon cream of tartar
- 2 teaspoons nutmeg
- 2 teaspoons baking powder
- 2 cups currants

Cream together first three ingredients. Stir in milk. Add one egg at a time and mix well. Sift dry ingredients together and add to butter mixture. Stir in currants. Roll out ½" thick and cut into 2" to 3" rounds. Bake on griddle at medium heat, making sure to turn to cook on both sides. May be dusted with powdered sugar when cool.

yield: 2 dozen
LAURA PECK

CHRISTMAS GINGERBREAD MEN TO HANG ON TREE

- 1 cup molasses
- ½ cup sugar
- 1 cup butter or margarine
- 2 cups whole wheat pastry flour
- 2 cups unbleached flour
- 1 teaspoon baking soda
- 1 teaspoon salt
- 1 teaspoon ground cloves
- 1 teaspoon cinnamon
- 1 teaspoon nutmeg
- 1 teaspoon ginger

Pre-heat oven to 375°F. Heat molasses to boil in large saucepan. Remove from heat. Add sugar and shortening to heated molasses. Sift dry ingredients together and add to molasses mixture. Chill several hours or overnight. Dust counter with sifted confectioners sugar so dough will not stick and get tough. Roll out to ⅛" to ¼" thickness. Cut into gingerbread man shape. Put on greased cookie sheet. Bake for 5 to 8 minutes. Make hole in head for hanging while still soft after removing from oven and insert either ribbon or ornament hanger to be used for hanging. Add raisin eyes and buttons before cooking, or decorate when cool with butter cream icing in different colors using pastry tube.

Butter Cream Icing:
- ¼ cup butter, or margarine if it will be hung on tree
- 2 cups confectioners sugar, well sifted
- 1 teaspoon vanilla
- 2 tablespoons cream
- Food color as desired

Cream butter and sugar. Combine vanilla and cream and add gradually to well creamed butter and sugar. Add food coloring as desired. Cover unused portions while using pastry tube so that icing will not get crusty and clog decorating tips.

yield: Depends on sizes and shapes of cookies

You can add hats, mittens, boots, overalls, hair, smiles, etc. with your butter cream icing. Your imagination is your only limit. These are a favorite family tradition for hanging on our Christmas tree.

ABBY PECK

ZUCCHINI MUFFINS

- 4 eggs
- 2 cups sugar
- 1 cup Wesson oil
- 1 teaspoon vanilla
- 3½ cups flour
- 1½ teaspoon baking soda
- 1½ teaspoon salt
- 1 teaspoon cinnamon
- ¾ teaspoon baking powder
- 2 cups zucchini, grated and drained

Pre-heat oven to 350°F. Beat eggs until frothy, then beat in sugar until mixture is thick and lemon colored. Beat in the oil and vanilla. Beat in remaining ingredients. Either line muffin tins with paper baking cups or grease well. Fill pans half full, and bake for 20 minutes or until tests done.

yield: 30 muffins

Very light and moist and they freeze beautifully.

SHARON WHITAKER

BROWN BREAD ✓ Excellent

Pre-heat oven to 350°F. Combine molasses and sugar. Combine milk and soda and add to molasses. Mix salt and whole wheat flour and add to liquid, stir well. Combine nuts, raisins and ¼ cup flour. Add to batter. Mix well. Put in greased 8" × 4" pan or 3 small 5" × 2" pans and bake for 1 hour for 8" × 4" loaf. If using smaller pans, check after 45 minutes for doneness. Toothpick inserted in loaf should come out clean when done. Great with baked beans. Also delicious with cream cheese for tea or dessert.

½	cup molasses
¼	cup sugar
1	cup milk
1	teaspoon soda
1	teaspoon salt
2	cups whole wheat flour
⅓	cup walnuts, chopped
1	cup raisins
¼	cup whole wheat flour

yield: One 8" × 4" loaf
or three (5 or 6) 5" × 2" loaves
JEANNE GEARHART

STREUDEL

Pre-heat oven to 350°F. Blend first three ingredients together thoroughly. If possible use food processor. Divide into four balls. Roll each out as thin as possible. Spread each with approximately 3 ounces of jam. Mix filling ingredients together and sprinkle ¼ of the filling on each streudel. Roll up as a jelly roll and close ends. Bake for one hour until brown. Sprinkle with confectioner's sugar. Slice on the diagonal while warm. This freezes very well and is even great served frozen when it is nice and chewy. It will keep for months in freezer.

Dough:
½	pound cream cheese
½	pound butter
2 ¼	cups flour

Jam Spread:
12	ounces apricot jam

Filling:
1 ½	cups chopped walnuts
1 ½	cups raisins
1 ½	cups sugar
4	Ritz crackers, crushed
¼	cup orange juice
	Confectioners' sugar

yield: 4 Streudels
15 pieces in each
JODI ROGALLA

PEANUT BRITTLE

2 cups granulated sugar
½ cup water
1 cup white corn syrup
3 cups raw whole peanuts
1 teaspoon salt
1 teaspoon vanilla
2½ teaspoons baking soda

In a large, heavy pan, combine sugar, water and corn syrup. Cook over medium heat, stirring occasionally until it reaches 250°F. on a candy thermometer. Add peanuts and salt. Boil over medium heat to 300°F. on a candy thermometer, stirring constantly. Remove from heat. Working quickly, stir in vanilla and baking soda. Mixture will foam. Immediately pour, spread, and pull the foamy hot mixture on a large, buttered marble slab, or use 2 buttered cookie sheets. Cool and break into eating-size pieces. Store tightly covered, at room temperature.

yield: 2 pounds

Friends and relatives in Dayton, Ohio continue to look forward to my mother, Betty Brundige's famous peanut brittle, which she has been making for many Christmases. We children think it is delicious and great fun to be a part of the process of making it!

BARBARA BRUNDIGE DECKER

TERRIBLE TRUFFLES

½ cup butter
6 ounces chocolate chips, more or less
1 teaspoon dry instant coffee
Confectioners' sugar
½ cup chopped pecans
Optional toppings

Melt butter over medium heat. Add chocolate chips and reduce heat to the lowest available. Add instant coffee. When chips are melted, stir. Mixture should be moderately thickened. Add confectioners' sugar one-quarter cup at a time, mixing after each addition until it reaches a paste-like consistency. Add chopped pecans. If mixture becomes too thick, add more butter and let it melt until stirring makes the mixture thinner. Roll between hands into small balls.

Balls may be served as is, or rolled in confectioner's sugar, cocoa, chopped coconut, finely chopped pecans, chocolate sprinkles or coated lightly with melted baking chocolate. Coating is most successful if balls are frozen before dipping. Unsweetened baking chocolate should be thinned with water, for the diet conscious, or butter for those who don't care. Add three tablespoons of water to three squares of chocolate or two tablespoons of butter to three squares of chocolate, melted over lowest heat. Again, these amounts may be varied according to the desires of the cook. Freezes well.

yield: 2 to 3 dozen, depending on how much sampling goes on during the rolling process!

These little darlings go right from the plate to your hips. They are far too easy to make with ingredients everyone has around the house, and making requires sampling. If preparer prefers them without pecans, the chocolate mixture should be chilled before rolling, otherwise preparer is forced to lick hands a lot. The amount of chocolate chips used depends upon the brand used. I prefer Hershey's because of the flavor and because they melt nicely. Some remain quite thick when melted, so fewer are needed or more butter should be added. Nothing is critical about this recipe. Amounts are flexible.

MOLLIE HEDGES

SUGARED WALNUTS

1 pound walnuts
1 cup sugar
   Oil
   Salt

Heat enough oil to 350°F. in frying pan to cover walnuts in one single layer so they can brown. While oil is heating, bring about 3 quarts of water to a boil in a 4 quart saucepan. Add nuts. Bring to a boil and boil for 1 minute. Drain. Put in large bowl and add sugar. Mix well. Fry in hot oil until golden brown. Drain well and add a good pinch of salt. Stir. Place on a cookie sheet until dry. If they stick together, break apart. Store in an air tight container. Good for weeks, if they last that long!

yield: 1 pound
LIANA WALSH

NEVER FAIL PEANUT BUTTER FUDGE

2 cups sugar
½ cup milk
   Dash of salt
1 7-ounce can marshmallow creme
1 cup peanut butter

Bring sugar, milk and salt to boil and simmer slowly for three minutes. Remove from heat and add marshmallow creme and peanut butter. Mix by hand all ingredients until well blended, 3–4 minutes. Pour into greased 9" cake pan. Cool completely. This candy keeps well if covered, and does not have to be refrigerated.

yield: 20–25 pieces
JANET DOBSON

ZUCCHINI PICKLES

4 quarts zucchini, cut in ½" slices
6 onions, chopped
2 green peppers, chopped
2 cloves garlic, chopped
4 teaspoons salt
1½ teaspoons turmeric powder
1½ teaspoons celery seed
2 tablespoons mustard seed
4 cups sugar
3 cups vinegar

Mix first five ingredients and let stand 3 hours, covered. Drain zucchini mixture. Add remaining five ingredients to zucchini and bring to a boil. Boil one minute. Put in prepared jars and seal.

yield: 8 pints
DOROTHY MOFFAT

PICKLED PEPPERS

6 red bell peppers
6 green bell peppers
  Salt
4½ cups sugar
4½ cups vinegar
1 cup water

Cut peppers into strips and let stand overnight in weak solution of salt water: 1 part salt to 12 parts water. Combine sugar, vinegar and water and cook over medium heat until sugar dissolves. Drain peppers, add to sugar-vinegar mixture. Bring to a boil. Pack in jars and seal.

yield: 3 pints
JANET HEALY

SPICED CRAB APPLES

24 ripe crab apples
3 cups cider
2 cups sugar
2 sticks cinnamon
6 whole cloves
6 whole allspice
½ teaspoon ginger
½ teaspoon grated nutmeg
1 cup sugar
¼ cup lemon juice

Wash whole crabapples. Boil cider, two cups sugar, and spices for 10 minutes. Add the crabapples a few at a time and cook until soft but not broken. Remove to a dish as soon as they are tender. Add remaining cup of sugar and lemon juice to the syrup and boil until thick. Strain and pour clear syrup over crabapples. Jar and seal.

yield: 8 pints

We had a crab apple tree in the back yard and mother, Mrs. George M.D. Lewis, made these spiced crab apples which are very good.

JOANNE LEWIS TODD

JALAPEÑO JELLY

1 cup canned Jalapeño peppers
1 medium bell pepper, chopped
1¼ cups vinegar
6 cups sugar
3-4 drops green food coloring
8 ounces Certo, 1⅓ bottles

Blend peppers in blender or processor with ¼ cup vinegar. Mix 1 cup vinegar with sugar in saucepan. Add pepper mixture. Bring to a boil and stir constantly for 15 minutes, skimming foam. Add certo and bring to boil again. Remove from heat. Add food coloring. Pour into jelly glasses and seal.

yield: 4 cups
PATTI SCHRECKENGAUST

Dinner Before the Christmas Dance

Fourteen fragrant evergreen wreaths are tied with red ribbon bows. They are hung in each front window and on the big white front door of the Waverly Community House. And there is one for the township pump house that faces Abington Road and Waverly travelers coming home from Scranton or Clarks Summit. They are real pine, spruce and hemlock boughs, fashioned into traditional wreaths by loving village hands. Old hands teach those new to the prickly, pungent task. All who can be there gather in the scout room on a morning in early December. Christmas carols mingle with greetings and chatter; we sip hot coffee; we share know-how and special decorative snippets of boxwood or juniper, laurel or ground pine.

Huge mounds of greens are cut from neighbor's woods and landscapes; Fordhams, Belins, Von Storchs, Hulls, Gearharts prune generously, and the wreaths grow. "One for the Comm and then make what you need for your own house." Rhoda Warren or Joanna Estep make the extra large and sturdily wired beauty for the front door. Helen Von Storch is surrounded by a tumble of perfectly tied bows. The floor is swept clean, a minute or two ahead of the Girl Scouts' meeting, all the wreaths are hung, and Waverly is dressed to celebrate the Christmas holidays.

A favorite celebration for many years was the Christmas pageant at the Community House. It had its beginnings in the late 1940's in the dramatic imagination of Carol Green. The wings for the first Angel Gabriel were fashioned by Bud Green from coat hangers and cheese cloth. Over the succeeding years, the tableaux depicting the Biblical Christmas scenes multiplied and were embellished with children from many lands and more elaborate music.

Rehearsals were held on December afternoons after school hours. Foddy Vipond and Peg

Lewis demonstrated patience of truly heroic proportions as they struggled with vibrating eight-year-old energy, shrunken attention spans, penny candy and ice cream cones, wriggling in the bleachers, rampant exhibitionism, explosive exuberance and the dozens of distractions possible only when a hundred or more children are gathered in one room.

But there is a power in a costume and a darkened auditorium which can enlarge a group of actors into a total considerably more than the sum of the parts. When the performance actually began, one evening close to Christmas, red-robed choirs filed into the dimly lit hall, filling the air with sweet carols. The familiar faces were rapt in the rays of small flashlights. Robed in yards of drapery fabric, a neighborhood terrorist was transformed into a solemn king. Self-conscious kid brothers became awe-struck shepherds and little sisters in kimonos shyly profferred gifts to the small child.

One year, this magical power endured a rigorous test. Mary knelt in blue-veiled devotion by the rustic manger, the glow of the flashlight reflected up on her concentrated young face. Joseph stood above her, within the protective cover of a small log evocation of the Bethlehem stable. The beautiful voice of Myra Evans filled the hall with the elegant cadences of Luke and Matthew. Shepherds came and bowed. Kings entered bearing gifts. Pairs of representatives of many nations filed past as carols of their lands rang out. Nobody, but his mother and Mary, noticed that Joseph, coming down with the measles, had wobbled, lost his supper into the manger and quietly fled the stage.

The inspiration of performance and the spirit of the season had transformed Waverly's children into celebrants. Parents and grandparents were touched by the transformation. Teachers and babysitters recognized the magic. The gym resounded to "Adeste Fidelis" and the joy of the season was among us all.

Today, the pageant continues with young performers choreographed and encouraged by Cassie Devine Coviello's talent and patience. The Community House salutes the season with dancing and dining. It is a chance to dress up ourselves, our homes and our tables with our brightest and best. It is an opportunity to extend ourselves for those we love, to show them the gifts of beauty, of welcome and of good tastes.

Dinner Before the Christmas Dance

MENU I
TOMATO/CELERY CONSOMMÉ
BEEF RICHELIEU WITH MADEIRA SAUCE
FLORENTINE CREPE CUPS
WATERCRESS SALAD WITH LEMON VINAIGRETTE
LAYERED CHOCOLATE MOUSSE

MENU II
SHRIMP HOSTARIA Del ORSO
PORK SLICES WITH ASPARAGUS AND SORREL SAUCE
ARMENIAN RICE PILAF
AVOCADO MUSHROOM SALAD
CHESTNUT ROLL

MENU I

TOMATO/CELERY CONSOMMÉ

4–5	pounds tomatoes
2	large bunches, celery
4–5	egg whites
	Salt to taste

Coarsely chop tomatoes and celery, including celery leaves. Place in a large stockpot with about 5 to 6 quarts of water. Boil 8 to 10 minutes, then simmer until celery is very tender and stock has reduced somewhat. Strain through 2 thicknesses of linen towel or 2 thicknesses of cheese cloth. Twist towel tightly to get all the juice you can. Clarify, using 4 or 5 egg whites and shells. Salt, if at all, to taste. Garnish as desired. Can also be used for aspic of vegetables, etc.

yield: 12 servings
JOE MOONEY

BEEF RICHELIEU WITH MADEIRA SAUCE

- 2 pounds potatoes, peeled and shaped into ovals, approximately 1½" in diameter
- 1 4-pound beef fillet
- 1 tablespoon oil
- 12 medium tomatoes
- ¼ cup butter
- 12 whole mushrooms, approximately 1½" in diameter
- 3 tablespoons butter
- Parsley sprigs

Madeira Sauce:
- 1 cup beef broth
- ¼ cup dry Madeira
- ¼ cup butter
- 2 tablespoons chopped truffles, or finely chopped mushrooms
- 2½ teaspoons arrowroot
- Salt and freshly ground pepper

Pre-heat oven to 375°F. Cook potatoes in enough boiling salted water to cover until barely tender, about 8 to 12 minutes. Drain well and set aside.

Brown fillet in 1 tablespoon oil in large skillet over high heat. Transfer to roasting pan and bake 25 minutes for rare. Meat thermometer should register 125°F to 130°F. When meat is done, remove from oven, cover loosely with foil and keep warm.

While meat is roasting, cook tomatoes in enough salted water to cover over medium-high heat until tender, 5 to 8 minutes. Do not overcook. Drain; let cool slightly and peel. Cover and keep warm. Melt ¼ cup butter in large skillet over medium-high heat. Add mushrooms and sauté until lightly browned. Remove from skillet and keep warm. Add remaining 3 tablespoons butter to same skillet and heat over medium-high. Add potatoes and sauté until evenly browned.

Madeira Sauce: This can be made up to 3 days ahead and refrigerated. Combine first four ingredients in small saucepan and bring to boil. Reduce heat and simmer 3 minutes. Mix some of sauce with arrowroot and then stir into pan. Continue simmering, stirring frequently, until sauce is consistency of whipping cream, about 20 to 25 minutes. Season with salt and pepper.

To serve, transfer meat to heated platter and surround with vegetables. Degrease pan drippings with paper towel or spoon, add to Madeira sauce and reheat. Spoon some of sauce over meat, reserving remainder to pass separately. Garnish with parsley sprigs.

yield: 6 servings

It is an easy and elegant dinner - impressive main course. You will need to use two 4-pound fillets and double all other ingredients for 12 servings.

HILDA BARAKAT

FLORENTINE CREPE CUPS

Crepe:
- 3 eggs, slightly beaten
- ⅔ cup flour
- ½ teaspoon flour
- 1 cup milk

Filling:
- 1½ cups shredded Cheddar cheese
- 3 tablespoons flour
- 1 4-ounce can mushrooms, drained
- 3 eggs, beaten
- 10 ounces frozen chopped spinach, thawed and drained

Topping:
- 6 slices cooked bacon, optional

Combine ingredients for crepe mix and let stand 30 minutes, then make crepes. Pre-heat oven to 350°F. Fit crepes in 12 greased muffin cups and trim edges. Combine filling ingredients and fill crepes with filling. Bake for 40–45 minutes. Cooked bacon may be crumbled on top before serving.

yield: 12 servings
BARBARA KIMMICK

WATERCRESS SALAD WITH LEMON VINAIGRETTE

Salad:
- 4 bunches watercress

Dressing:
- 2 egg yolks, lightly beaten
- 2 ounces fresh lemon juice
- 1½ cups vegetable oil
- 2 tablespoons chopped parsley
- Grated zest of one lemon

Rinse and trim watercress. Refrigerate. Combine dressing ingredients, mixing well. Just before serving, lightly dress the watercress with lemon vinaigrette and arrange on salad plates.

yield: 12 servings
THE RYAH HOUSE

LAYERED CHOCOLATE MOUSSE

Mousse:
- 12 eggs, separated
- 2 cups sugar
- 8 ounces unsweetened chocolate, melted
- ¼ cup rum or Cognac
- 1 cup heavy cream, whipped

First Layer:
- 1 cup heavy cream, whipped
- ¼ cup sifted confectioners' sugar
- 1 teaspoon vanilla

Second Layer:
- ½ cup heavy cream, whipped
- 1½ ounces unsweetened chocolate, shaved

Third Layer:
- 1 cup heavy cream, whipped
- ¼ cup sifted confectioners' sugar
- 1 teaspoon vanilla

Beat yolks until thick and light in color. They will form a heavy ribbon after about five minutes. Add sugar gradually, continuing to beat well. Gradually add melted chocolate, followed by rum or Cognac. Beat egg whites with a pinch of salt until stiff peaks are formed. Fold whipped cream into egg-yolk mixture, then fold in egg whites immediately, just to the point when mousse is evenly blended. Do not fold too much.

Spread half of mousse mixture in the bottom of a large bowl or mold. Chill briefly. First layer: top with sweetened and flavored whipped cream. Second layer: mix whipped cream with shaved chocolate and spread over first layer. Third layer: spread sweetened whipped cream over second layer. Top with remainder of chocolate mousse. Smooth top with spatula. Chill thoroughly. Garnish with chocolate shavings or rosettes of whipped cream. Does not freeze well.

yield: 16 servings

In our family of chocoholics, this variation of chocolate mousse has become a favorite dessert for special family celebrations. Served in a large glass bowl to show off the contrasting layers, the mousse makes a spectacular presentation. You'll need a bowl that holds at least 14 cups or 3½ quarts, and people who are not bashful about indulging in a rich, creamy dessert.

SUSAN BELIN

MENU II

SHRIMP HOSTARIA Del ORSO

Cooked shrimp: 6–8 per person, depending on size

Combination of Boston lettuce, iceberg lettuce, Belgian endive: enough to make ½" bed on bottom of individual serving dishes

Finely diced celery, zucchini, scallion, cucumber, carrots; enough to make ½" layer over lettuce

Sauce:
- 3 parts mayonnaise
- 1 part catsup or chili sauce
- Heavy cream to thin slightly
- Salt to taste
- Tabasco to taste
- 1 teaspoon each marjoram, chervil, tarragon

Early in day put layer of lettuce on individual plates. Salt vegetable mixture; cover and put in refrigerator. Pour off water that forms; put vegetables over layer of lettuce. Add shrimp in layer on top of vegetables. Mix sauce. It should be thin enough so that it penetrates vegatables and lettuce. If it is too thick, thin with milk. Spoon sauce over shrimp and vegetables just before serving.

yield: 12 servings

This recipe from the well-known Hostaria Del Orso restaurant in Rome was given to us by a friend who lived in Italy for many years.

CORINNE O'DONNELL

PORK SLICES WITH ASPARAGUS AND SORREL SAUCE

1	package frozen whole asparagus spears, thawed, or 1½ pounds fresh thin asparagus spears
1	cup chicken stock
8	tablespoons unsalted butter
2½	cups heavy cream
	Salt and Pepper
¼	cup drained cooked sorrel, pureed, or ¼ cup sorrel puree, available at specialty stores
12	butterflied slices of pork, ½" thick
2	eggs, slightly beaten
2	cups fresh bread crumbs
1	tablespoon cooking oil
2	tablespoons fresh lemon juice

Pre-heat oven to 350°F. Cut 2 inches of the asparagus tips from the stems and boil them until just tender: 5 minutes for fresh asparagus, 1 minute for thawed. Remove from boiling water with a slotted spoon, hold under running cold water to stop the cooking. Drain on paper towels and set aside. Cut the asparagus stems into 1 inch pieces, measure 1 cup of them. Use the remainder for another recipe. Boil the 1 cup of stems until very tender: 8 minutes for fresh asparagus, 4 minutes for thawed. Drain and set aside.

In a small saucepan reduce the chicken stock to 1 teaspoonful. In a 2 quart saucepan melt 3 tablespoons butter, cook it slowly until it turns golden brown. Stir in the reduced stock, 1½ cups cream, salt and pepper. Boil slowly for 3 minutes.

In a food processor puree the asparagus stems, sorrel and cream mixture. Return the sauce to the saucepan and set aside.

Season the pork slices with salt and pepper, dip them in the beaten egg and then coat them with bread crumbs. In a large skillet melt 2 tablespoons butter and the oil over moderate heat. Brown the pork slices being careful they do not get too dark. Add more butter if necessary. Butter a baking dish large enough to hold the slices in one layer. Put the slices in the baking dish.

Stir together 1 cup cream and the lemon juice. Pour it over the meat slices. Cover the baking dish with foil. Bake at 350°F. for 25 minutes.

When the meat is almost done, heat the asparagus tips in 2 tablespoons butter in a small skillet over low heat.

Remove the meat from the baking dish to a heated platter and keep it warm. Remove any fat from the baking dish, pour the defatted contents in the asparagus sauce. Bring to a boil, correct seasoning.

Place a slice of pork on each heated dinner plate, spoon some sauce over each slice and garnish with the asparagus tips.

yield: 12 servings

For 6 slices of pork - make a full recipe of the sauce to the point of adding the juices and cream from the baking dish. Freeze half of it to use at another time. The sauce freezes well, in small plastic containers, for up to three months.

MARY RHODES

ARMENIAN RICE PILAF

Melt butter in 3-quart sauce pan, add noodles and let fry until golden brown, stirring constantly. Remove from stove. Wash rice and drain well, add to noodles and mix well. In separate pot bring broth to a boil. Add slowly to rice and noodles; then add salt. Return to stove, bring to boil, stir once, cover and let simmer for 20–25 minutes. Remove from stove and let stand, covered for 20 minutes, before serving.

yield: 12 servings
JEAN C. MORI

- 4 tablespoons butter
- ½ cup fine noodles, broken up
- 1½ cups long grain rice
- 4 cups clear chicken broth
- 1 teaspoon salt

AVOCADO AND MUSHROOM SALAD

Chill mushrooms in marinade for one hour. Arrange sliced avacados on salad plate. Spoon mushrooms on top. Garnish with chopped parsley.

yield: 12 servings

This recipe was one of my mother's, Mrs. George M. D. Lewis.

JOANNE LEWIS TODD

- 1 pound mushrooms, thinly sliced
- 4 avocados, thinly sliced

Marinade:
- ½ cup olive oil
- 2 tablespoons white wine vinegar
- 1 tablespoon chopped parsley
- 1 clove garlic, halved
- 1 teaspoon salt
  Fresh ground pepper
  Juice of a lemon

Garnish:
- ½ cup chopped parsley

CHESTNUT ROLL

Chestnut Rum-Filling:
- 1   17½-ounce can creme de marrons (chestnut purée)
- 2   tablespoons dark rum
- 1   cup whipping cream

Garnish:
- Bitter chocolate curls

Cake:
- ¾   cup sifted cake flour
- 1   teaspoon baking powder
- ¼   teaspoon salt
- 4   eggs
- ¾   cups sugar
- 1   teaspoon vanilla
- Confectioners' sugar

Filling: Combine chestnut purée and rum in mixing bowl and blend well. Whip cream separately until soft peaks form. Gently but thoroughly fold into purée.

Pre-heat oven to 400°F. Line bottom of a 10½" x 15½" jelly roll pan with well buttered waxed paper or foil. Sift together flour, baking powder and salt. Set aside. Beat eggs until light and foamy. Continue beating, adding sugar gradually, until mixture is thick and at least doubled in volume. Sprinkle flour mixture over batter and fold gently to combine. Fold in vanilla. Pour into prepared pan and bake 12 to 15 minutes or until cake is delicately browned and top springs back when lightly touched with fingertip. Lay large towel flat on a surface, and generously dust with confectioners' sugar and lossen cake around edges with knife and turn out onto cloth. Carefully remove paper. Cut off any crisp edges of cake and discard. Beginning on long side, gently roll up cake and cloth. Transfer to rack and cool completely. When cool, unroll cake and remove towel. Spread top with half of filling and re-roll. Place on serving platter and frost with remaining cream filling. Decorate with chocolate curls.

yield: 10 to 12 servings

Easy dessert but very different. Could make cake and cream a day ahead but assemble 1½ hours before serving and refrigerate.

HILDA BARAKAT

Newcomers' Coffee

New neighbors are always exciting. The moving van is a signal of change and the children bring home reports of bicycles, high chairs, skis, a piano and a doll house. Each clue is a peek into the nature and potential of new friends. A welcoming visit with a cake or casserole is a time-honored tradition in the upheaval of new beginnings.

When Polly and John Miller came into the clearing at Deacon William Clark's cabin in 1802, she carried their eighteen-month-old son; and he carried his gun, his axe, his sap bucket, a bag with cheese and bread, and two bushels of wheat he had just bought at Slocum's mill at Roaring Brook with his last two dollars. The Clarks offered land, and John Miller cleared trees and built a sixteen-foot log hut with a hearth in one corner and a split basswood floor. They lived there until they could buy, clear and build on land of their own on the south-facing slope below today's Hickory Grove Cemetery. This was part of a three-hundred acre parcel purchased from John Phillips for $40. He paid for it with $20 cash, $10 worth of maple syrup and $10 worth of tinware.

John Miller recorded: "We had one towel, one linen sheet, a blanket and a bedtick loaned us by good sister Parker. I made a bed-stead of bound sticks corded with elm bark. The bed tick I filled with dry leaves. Our pillows were of hemlock boughs. Good sister Parker also loaned us an iron kettle, two plates, two cups and two pewter spoons. We began life anew and happy as the birds in yonder forest."

When it was time for the "moving van" to bring up their household goods which had come from his home in Connecticut and Polly's home in Plainfield, New York, John Miller describes the move in his diary:

"I borrowed $20 of a friend. I went back after our goods left at Harpersville on the Susquehanna River. The river was too low for a raft to run. I bought a large canoe and loaded the things into it, and hired two men to row the cargo which landed safely at Pittston in due time. From there the goods were brought to Providence by wagon and team. To get the load from Providence through the notch to Clarks Green, took one team of horses and all day labor of myself, Robert Stone and Stephen Parker. There was an ox-sled path through the mountain gorge, but no wagon had passed through the Narrows. By attaching a rope we were able to prevent it from upsetting by pulling on the rope in the opposite direction. Laid poles against rocks and logs and then lifted the wheels to get the load over."

Those early settlers in the wild beech woods of Abington served each other as teachers, preachers, trading center, library, post office and canteen, as well as nurse, midwife, drugstore, counselor and friend. At the Waverly Community House, the annual Newcomer's Coffee is a symbol and a reminder of the true meaning of community in these times when specialization robs us of confidence in the threads with which we each weave human relationships.

Newcomers' Coffee

LEMON BREAD
APPLE COFFEE CAKE
ANZACS
LINZER BARS
ORANGE COOKIES
CHOCOLATE TEA COOKIES
ALMOND MACAROONS
GINGER COOKIES
PEPPARKAKOR
REAL MAINE DOUGHNUTS
CIAMBELLOTO

LEMON BREAD

- 1 cup sugar
- 6 tablespoons margarine
- 1 tablespoon grated lemon rind
- 2 eggs
- 1½ cups sifted all purpose flour
- ½ teaspoon salt
- 1 teaspoon baking powder
- ½ cup milk
- ½ cup chopped nuts

Topping:
- ¼ cup sugar
- 3 tablespoons lemon juice, heated until sugar melts

Pre-heat oven to 350°F. Cream margarine and sugar well. Add lemon rind and eggs. Stir. Add dry ingredients alternately with milk, beginning and ending with flour. Add nuts. Pour into greased 9" × 5" loaf pan. Bake 35 to 45 minutes or until done when tried with toothpick. Do not remove from pan. While hot, pour topping over loaf and let stand until cool. This recipe can be baked and then frozen for serving at a later date.

yield: 1 loaf
JACKIE SHOEMAKER

APPLE COFFEE CAKE

- 1 cup flour
- 1 cup sugar
- 1 teaspoon baking soda
- ⅛ teaspoon salt
- ½ teaspoon baking powder
- 1 teaspoon cinnamon
- ¼ cup butter
- 1 egg, beaten
- 1 teaspoon vanilla
- 2 cups apples, diced
- ½ cup raisins
- ½ cup walnuts or pecans, chopped

Pre-heat oven to 375°F. Sift dry ingredients together. Melt butter, add to beaten egg along with vanilla. Add dry ingredients, fruit and nuts. Put in 9" × 9" pan. Bake for 30 minutes. May also be served as a dessert with lemon flavored whipped cream

yield: 9–12 servings
PAT ATKINS

ANZACS

½	cup butter
1	tablespoon maple syrup
1	cup flour
½	teaspoon baking powder
½	cup rolled oats
½	cup coconut, angel flake
¼	cup sugar

Pre-heat oven to 350°F. Soften butter slightly, then cream with syrup. Add remaining ingredients. Roll into small balls. Place well apart on greased cookie sheets. Bake at 350°F. for 15 minutes. Cool before removing.

yield: 2 dozen

These biscuits (cookies) were named after the Australian and New Zealand Army Corps, a combined force of volunteer soldiers formed in Egypt during World War I. They were involved in the largest military landing in history at Gallipoli, Turkey in 1915. These cookies keep their memory alive in the kitchen.

HELEN HYDE

LINZER BARS

2½	cups flour
1½	cups sugar
½	pound butter
2	egg yolks
1	6-ounce jar raspberry jam, seedless is better
4	egg whites
1½	cups ground walnuts or pecans

Pre-heat oven to 350°F. Make a dough of flour, ½ cup sugar, butter and egg yolks blending with your fingers. Pat into a 10" × 15" pan. Prick with a fork and bake for 15–20 minutes until golden. Remove from oven and spread with jam. Beat egg whites stiff with 1 cup sugar, fold in nuts. Spread over jam. Return to oven for 25 minutes. Cut into bars when cool.

yield: 3 dozen bars

MARY BENJAMIN

ORANGE COOKIES

- ½ teaspoon salt
- 3 cups flour
- 1½ teaspoons baking powder
- ½ teaspoon baking soda
- 1½ teaspoon vinegar
- ½ cup milk
- ¾ cup shortening
- 1½ cup sugar
- 2 eggs
- 1 teaspoon vanilla
- 1½ teaspoon grated orange rind

Topping:
- 1 teaspoon granted orange rind
- ¼ cup orange juice
- ½ cup sugar
- Chopped nuts, optional

Pre-heat oven to 375°F. Sift dry ingredients together. Add vinegar to milk and let stand. Cream shortening and sugar. Add eggs, one at a time, and then vanilla, rind and milk mixture alternately with flour mixture. Drop from spoon onto greased cookie sheet. Bake for about 10 minutes. While cookies are baking, prepare topping. Watch for browning of edges. While warm, remove cookies from sheets; spread center of each cookie with orange-sugar topping and optional nuts.

yield: 5 dozen

In 1936 this recipe was given me by a longtime Waverly resident, Mrs. Oswald Strauch, whose forebears, the Stevensons, where early settlers here. These are delicious cookies. They freeze well.

CONSTANCE R. BELIN

CHOCOLATE TEA COOKIES

- ¼ cup butter
- 2 ounces baking chocolate
- 2 eggs
- 1 cup sugar
- 1 teaspoon vanilla
- 1 cup flour
- 1 teaspoon baking powder
- Confectioners' sugar

Pre-heat oven to 375°F. Melt butter and chocolate together over hot, not boiling water. Add the eggs, sugar and vanilla. Sift flour and baking powder together. Mix all ingredients. Chill several hours in refrigerator. Form into small balls and roll in confectioner's sugar. Bake 5-8 minutes.

yield: 2 dozen cookies

My mother used to make these cookies frequently when I was younger and I had never seen them anywhere else until they were served one night at friend's home in Clarks Green right before we moved here from New York City. These freeze very well.

LESLEE J. DOHERTY

ALMOND MACAROONS

½ pound almond paste
1 cup sugar
2-3 egg whites
¼ teaspoon almond extract
⅛ teaspoon salt

Pre-heat oven to 325°F. Cut almond paste into ½ inch pieces and place in food processor. Add sugar, 2 egg whites, almond extract and salt. Process until smooth. Add more egg white, 1 teaspoon at a time, if the dough seems too stiff. Scrape it into a bowl and beat it until smooth. Line a cookie sheet with brown paper.

Drop dough onto the paper by spoonfuls or use a pastry bag with a plain or star tip. Flatten the macaroons slightly. Bake for 30 minutes or until lightly browned. Cool on a rack. Invert paper, brush it with water to dampen paper until the macaroons can be easily removed.

yield: 2 dozen
MARY RHODES

GINGER COOKIES

¾ cup butter
1 cup sugar
¼ cup molasses
1 egg
2 cups flour
2 teaspoons baking soda
1 teaspoon ginger
1 teaspoon ground cloves
1 teaspoon cinnamon
Small dish granulated sugar

Pre-heat oven to 350°F. Cream butter and sugar, add molasses and egg and beat well. Add flour, baking soda and spices. Mix well. Chill one hour.

Roll with hands to walnut size, dip top in granulated sugar. Place on ungreased cookie sheet two inches apart. Bake approximately 10 minutes or until edges brown. Tops will be crinkled. Cool on racks.

yield: 3 dozen

One of my family's favorites and I make them often for a hostess gift.

DEANNA I. SMITH

PEPPARKAKOR

Cookie Dough:
- 3½ cups unsifted all-purpose flour
- 1 teaspoon baking soda
- ¼ teaspoon salt
- 1½ teaspoons ground ginger
- 1½ teaspoons ground cinnamon
- 1 teaspoon ground cloves
- ½ cup butter or regular margarine, softened
- ¾ cup granulated sugar
- 1 egg
- ¾ cup light molasses
- 1 teaspoon grated lemon peel

Frosting:
- ⅓ cup egg whites
- 3¾ cups sifted confectioners' sugar

Make dough: measure unsifted flour, and sift with baking soda, salt, ginger, cinnamon and cloves onto large sheet of waxed paper. In large bowl of electric mixer, with the mixer at high speed, beat the butter, granulated sugar and 1 egg until light and fluffy.

Add molasses and lemon peel; beat until well blended. With wooden spoon, stir in flour mixture; mix with hands until well blended and smooth. Divide the dough into four parts. Wrap each part separately in waxed paper or foil, and refrigerate overnight.

Pre-heat oven to 375°F. Lightly grease cookie sheets. Roll one part of cookie dough at a time; keep rest refrigerated until ready to roll out. With a stockinette-covered rolling pin, roll out the dough ⅛ inch thick on lightly floured pastry cloth.

Use cutters (hearts, stars, bells, trees, animals, people, houses) 2 to 3 inches in diameter, to cut out cookies. Place cookies 1 inch apart on cookie sheets. Bake 6 to 8 minutes, or until lightly browned. Remove to wire rack to cool.

Meanwhile, make white decorating frosting: in medium bowl, with portable electric mixer at medium speed, beat the egg whites with the confectioners' sugar to make a smooth, stiff frosting. Cover with a damp cloth until ready to use, to prevent drying out.

To decorate: fill pastry bag with a number 3 or 4 small tip for writing with frosting. Pipe on frosting following outline of cookies. Let frosting dry. Store in a covered tin at room temperature. This is a Swedish recipe for traditional Christmas cookies.

yield: 7 to 10 dozen
HEATHER M. ACKER

REAL MAINE DOUGHNUTS

Cream together eggs with sugar. Sift together dry ingredients and add to egg mixture alternating with milk and shortening. Chill overnight to firm dough. Roll or pat to ¼" thickness. Cut into desired shapes. Fry in deep fat heated to 370°F.-375°F.

yield: 3 dozen

The ginger is added "so they don't soak fat, deah!"

JAMIE PECK

2	eggs
1	cup sugar
3	cups flour
½	teaspoon baking soda
1	teaspoon baking powder
1	teaspoon salt
1	teaspoon nutmeg
1	teaspoon ginger
1	cup buttermilk or sour milk
2	tablespoons shortening, melted

CIAMBELLOTO

Pre-heat oven to 350°F. Cream butter and sugar. Add lemon rind and next four ingredients. Add eggs one at a time; then add flour and baking powder alternately with milk. Pour into well-greased 10" bundt or tube pan. Bake for 45 minutes.

Topping: Grate orange rind and squeeze juice. Add powdered sugar to make a glaze. Spoon on cake while hot.

yield: 8-10 servings

A most interesting cake with the pleasant blending of refreshing extracts and flavorings

MADALINE LORI

Cake:
½	pound butter
1½	cups sugar
1	whole lemon rind, grated
1	teaspoon vanilla
½	teaspoon anise seeds
1	teaspoon lemon extract
1	teaspoon anise flavoring
4	eggs
3	cups flour
3	teaspoons baking powder
1	cup milk

Topping:
1	orange
	Confectioners' sugar

Mid-Winter Blues Chasers

> . . . The way was a desert of white,
> dunes whirling in the street where cars
> lay buried, humped and sleeping like camels . . .

The streets in Jay Parini's poem "Beginning the World," are the sculpture of a snow storm, before the plows and the salt and cinders create a corridor for the stream of traffic and slush to flow through. Civilization depends on traffic, on sharing and distributing goods and services. Winter snows may slow us down, but the roads continue to be a tangible testament to our interdependence. Among the earliest Yankee settlers in Northeastern Pennsylvania in the 1770's, Isaac Tripp and his son made regular trips to Hartford in order to represent the Lackawanna and Wyoming Valleys in the Connecticut Assembly. In the summer of 1799, some of the first men to come to Abington, William Clark, Ephraim Leach and Thomas Smith, each labored thirty days to clear and improve a path from Providence on the Lackawanna River, through a notch at Legget's Gap and into the beech-covered Abington hills.

After the Revolutionary War, the 1783 Trenton Decision awarded jurisdiction of this area to Pennsylvania. Philadelphia speculators Meredith, Clymer, Drinker and Cadwallader bought up veterans' land warrants giving them control of vast tracts of land in the unsettled Northeastern endless mountains. Hoping to expedite settlement, they organized the Philadelphia and Great Bend Turnpike Company. In 1819, they obtained a charter and began construction with $12,000 appropriated by the legislature. Built with a rock base, the road was largely constructed by local labor. Henry Drinker came from Philadelphia to survey and sell parcels of land. He was encouraged by the Clarks, stockholders in the Company, who received the first license for a tavern along the northern end of the route from Mt. Pocono. This Turnpike, today's Abington Road, followed the old Indian path from the Lackawanna River at Providence, through Clarks Green and

Waverly, to the Susquehanna River at Great Bend. Finished in 1826, it connected with other turnpikes to become part of the growing network of roads uniting the states. In 1823 the Abington-Waterford Turnpike was chartered from Clarks Green, along today's Glenburn and Waterford Roads, through Montrose to reach Waterford, Connecticut. Plank roads, developed in Russia, were introduced in the 1850's and their improved surfaces expedited the passage of goods to markets.

Life along the turnpike was lively in the nineteenth century. The Philadelphia and Great Bend Turnpike became a mire of muddy ruts under the wheels of great canvas covered wagons. Four-horse teams strained, pulling the creaking load of products from local farms and forests, and returning with goods from the cities' manufactories. Passengers and mail rode in gaily colored stagecoaches. A trip to Philadelphia was made via Providence three times a week, and was accomplished in two days of unvarying jolting. Private carriages and individuals on foot or horseback welcomed the early road with hotels or inns about every twenty miles.

Dr. Andrew Bedford established a medical practice in Abington Center in 1824. His two-hundred-square-mile practice took him as far as Greenfield, Factoryville, Glenwood and Slocum Hollow, and he appreciated the few roads that eased his way. Ministers traveled far on these roads and interconnecting paths. Livestock herds were driven along the turnpike, filling the air with smells and sounds of cattle, mules, horses, sheep, hogs, turkeys and geese on their way to market. And when the circus traveled through, the elephants paused in Fleetville at the roadside watering troughs and drank them dry.

On September 11, 1871, the Providence reporter noted: "Abingtonians poured down upon us Monday with a rush . . . Brown and Carpenter, cattle dealers, driving a span of bays pell-mell and raising a great dust. The reason of their unusual haste was soon apparent — they were racing; yes, racing through Providence! Immediately behind them was John Stone, with a nimble-footed nag, driving like Jehu. At the top of Winton's hill the bays hauled off the course, but Stone went whirling down toward Scranton, raising a cloud of dust and bringing many to their doors, exclaiming, 'What's up?' Then followed a drove of beef cattle on a stampede, to the great peril of pedestrian women and strolling children, sending still higher and wider the cloud of dust, to the great annoyance of shopkeepers. Then came other farmers, followed by John Miller, also driving cattle, but slowly and gently, like a man of moderation and good sense. Other Abingtonians such as Knight, Nichols, O'Malia and Scanlon, also drive cattle through our streets almost daily, some driving slowly and cautiously and some furiously, indicating the temperament of the different men. Cattle are often driven by boys without discretion, who pelt them with stones rendering them wild and unmanageable. We always think such boys need pelting, welting or wisdom. Anyone who has taken the trouble to count the number of teams which pour . . . through the Abington notch daily, will come to the conclusion that turnpike stock must be valuable, especially if he knows anything about the rate of toll charged at the gate."

Nights were dark and unlighted and these travelers needed lodgings. Many stopped at the tavern of Jeremiah Clark. This large and handsome inn dominated the hill overlooking the Green, near the toll booth and the beginning of the Waterford Pike. Jeremiah, following religious scruples, did not allow his guests to drink alcoholic beverages or to play cards, so some preferred to travel further on to George Parker's "Wayside Inn" beside the Turnpike north of the intersection with Carbondale Road. In 1832 his cousin, Alvah Parker, built a competitive tavern on the northeast corner of Academy and Turnpike; and in 1850 Alvah Parker joined Dr. Bedford and Lemuel Stone in operating Waverly House across the corner on Turnpike and Clinton Street. There were always ample stables and pens for livestock out back, and a cheery hearth with food and drink for the traveler inside.

Today's network of roads and interstate highways still brings travelers here. In 1980, 25,800 vehicles passed through Clarks Summit each day on the Abington's main thoroughfare. And there are many fine modern counterparts of yesterday's taverns. Our traveling friends and families come here with fond anticipations of a bright, warm welcome, no matter what the weather or season.

We are all very much affected by the weather. "If you don't like the weather, just wait a bit. It will change." We are lucky to live where we still have weather and not just an air-conditioned comfort zone. The dull days present their pleasant surprises. A cardinal is much brighter and more welcome at the bird feeder on a grey morning. If the sun shone every day, the pewter gleam of a bare wet branch would never be noticed. And feeling a little dull and lonely just whets our appetites for getting together with friends, to eat, drink and be merry and dispel cabin fever.

Mid-Winter Blues Chasers

MENU I
MOUSSAKA
CONFETTI BROWN RICE
GREEK SALAD
FOOLPROOF COFFEE SOUFFLÉ

MENU II
SEAFOOD CASSEROLE
SPINACH MALFATTI
WILD RICE WITH MUSHROOMS AND ALMONDS
APRICOT MOUSSE

MENU III
SAUCY STUFFED CHICKEN
HAY AND STRAW
BUTTERNUT SQUASH, SNOW PEA AND ENDIVE SALAD
WITH GINGER-SESAME DRESSING
FROZEN CHOCOLATE PECAN PIE

MENU I

MOUSSAKA

Pre-heat oven to 350°F. Meat Sauce: In hot butter or margarine sauté onion, ground meat and garlic stirring until brown (8–10 minutes). Add herbs, spices and tomato sauce; bring to boil, stirring constantly. Reduce heat. Simmer, uncovered for ½ hour. Meanwhile, halve un-pared eggplant lengthwise. Slice crosswise ½ inch thick. Place in broiler pan, sprinkle with salt. Brush with melted butter. Broil 4 minutes each side. Set aside.

Cream Sauce: In saucepan, melt butter. Stir in flour, salt, pepper. Add milk, heat to boil, stir until thickened. Remove from heat. Add beaten eggs. Mix well.

Place eggplant in shallow 12" × 7½" × 2" casserole, over-lapping slightly. Sprinkle with 2 tablespoons Cheddar and Parmesan. Stir bread crumbs into meat sauce. Spoon over eggplant. Sprinkle 2 tablespoons Parmesan and Cheddar. Layer rest of eggplant. Pour cream sauce over all. Sprinkle top with rest of cheese. Bake for 35–40 minutes until golden brown and top is set. Cool slightly. Cut into squares. Looks complicated - not so.

yield: 12 servings
MARGOT W. McDONALD

Meat Sauce:
- 2 tablespoons butter or margarine
- 1 cup finely chopped onions
- 1½ pounds ground chuck or lamb
- 1 clove crushed garlic (optional)
- ½ teaspoon oregano
- 1 teaspoon basil
- ½ teaspoon cinnamon
- 1 teaspoon salt
- Dash of pepper
- 2 cans (8-ounces) tomato sauce
- 2 eggplants, washed and dried
- Salt
- ½ cup butter or margarine, melted

Cream Sauce:
- 2 tablespoons butter or margarine
- 2 tablespoons flour
- ½ teaspoon salt
- Dash of pepper
- 2 cups milk
- 2 eggs, beaten
- ½ cup grated Parmesan cheese
- ½ cup grated Cheddar cheese
- 2 tablespoons bread crumbs

CONFETTI BROWN RICE

- 1/3 cup vegetable oil
- 1 medium onion, chopped
- 2 cups mixed dried fruit, chopped
- 1 1/2 cups mixed nuts, chopped
- 2/3 cup sesame seeds
- 1/2 teaspoon ground cloves
- 1 teaspoon salt
- 3 cups brown rice, cooked
- 1/2 cup butter, melted

Pre-heat oven to 350°F. Heat the oil in a skillet and sauté the onion, fruit, nuts, and sesame seeds until the onion is translucent, about 5 minutes. Add the cloves and salt to the onion mixture and stir. Add the cooked rice and mix well. Place the rice in a buttered casserole dish and pour the butter over all. Bake for 15-20 minutes to heat through. Serve immediately.

yield: 12 servings
BARBARA PLATT

GREEK SALAD

- 1 garlic clove
- 1 pint basket cherry tomatoes
- 1 cup Greek olives, pitted
- 1 cup Feta cheese, crumbled
- 2 large heads Romaine lettuce

Dressing:
- 1/2 cup olive oil
- 4 tablespoons lemon juice
- 1/2 teaspoon oregano
- Pinch thyme, salt, pepper

Rub salad bowl with garlic. Add cherry tomatoes, pitted olives and cheese. Mix dressing and pour over salad. Refrigerate for at least 4 hours. Bring to room temperature. Tear lettuce into bite-size pieces. Add to salad bowl and toss well.

yield: 12 servings
JANE STEVENS

FOOLPROOF COFFEE SOUFFLÉ

- 1 1/2 cups strong coffee
- 1/2 cup milk
- 2/3 cup sugar
- 1 tablespoon unflavored gelatin
- 1/4 teaspoon salt
- 3 egg yolks, slightly beaten
- 3 egg whites, beaten stiff
- 1/2 teaspoon vanilla
- Whipped cream

Mix coffee, milk, sugar, gelatin, salt and egg yolks. Cook in double boiler stirring constantly until mixture coats a silver spoon. Remove from heat. Fold in egg whites and vanilla. Pour into 1 quart mold which has been rinsed in cold water. Chill; unmold and serve with whipped cream.

yield: 6-8 servings

This was a favorite of my great-grandmother and always a birthday special request for my mother and for me. The soufflé will separate into two layers: a strong coffee jelly and a coffee flavored sponge - pretty, cool and delicious. It's really a Spanish cream.

LUCY PECK EYSENBACH

SEAFOOD CASSEROLE

1	pound bay scallops
1	cup dry white wine
2	teaspoons lemon juice
6	tablespoons butter
1/3	cup flour
2	cups light cream
1/3	cup Cognac
3/4	cup Parmesan cheese
	Salt
	Pepper
2	beaten egg yolks
3/4	pound cooked, sliced mushrooms
1	pound cooked lobster
1	pound cooked crab
1	pound cooked shrimp
1	tablespoon chopped parsley
1 1/2	cups soft bread crumbs, tossed with 1/2 cup melted butter

Pre-heat oven to 350°F. Cook scallops in 1 cup dry white wine with lemon juice for 3 to 5 minutes. Drain scallops and reserve 3/4 cup of the liquid. Melt butter and add flour to make a roux. Stir in scallop liquid, cream and Cognac and stir over heat until thickened. Add 1/4 cup Parmesan cheese and salt and pepper to taste. Put small amount of sauce into beaten egg yolks and slowly combine egg yolk mixture into the remaining sauce. Add mushrooms, lobster, crab, shrimp, and parsley.

Pour into buttered casserole and top with buttered bread crumbs and remaining Parmesan cheese. Bake for 25–30 minutes.

yield: 12 servings
LINDA SPROUL

SPINACH MALFATTI

1	8-ounce package frozen chopped spinach
5	ounces ricotta cheese
4	tablespoons Parmesan cheese
1/2	cup fresh bread crumbs
2	eggs
1	clove garlic, finely chopped
	Salt to taste
1/4	cup flour
2 1/2	pints chicken stock

Pre-heat oven to 350°F. Cook spinach according to package directions; drain and squeeze out as much water as possible. Combine spinach, ricotta, Parmesan, bread crumbs, eggs, garlic, and salt. This should be a very firm mixture. Form into egg shaped ovals. Bring the chicken stock to a simmer. Roll the spinach ovals in the flour and drop a few at a time into the stock. Keep at a gentle simmer. The spinach malfatti will float to the top. Cook them only another minute after they float up, lift out with a slotted spoon and drain on paper towels. Place in a buttered ovenproof baking dish and top either with your favorite tomato sauce, or melted butter flavored with sage. Sprinkle with additional Parmesan cheese. Bake for 10 minutes to reheat. May be made ahead and refrigerated until reheating.

yield: 6 servings
JEAN COLOMBO

WILD RICE WITH MUSHROOMS AND ALMONDS

- 2 tablespoons butter
- ½ cup raw wild rice
- ¼ cup blanched, slivered almonds
- 1 tablespoon chopped green onion or chives
- 1 7-ounce can mushroom pieces, or fresh sliced mushrooms, sautéed
- 1½ cups chicken broth

Pre-heat oven to 300°F. Put all ingredients except broth, and fresh sauteed mushrooms if using instead of canned mushrooms, in heavy skillet; cook over low heat about 20 minutes or until almonds are slightly brown, stirring often. When almonds are brown, add chicken broth and fresh mushrooms. Pour mixture into 1 quart baking dish. Cover tightly and bake for about 2 hours. Can also add some chopped sautéed celery to casserole if you like.

yield: 4 servings
SHERRY W. CONNELL

APRICOT MOUSSE

- 1 14-ounce can apricots
- 1 3-ounce package orange gelatin
- 1 8-ounce package cream cheese
- 1 cup heavy cream, whipped
- 1 can Mandarin oranges, drained

Drain apricots and reserve juice. Bring apricot juice to a boil and mix with gelatin, stirring well until dissolved. Cool. Combine gelatin, cream cheese and apricots in blender or mixer. Blend until smooth and chill until partially set. Fold in whipped cream and oranges. Turn into 6-cup mold and chill until firm.

yield: 6 servings
PAULA STAVISKY

MENU III

SAUCY STUFFED CHICKEN

3	whole chicken breasts, boned and skinned
2	pounds fresh spinach, washed and stemmed or 1 10-ounce package frozen spinach
1	large onion
8	tablespoons butter
	Salt and freshly ground black pepper to taste
6	slices cooked ham
6	slices Swiss cheese
½	cup chicken broth
½	cup dry white wine
2	tablespoons flour
	Juice of two lemons
1	cup heavy cream
1	pound mushrooms, sliced
	Parsley for garnish

Pre-heat oven to 350°F. Split the chicken breasts in half and pound them between two pieces of wax paper with a mallet or rolling pin. Blanch the fresh spinach or cook the frozen spinach and drain it thoroughly. Dice the onion and sauté it with 4 tablespoons of the butter. Add the drained spinach to the onions and stir in the salt and pepper. Let the mixture cool. Place a slice of ham and a slice of cheese on top of each pounded chicken breast. Top with a mound of the spinach filling. Carefully roll the chicken breasts and place them in a buttered baking dish, seam side down. When all the breasts are filled and rolled, pour the chicken broth and ¼ cup of the white wine over them. Place the chicken in the preheated oven for 20–25 minutes. Remove it from the oven and carefully strain off the liquid. Set the liquid aside. Keep the chicken breasts warm while you make the sauce.

Make a roux with the remaining 4 tablespoons butter and the flour and gradually add the reserved liquid, the rest of the wine, the lemon juice, and the cream, stirring until the sauce thickens. Add the sliced mushrooms and continue simmering the sauce until the mushrooms are soft. Pour the sauce over the chicken breasts and garnish with fresh parsley.

yield: 6 servings
VIRGINIA CHAMBERLIN

HAY AND STRAW

6	ounces green noodles
6	ounces yellow noodles or spaghetti
	boiling water, salt
3	tablespoons olive oil
1	clove garlic, halved
1	medium onion, chopped
¾	pound fresh mushrooms, sliced
¼	pound sweet butter
	Salt and pepper to taste
¼	pound Parmesan cheese, grated

Cook yellow and green noodles in boiling water in separate saucepans, each with ¾ teaspoon salt, half a tablespoon olive oil, for time specified on each package, usually 10–12 minutes. Drain; rinse in hot water; keep hot. Meanwhile, sauté garlic in 1 tablespoon oil for 3 minutes. Remove garlic. Add to the oil the chopped onion and sauté until tender, about 5 minutes. Remove. Add remaining oil and mushrooms. Sauté 5 minutes or longer, stirring constantly. Have ready a large earthenware, enamel, or glass bowl containing the butter, which has been cut into 6 or 8 chunks. Add noodles, onions, and mushrooms. Toss, as you would a salad, to mix. Add salt to taste, as well as black pepper, then add half the grated cheese. Toss again to distribute thoroughly. Pass remaining cheese to be added as desired.

yield: 4–6 servings
MARY ANN LA PORTA

BUTTERNUT SQUASH, SNOW PEA AND ENDIVE SALAD WITH GINGER-SESAME DRESSING

Salad:
- 1 small butternut squash (¾ to 1 pound)
- ½ pound snow peas, strings removed and cut lengthwise into ¼" julienne
- 3 large Belgian endives, halved crosswise, then cut lengthwise into ¼" julienne
- 6 large radishes, trimmed and cut into ¼" julienne
- ¼ teaspoon salt
- ⅛ teaspoon pepper

Dressing:
- 1 small garlic clove, crushed
- 1½ teaspoons peeled and grated ginger root
- ¼ teaspoon finely grated orange zest
- 1 tablespoon honey
- 2 tablespoons soy sauce
- 3 tablespoons oriental sesame oil
- 1 tablespoon peanut oil
- 3 tablespoons fresh lemon juice

Halve the squash lengthwise, scoop out all seeds and stringy portions. Cut crosswise in half. Peel squash and cut into matchstick julienne, about 1½" × ¼". Put squash in a strainer and dip into a large pot of boiling, salted water and blanch until crisp-tender, about 20 seconds. Rinse under cold running water. Drain well. In the same water blanch the snow peas about 5 seconds, only to turn them bright green. Run under cold water and drain well. In a large serving bowl, combine squash, snow peas, endives and radishes. Season with salt and pepper. Make dressing in a small bowl. Whisk together the garlic, ginger, orange zest, honey, soy sauce, and oils. Let stand at room temperature 20 minutes to allow flavors to blend.

To assemble, drizzle dressing over the salad and toss lightly to mix. Let stand at room temperature for 10 minutes. Add lemon juice, toss again and serve.

yield: 6 servings
SALLY MARQUARDT

FROZEN CHOCOLATE PECAN PIE

Crust:
- 2 cups chopped pecans, toasted
- 5¼ tablespoons packed brown sugar
- 5 tablespoons chilled butter, cut into small pieces
- 2 teaspoons dark rum

Chocolate Filling:
- 6 ounces semisweet chocolate
- ½ teaspoon instant coffee
- 4 eggs
- 1 tablespoon dark rum
- 1 teaspoon vanilla
- 1½ cups whipping cream

Crust: Mix all ingredients in blender or food processor until mixture holds together. Press into bottom and sides of 9 inch pie plate. Freeze for 2 hours.

Filling: Melt chocolate with coffee in top of double boiler over hot water. Remove from heat. Beat in eggs, rum and vanilla until mixture is smooth. Cool. Whip 1 cup cream and gently fold into chocolate mixture. Pour into crust and freeze. Just before serving whip remaining ½ cup cream and pour over pie.

yield: 6–8 servings
LINDA SPROUL

Cross Country Ski Supper

When snow blankets the Abington hills, it is an invitation to play, whatever your age. A beckoning chain of fields, woods, lakes and swamps augments the more manicured realm of the backyard hill, the golf course and the State Park. Snow sifts in a veil across the dark woods beyond, and piles up in generous dollops on the hemlock boughs. Puddles of late afternoon sunlight spill through the branches onto dimpled snow. Beech leaves rattle, pale pennants on silvery branches. Singular dark seed pods and grasses stand in elegant relief against the white expanse. Cheeky and tenacious, chicadees glean the winter branches.

Frozen lakes and ponds become magnets for skaters. Double runners and kitchen chairs aid beginners who wonder if they will ever be part of the hockey games or crack-the-whip. Ominous groans and cracking sounds are a reminder that we are enjoying a temporary condition; plenty of cold dark water is just below this slippery new playground. In the rare times of "black ice," this is abundantly clear as swaying reeds and suspended fish can be seen, magically, right through the dark ice. It is a treat to sweep on singing blades from shore to shore, through the swamp and back again to outstretched, mittened hands. Some winters we achieved terrifyingly wonderful speeds with Bud Green's skate sail. But, inevitably, aching ankles, cold toes and the smell of cocoa draw us ashore, and into cold plodding boots.

The ice and snow of winter are not an undiluted pleasure. The Blizzard of 1893 piled six-foot drifts on Carbondale Street "and the narrow passage shoveled between them is like a canyon between walls of white marble." S.S. Kennedy went on to observe in the Scranton *Republican,* "There are three toboggan slides in Waverly where sleds go down the streets with a mighty swish to the imminent peril of all pedestrians who are obliged to cross where they fly. We are praying the ice is melting and hope soon to have a rest from the coasting nuisance."

Joe Miller remembers bob-sled rides from the top of Academy Hill to Dean Road — halfway to Dalton with a memorable swoop across Main Street — and a long walk back. That long walk back was uppermost in the mind of Searle Von Storch in 1949 when he hooked up a motor and rope to make a ski tow. In the orchard on the hill between the school pines and Belin's woods, short winter afternoons were filled with speed and tumbles. The Fullers also set up a tow in a gentle field, overlooking Lily Lake, where tobogganers and skiers could ride back up again. What a luxury to ride up instead of unstrapping the skis and trudging up along the edges! It was a foretaste of the development of recreational downhill skiing at Montrose and then at Elk Mountain and Montage. Chairlifts and lodges offer comforts, while steep slopes, moguls, ice and other skiers offer challenges and excitement.

A very different world opens to the cross-country skier. With each stride, the carefully waxed skis offer a gift of glide. These slender sibilant skis carry us into the secret heart of winter and bring us home, rosy-cheeked and jubilant. With a towering thirst for a cold drink, the relaxing skier enjoys the warmth, food, company and recollections of adventure.

Cross Country Ski Supper

MENU I
HAM, CHEESE AND ONION CHOWDER
BLACK BEAN SOUP
MUSHROOM VEGETABLE SOUP
HERB BREAD
SWEDISH LIMPA MUFFINS
RICE KRISPIE COOKIES
PECAN SURPRISE BARS

MENU II
FISH CHOWDER
TUSCAN BEAN SOUP
JAMAICA PEPPERPOT SOUP
ITALIAN CHEESE BREAD CRESCIA
ANADAMA BREAD
BLACK BOTTOM CUPCAKES
LACY OATMEAL COOKIES

MENU I

HAM, CHEESE AND ONION CHOWDER

Cook cubed potatoes in water until tender, approximately 10 minutes. Drain, reserving liquid. Add enough water to reserved liquid to make 1 cup. In sauce pan cook onion in butter until tender, not brown. Blend in flour and pepper. Add milk, potatoes, and water all at once. Cook and stir until it thickens and bubbles. Add ham and cheese, stir until cheese melts.

yield: 4-6 servings

Great soup for all those cold and snowy days. These ingredients you can always keep on hand for emergency dinners.

JODI ROGALLA

- 2 medium potatoes, pared and cubed, approximately 2 cups
- ½ cup boiling water
- 1 cup chopped onion
- 3 tablespoons butter
- 3 tablespoons flour
  Dash pepper
- 3 cups milk
- ½ cup cooked ham, chopped
- 1½ cups shredded sharp cheese

BLACK BEAN SOUP (SOPA de CAROATAS NEGRAS)

Place beans in large pot. Cover with water plus one inch. Simmer, covered for 2 to 3 hours, until beans are tender. Heat oil in another large saucepan. Sauté leeks, onions and garlic until golden. Add beef broth. Drain beans and force through sieve or blend in processor or blender. Add to vegetables and broth. Stir in butter and simmer 2 minutes. Add croutons and brown sugar. Serve immediately. Garnish with lemon slices.

yield: 6 servings
KAREN SHUPTAR KELLAND

- 1 cup black beans, soaked overnight and drained
- 2 tablespoons oil
- 1 leek, sliced into rings
- 1 yellow onion, finely chopped
- 1 clove garlic, crushed
- 6 cups beef broth
- ½ teaspoon salt
- 2 tablespoons butter
- 1 cup toasted croutons
- 1 tablespoon brown sugar
  Sliced lemon

MUSHROOM AND VEGETABLE SOUP

- ¼ pound butter
- 1 cup onion, chopped
- 1 cup celery, diced
- 1 cup carrot, diced
- ¼ cup white turnip, diced
- 1 pound mushrooms, sliced
- 1 cup potatoes, diced
- 1 cup canned tomatoes, drained
- 4 cups boiling chicken broth
- ½ teaspoons thyme, dried
- 1 tablespoon fresh parsley, chopped
- Salt and pepper

Melt butter in heavy kettle. Sauté onion over low heat until tender but not brown. Add celery, carrot and turnip and cook 5 minutes. Add mushrooms and potatoes and cook 3 minutes longer. Add remaining ingredients and salt and pepper to taste. Simmer, covered until vegetables are tender, but not mushy, about 5 minutes.

yield: 6 servings
JANET WRIGHTNOUR

HERB BREAD

- 1 package yeast
- 1¼ cups warm water
- 2 tablespoons shortening
- 2 teaspoons salt
- 2 tablespoons sugar
- 3 cups flour
- 1 teaspoon dried parsley
- ½ teaspoon dried basil
- ½ teaspoon dried oregano
- 2 tablespoons Parmesan cheese

Preheat oven to 400°F. Mix yeast with water in large bowl. Add shortening, salt, sugar, and one-half of flour. Beat two minutes. Add remaining ingredients. Beat until smooth. Cover and let rise one-half hour. Stir down. Put into greased 9½" × 5½" loaf pan. Let rise until doubled. Bake for 35 minutes. Makes great toast. Freezes well.

yield: 1 loaf
ELLIE HYDE

SWEDISH LIMPA MUFFINS

1	cup rye flour
¾	cup all-purpose flour
¼	cup firmly packed brown sugar
4	teaspoons baking powder
½	teaspoon salt
1½	teaspoons caraway seed *or*
1½	teaspoons grated orange peel *or*
1	teaspoon of each of the above
1	egg
¾	cup milk
¼	cup oil
¼	cup molasses

Pre-heat oven to 400°F. Line muffin tin with paper baking cups or grease tin well. In large bowl, combine flours, sugar, baking powder, salt and caraway seed/orange peel. With wooden spoon make well in center of dry ingredients. In small bowl, slightly beat the egg and add the milk, oil and molasses to it. Pour liquids all at once into well in dry ingredients. Stir gently only until dry ingredients are thoroughly moistened. Fill prepared muffin cups about half full. Bake for 15 to 20 minutes until golden brown. Serve warm.

yield: 12 muffins
MARTHA ADAMS

RICE KRISPIE COOKIES

½	cup margarine
½	cup brown sugar
½	cup granulated sugar
1	teaspoon vanilla
1	egg
1	cup all purpose flour
½	teaspoon baking powder
1	teaspoon baking soda
¼	teaspoon salt
1	cup Rice Krispies

Pre-heat over to 350°F. Cream margarine well with sugars and vanilla. Add egg, mix well. Sift dry ingredients and add to creamed mixture. Stir in Rice Krispies. Place heaping teaspoon of mixture on greased cookie sheet. Do not place cookies too close together - they spread. Bake for 8 minutes or until golden brown. Remove immediately from cookie sheet - do not allow to cool or they will stick. Yield may vary, depending on how large you desire cookies. These keep well for weeks in a tight container.

yield: Approximately 2 dozen
BARBARA VON STORCH

PECAN PIE SURPRISE BARS

Crust:
- 1 package yellow cake mix: reserve 2/3 cup for filling
- ½ cup butter, melted
- 1 egg

Filling:
- ⅔ cup reserved cake mix
- ½ cup firmly packed brown sugar
- 1½ cups dark corn syrup
- 3 eggs

Topping:
- 1 cup chopped pecans

Pre-heat oven to 350°F. Crust: Grease bottom and sides of 13" × 9" pan. Reserve 2/3 cup dry cake mix for filling. In a large bowl, combine remaining dry cake mix, butter and one egg. Mix until crumbly. Press into greased pan. Bake for 15 to 20 minutes. Filling: In a large bowl, combine all ingredients. Beat at medium speed for 2 minutes. Pour over partially baked crust. Sprinkle with chopped pecans. Return to oven and bake 40–50 minutes until light golden brown. Cool, cut.

yield: 36 bars
BARBARA SCHEUER

MENU II

FISH CHOWDER

- 1 1-pound 4-ounce can tomatoes, put through strainer
- 1 large clove garlic, minced
- 6 onions, sliced
- 6 potatoes, diced
- 1 small can peas
- 3 cups water
- 2 pounds haddock or halibut fillet, fresh or frozen
- 1 tablespoon salt
- Pepper to taste
- ¼ teaspoon thyme
- ½ teaspoon rosemary
- 1 pint light cream
- ¼ pound butter

Prepare all the vegetables and put in large kettle with water. Put fish on top. Add salt, pepper and spices. Cook for 1½ hours over low heat. Before serving, add butter and cream and heat for fifteen minutes, without boiling. This can be a meal in itself with a salad and french bread before a meeting or the theater.

yield: 8 servings
MARY BELIN

TUSCAN BEAN SOUP

2½ cups dried white beans, soaked overnight
2-3 tablespoons olive oil
1 clove garlic, finely chopped
1 onion, finely chopped
1 carrot, finely chopped
1 stalk celery, finely chopped
2 leeks, finely chopped
1 teaspoon Rosemary, crushed
½ teaspoon hot pepper flakes
1 ham bone
Salt, pepper, water

Garnish:
½ cup olive oil
2 cloves garlic, crushed
Pinch thyme
8 slices of bread, toasted
¾ cups grated Parmesan cheese
1 onion, thinly sliced

Drain beans. Heat olive oil in soup kettle and gently sauté garlic, onion, carrot, celery, leeks, rosemary, and hot pepper flakes until they begin to brown. Add the beans and ham bone, cover with water, season with salt and pepper and simmer gently for about 2 hours or until the beans are tender. It may be necessary to add a bit more water from time to time. Remove the ham bone and rub about half the beans through a seive, or purée in a blender. Return the purée to the soup. The soup may be served now, or with garnish.

Garnish: Pre-heat oven to 375°F. Heat olive oil and sauté the garlic and thyme until golden. Strain half the oil into the soup and stir well. Discard the garlic. Arrange the slices of toast in the bottom of an ovenproof tureen, sprinkle with half the Parmesan cheese, and pour the soup over the top. Cover with the onion slices, add the rest of the oil and grated cheese. Cook in oven for about ½ hour.

yield: 6-8 servings
JEAN COLOMBO

JAMAICA PEPPERPOT SOUP

1½	pounds soup meat
¾	pound pigs tail or any salted meat
½	pounds coco or yam
2½	pounds fresh spinach, chopped fine
1½	pounds kale, chopped fine
1	medium onion, chopped
1	clove garlic, crushed
3	large scallions, chopped fine
1-2	sprigs thyme
1	whole unbroken green hot pepper
1	pound shrimp, cooked
½	cup coconut milk
1	egg, hard cooked and chopped coarsely

Place soup meat and pigs tail in a large soup kettle with about 4 quarts of cold water. Boil slowly until meat is nearly cooked, then add coco or yam. In a separate saucepan, place all chopped greens, onion, garlic and scallions and steam covered until cooked, about ten minutes. Rub all vegetables through a coarse strainer or colander into soup kettle.

Add thyme and green hot pepper. Taste for flavor and if more salt is needed, add now. If more boiling water is needed, add now. Simmer until soup appears to have thickened, then add shrimp. Lastly, add coconut milk and cook for only five minutes after last addition. Garnish with chopped egg.

yield: 12 servings
LARRY THEILGARD

ITALIAN CHEESE BREAD CRESCIA

½	pound butter
½	pound margarine
12	cups flour
6	cups locatelli or Romano cheese, grated
1	jigger olive oil
8	teaspoons pepper (or less to taste)
15	eggs, well beaten (5 minutes)
5	large compressed yeast cakes
1½	cups lukewarm water
1	egg, diluted with 1 tablespoon water

Cream butter and margarine with 1 cup flour. Add cheese, oil, pepper, eggs. Dissolve yeast with 1½ cups lukewarm water. Add to creamed mixture and add remaining flour. Grease five 9½" × 5½" loaf pans; fill halfway with batter and place in warm oven. When doubled in bulk, leave in oven and brush tops with egg diluted with water. Turn oven on to 325°F. Bake for 45 minutes or until golden brown.

yield: 5 loaves

This is a traditional Easter bread. The custom was to put a small piece of palm from Palm Sunday into the top of the bread before baking and then the bread was taken in baskets to church were the priest would say a blessing.

Makes a wonderful snack by slicing very thin, brushing with butter and sprinkling with herb-cheese mixture and then baking slowly in 250 F.° oven for an hour. Freezes well.

CORRINE O'DONNELL

ANADAMA BREAD

1	cup water
1	teaspoon salt
¾	cup cornmeal
2	tablespoons safflower or sunflower oil
⅓	cup molasses
1⅓	cups warm water
2	tablespoons yeast
5–6	cups whole wheat flour

Bring 1 cup water and salt to boil. Stir in cornmeal, oil and molasses until smooth. Remove from heat and let cool so it will not kill the yeast. Dissolve the yeast in 1⅓ cups warm water. Add to cooled cornmeal mush. Add 2 cups flour and stir vigorously until the dough is stringy, to indicate the gluten in the flour is activated. Knead in the rest of the flour until the dough is smooth and forms ball. Oil ball, cover, let rise until double in bulk. Punch down, divide into two 1½ pound balls. Roll out air bubbles. Shape into loaves and place in greased 8" × 4" pans. Let rise until double. Pre-heat oven to 375°F. Bake thirty minutes. Remove from pan to cool.

yield: Two 1½ pound loaves
ROSAMOND PECK

BLACK BOTTOM CUPCAKES

1	8-ounce package cream cheese
½	cup sugar
1	egg
	salt
1	cup chocolate chips
1½	cups flour
¼	cup cocoa
1	cup sugar
½	teaspoon salt
1	teaspoon baking soda
1	teaspoon vinegar
1	teaspoon vanilla
½	cup oil
1	cup water

Topping:
½	cup chopped walnuts
	Sugar

Pre-heat oven to 350°F. In small bowl beat cream cheese, ½ cup sugar, egg and pinch of salt until creamy. Add chocolate chips and set aside. In large bowl beat together other ingredients, except nuts and sugar for topping. Fill paper-lined muffin tins ⅓ full. Spoon the cream cheese mixture over chocolate batter. Sprinkle each cake with some nuts and sugar. Bake for 20–25 minutes, but no longer.

yield: 2 dozen

Freezes well. For best taste store in refrigerator. Given to me by a Scranton friend, this is a family favorite and great for school lunches.

JULIA MUMFORD

LACY OATMEAL COOKIES

- 1 cup oil
- 1 cup sugar
- 2 eggs
- 2 cups oatmeal
- 1½ cups flour
- 1 teaspoon cinnamon
- 1 teaspoon salt
- 1½ cups raisins
- 1 teaspoon soda
- 1 tablespoon vinegar

Pre-heat oven to 400°F. Beat oil and sugar together until frothy. Beat eggs and add to oil mixture. Stir in oatmeal. Sift flour and spices together and stir into batter. Add raisins, soda and vinegar, stir until well blended. Drop by spoonfuls onto cookie sheet and bake for 10 minutes.

yield: 5 dozen
LUCY PECK EYSENBACH

205

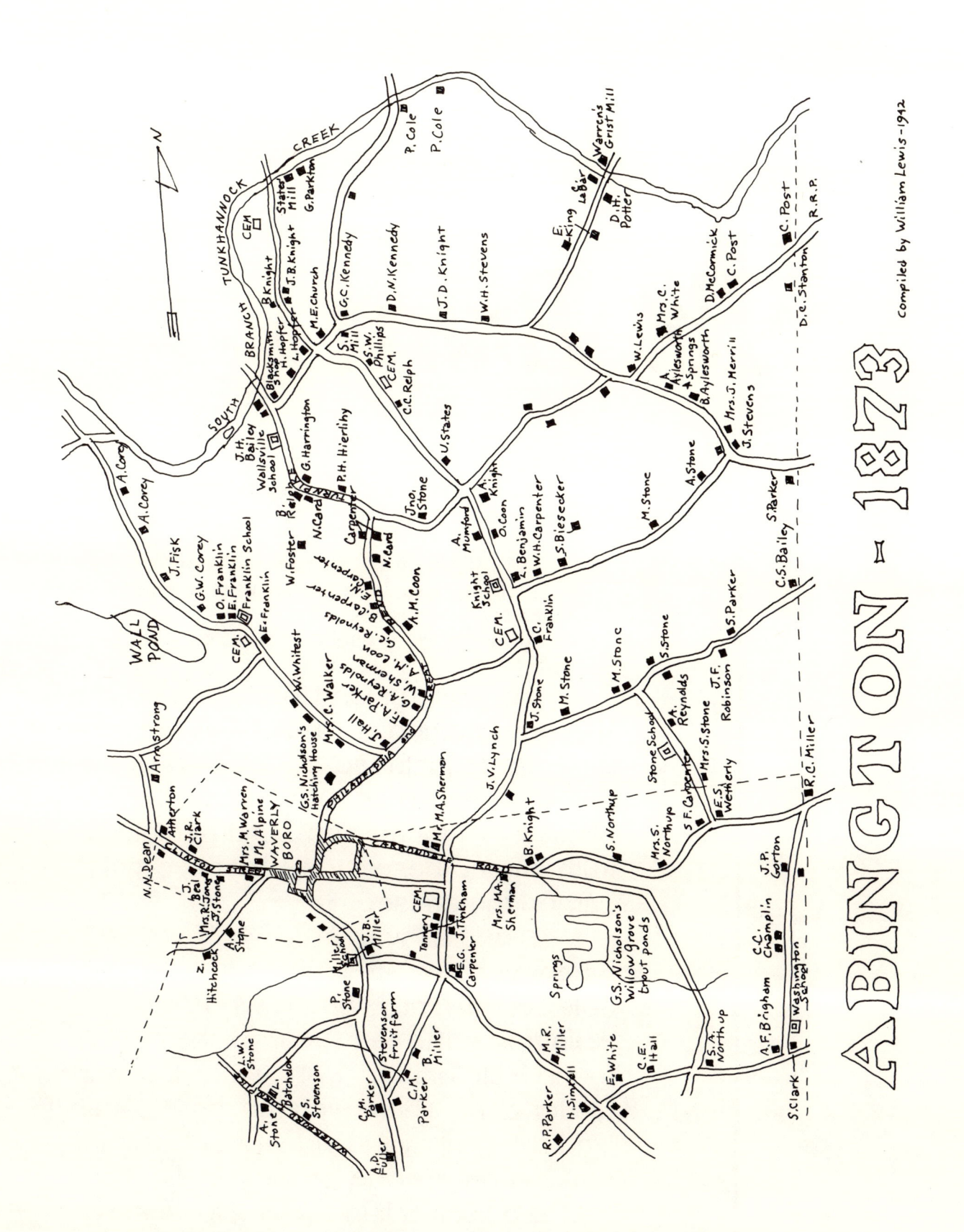

Pot Pourri

...Happy the homes where they are
found;
Happy the land where such abound;
Happy the mothers who can share
Kindly aid of such daughters fair;
Happy the brothers, who, with pride,
Walk with such sisters by their side;
Happy the lovers who have won
Rosy-cheeked girls of Abington...

The Milkmaids Convention at the Waverly Methodist Church, in December, 1871, included a recitation of this poem, written in 1850. Although the verbiage is Victorian and sentimental, the truth is that those "rosy-cheeked girls" earned the praise.

Pioneer women, wherever and whenever they are found, are a remarkable breed. The women who settled in Abington in the early years of the 1800's found a life of hard work, with little margin for error. There were no institutionalized safety nets; individual responsibility was a cornerstone of their lives. They had to be self-reliant, willing to tackle an exhausting variety of chores and chal-

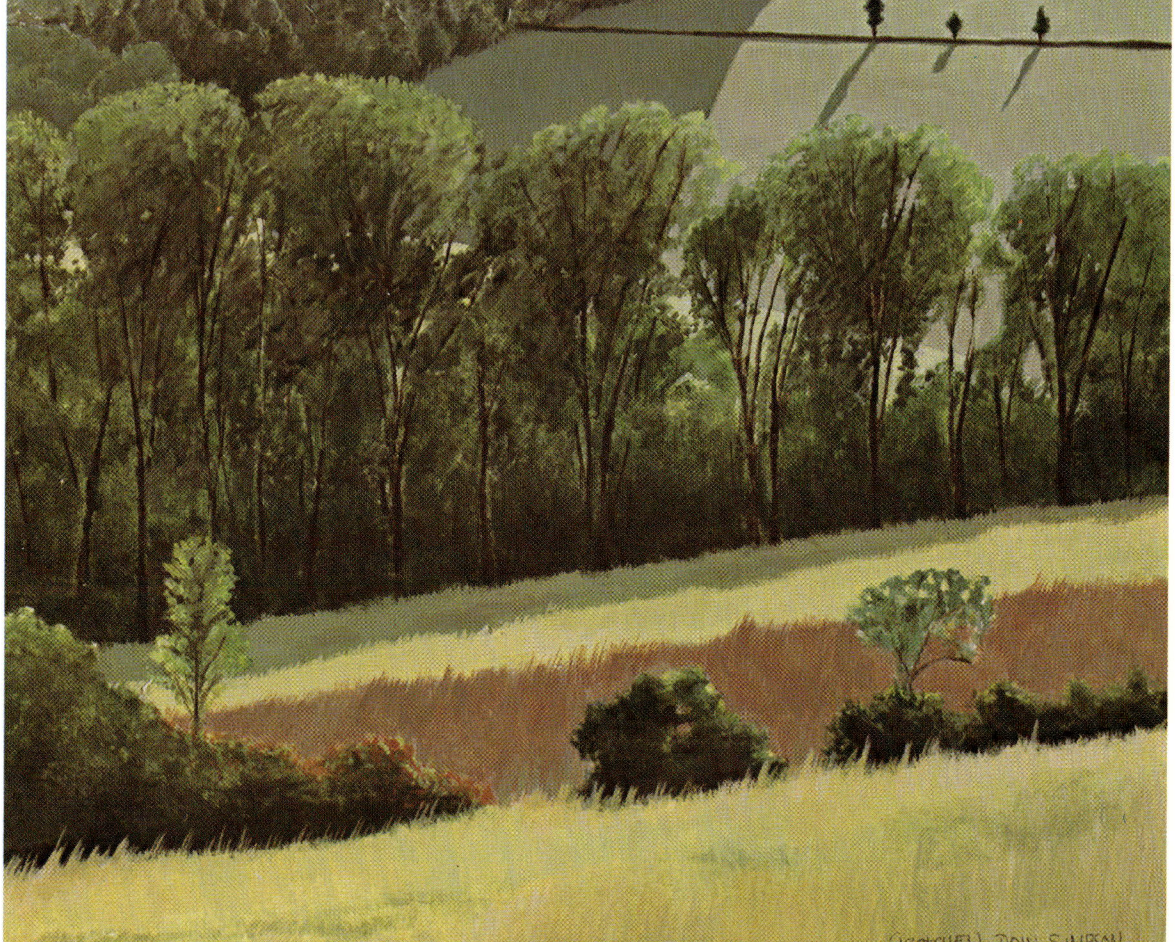
GRETCHEN DOW SIMPSON

lenges. That work was indoors and out, skilled and arduous, from sun to sun, and never done. Add to this the harsh dangers of child-bearing at that time, and it is clear that this life was especially hard on women. This can be seen in the wry poem attributed to Tom Hall and said to describe Deacon Lora W. Stone:

> The Deacon lay on his first wife's bed;
> His second wife's pillow under his head;
> His third wife's coverlet over his hide;
> While his fourth wife slumbered by his side.

The women's work also included, traditionally, that of teaching, sensitizing, refining. It is certain that Jonathan Hall's widowed mother was very influential in the construction of the first plank house in the township. Though her husband died before he could bring his family back to the land he had selected in Abington, she carried out their resolve, and arrived with their children in 1801. A log cabin was adequate shelter, but in 1802, work began on an ambitious project. Six years' work produced the handsome house with five upstairs bedrooms, that overlooks today's Church Street hill from the upper edge of Waterford Road in Glenburn.

There were no roads in 1811, but on a nearby hilltop, in what is now Clarks Green, William Clark and his wife were ready to leave the cramped log house near the burying ground. The elegant plank house they built has a large central hall and is decorated with four graceful doorways with fanlights and sidelights. Such adornment of a house in the wilderness was beyond useful purpose and can only have been done to satisfy the love of beauty.

In 1820, the Turnpike project promised prosperity and sparked more construction of graceful houses. Jeremiah Clark's home was a double house, to serve as an inn for turnpike travelers. It was just across the Green from his brother's house. Stephen and Mary Parker built, on the hillside farther north along the turnpike route, a house that shows their New England heritage in its attached outbuildings.

But most of the young township was covered with trees, only rarely marked by a small clearing and a house, isolated and crude, with dark miles before the next clearing. Through these hard and lonely times, the women helped keep civilization in focus. And as neighbors move closer and mechanical assistants lighten the load, this intangible vision is even more important.

Women of the late twentieth century have a very different set of challenges and dangers to meet. Opportunities have expanded at an exponential rate, but we still live in a twenty-four hour day. Labor saving devices crowd our homes, so we venture into the marketplace to find new jobs and validity. Incredible varieties of foods are available, yet we find ourselves suspicious of ingredients that will not spoil, counting the calories in food that almost leaps to our lips, and struggling to resist that midnight snack, the pause that refleshes. There is a dazzling array of things we can do, but when we have done them, they are only done. Then what?

We must *be* something. We educate our minds and train our bodies. We must keep our heart-strings out where they can be tugged. With space-age communications we can be tuned to disaster on a world-wide scale; we have trained specialists in every area of political, social and medical intervention; but when it comes to our own backyard, too often, today, "We don't want to be involved" and we need a major corporation to urge us to "reach out and touch someone."

Our families teach us how to touch each other. At our dinner tables we learn basic social values and skills. And as we learn, so we go out to build our communities. At home we learn to listen, to notice, to discover what we want, to compromise, to accept responsibility. These skills need to be practiced on a human scale with real people, in real life, for peace begins with us; it is not just an idea.

Millions of dinner tables have been set in Waverly over the years, with a pot pourri of delicious foods and some superior teachings by our distinguished men and women. The values are not new; they are very old, but they have been *lived* here. By this living, we build humans, families, communities and nations. Of course, our community is unique. We must honor that. Of course, it has unnumbered counterparts. And we must honor that as well. And with these honors due, we celebrate the life, the history, the flavor of Waverly.

Pot Pourri

SOUP AND SALAD
PASTA
POULTRY
MEAT
FISH
VEGETABLES
BAKED GOODS
DESSERTS

SOUP AND SALAD

SENEGALESE SOUP

¼ cup minced onion
¼ cup minced celery
2 teaspoons curry powder
2 tablespoons margarine or butter
1 can cream of chicken soup
1 cup half n' half cream

Garnish:
　Chutney
　Chopped Chicken

Cook onion, celery and curry in margarine or butter until tender. Mix with soup and half n' half. Blend at low speed until smooth. Serve hot or cold with chutney or chopped chicken added to each soup bowl. Thin if desired with chicken broth.

yield: 4 to 6 cups
RHODA WARREN

COLD CREAM OF CARROT SOUP

1 cup carrots, sliced
1 medium onion, sliced
1 stock of celery with leaves, sliced
1½ cups chicken stock
1 teaspoon salt
　Generous pinch of cayenne pepper
½ cup cooked rice
¾ cup cream

Garnish:
　Diced pimento, chives or parsley

Place carrots, onion, celery and half of chicken stock in saucepan. Bring to a boil, cover, reduce heat and simmer 15 minutes. Transfer to electric blender and add salt, cayenne and cooked rice. Cover and turn on high speed. Remove cover and with motor running pour in remaining stock and cream. Chill and garnish with diced pimento, chives or parsley.

yield: 6 servings
IRENE REID

CARROT SOUP

3	tablespoons butter
2	pounds carrots, scraped and chopped
2	large onions, sliced
2	potatoes peeled and chopped, about 1 pound
1	bay leaf
½	teaspoon dry sage
½	teaspoon dry dill
¼	teaspoon curry powder
6	cups chicken stock, or more
	Salt and freshly ground pepper to taste

Garnish:
　Minced fresh parsley, or dry

Melt butter in Dutch oven or other large pan over low heat. Add carrot and onion. Cover with lid or circle of waxed paper and let steam about 8 minutes. Take off lid and add potatoes, bay leaf, sage, dill, curry powder and chicken stock. Simmer, covered, until vegetables are tender, about 40 minutes. Discard bay leaf.

　Purée soup in batches in processor or blender. Return to pan and season with salt and pepper to taste. Place over medium heat and bring to boil, stirring occassionally. You can add some more chicken stock or even some dry white wine if thinner soup is preferred. Ladle into bowls and garnish with minced parsley.

yield: 8 servings

I slice the carrots and onions in food processor first and put them in the pan, then slice the potatoes in processor. The spices can be varied to taste.

SHERRY W. CONNELL

SPINACH EGG DROP SOUP

3	cups clear chicken stock
3	eggs, beaten
5	ounces spinach, cooked, drained and chopped

Bring stock to a full boil in medium size sauce pan. Pour in beaten eggs very slowly, stirring constantly just until eggs cook and separate into shreads. Add spinach and serve immediately. Easy, quick and delicious.

yield: 6 servings
NORA FOX

POTATO SOUP WITH SPINACH BALLS

- ⅓ cup chopped onion
- 1½ cups peeled, cubed potatoes
- 2 tablespoons butter
- 3 14-ounce cans chicken broth, or use homemade stock
- 1 cup frozen chopped spinach, cooked and well-drained
- 1 cup bread crumbs
- 1 egg white, slightly beaten
- ¼ teaspoon nutmeg

Cook onions and potatoes in butter over medium heat until tender, 10 to 15 minutes. Add chicken broth; reduce heat to low and cook 20 minutes more. Meanwhile, prepare spinach balls. Combine spinach, bread crumbs and egg white; let stand 15 minutes to firm. Shape mixture into balls the size of marbles. Add to simmering broth and cook 5 more minutes. Garnish with nutmeg.

yield: 4 servings
KATHY CESARE

LENTIL SOUP

- 2 cups lentils
- ½ pound each sweet and hot sausage
- 4 cups chicken broth
- 6 cups water
- 8 ounces pepperoni, thinly sliced
- 1 cup onion, chopped
- 1 16-ounce can of tomatoes
- ½ teaspoon salt
- ½ teaspoon oregano
- ¼ teaspoon sage
- ¼ teaspoon cayenne
- 2 carrots, sliced
- 2 stalks celery, sliced

Wash lentils; cut sausage into small pieces and fry in the soup kettle. Drain. Add lentils, chicken broth, water, pepperoni, onions, tomatoes, salt, oregano, sage and cayenne. Bring to a boil; reduce heat to a gentle simmer. Cover and simmer 30 minutes, stirring occasionally. Add carrots and celery, cover and simmer another 40 minutes.

yield: 8 servings
JEAN COLOMBO

MIMERER'S CABBAGE SALAD

- 1 medium cabbage
- 5 stalks celery
- ¼ cup lemon juice
- ½ cup oil
- Lowery's Seasoning Salt to taste

Chop cabbage and celery coarsely. Mix lemon juice, oil and seasoning salt. Pour over cabbage and celery. Toss well.

yield: 6 servings

My grandmother always made this to go with a roast for Sunday dinner. It is also very good with cottage cheese and apples for a light lunch.

KATHY POGUE

MA MAISON'S CHICKEN SALAD

1	3-pound chcken, simmered until tender
1	medium golden delicious apple
1	stalk celery
1	tablespoon capers
2	tablespoons Moutard de Meaux
½	cup mayonnaise
	Salt
	Freshly ground pepper
	Lemon juice

Garnish:
Sliced tomatoes, eggs or green beans

Remove the skin from cooled chicken. Peel meat from the bones and shred. Do not cut with a knife. Peel and core the apple. Cut into ¼" cubes. Cut celery stalk into ¼" cubes. Mix chicken, apple, celery, capers and mustard. Add enough mayonnaise to coat lightly. Taste and correct seasoning with salt, pepper and lemon juice. Add more mustard if desired. Serve without refrigeration.

Optional: Garnish with tomatoes, green beans and slices of hard boiled egg. Serve on a bed of lettuce.

The chicken should be torn apart and mixed with all the seasonings when still warm. It does not have to be refrigerated and should be served at room temperature.

yield: 6 servings

This recipe is from Wolfgang Puck, owner of Spago and Chinois, Los Angeles, California.

SUSAN SCRANTON

POPPY SEED SALAD DRESSING

1½	cups sugar
⅔	cup vinegar
2	teaspoons salt
2	teaspoons mustard, dry or prepared
1	tablespoon grated onion
	Scant 2 cups oil
2	tablespoons poppy seeds

Mix first five ingredients in blender. While blending, slowly add oil. Add poppy seeds and blend lightly. Store in jar in refrigerator.

yield: 4 cups

Whenever I serve this on salad, I am asked for the recipe. I usually only make half the recipe. It lasts several days.

JULIA MUMFORD

PASTA

RICE RING

1 cup rice
2 cups chicken stock
1 tablespoon salt
2 tablespoons butter or margarine
2 egg yolks
3 tablespoons cream or milk

Pre-heat oven to 350°F. Cook rice in stock ½ hour. Add salt and butter. Beat yolks with cream and stir into warm rice. Pack rice mixture firmly into 7" greased ring mold. Bake for 20 minutes. Let stand 10 minutes in warm place. Turn out on platter.

yield: 8 servings

Fill center of rice ring with any mixture. We like it with sautéed chicken livers.

DITTY QUIGG

PHILHARMONIC TORTELLINI SALAD

1 pound cheese tortellini
1 cup cherry tomatoes
4 cups crisp-steamed assorted vegetables (broccoli, beans, zucchini, cauliflower, snow peas artichoke hearts)
½ cup pitted olives, drained and sliced

Vinaigrette Dressing:
½ cup olive oil
4 tablespoons wine vinegar
¼ teaspoon dried basil
¼ teaspoon dried oregano
1 teaspoon Dijon mustard
½ teaspoon salt
¼ teaspoon cracked pepper

Cook tortellini as per directions. Drain and chill. Mix the tomatoes and steamed vegetables with tortellini. Add olives. Mix all ingredients for dressing. Toss with salad just before serving.

yield: 6 to 8 servings

In September of 1983, the Philharmonic Women's League of Scranton sold this salad at La Festa Italiana. In preparing our share of the salad, Marilyn Costa and I spent several hours "cleaning out" Jean and Chris Colombo's garden - multiplying the recipe at least 20 times by preparing about 20 pounds of freshly picked vegetables in addition to at least 20 cups of tomatoes!

NATALIE SOLFANELLI

PESTO PIZZA

1	10½" × 16" par-cooked pizza crust, store-bought, regular or whole wheat
1	cup pesto sauce
1	pound Mozzarella cheese, grated
4	ounces Cheddar cheese, grated
1	medium onion, sliced very thin
2	garden fresh ripe tomatoes, sliced thin

Pre-heat oven to 375°. Place pizza shell on a large cookie sheet sprayed with Pam. Spread pesto over the entire crust. Sprinkle ½ cup grated Mozzarella cheese over the sauce. Spread onions evenly over cheese. Place tomato slices in rows over cheese. Cover with remaining cheeses. Bake for 15-20 minutes until cheese is melted and crust is crispy. Cut into large squares for a meal with salad. Cut into small bite size pieces for hors d'oeuvres.

yield: 8 large or 24 bite-size pieces
CHERYL ROSE-WEAVER

LINGUINE WITH WHITE CLAM SAUCE

4	tablespoons olive oil
8	large cloves garlic, 4 whole, 4 minced
2	8-ounce bottles clam juice
2	8-ounce cans minced clams
½	cup dry white wine
1	pound linguine
¼	cup butter, melted
3	tablespoons minced parsley

Heat oil in frying pan. Add 4 whole cloves garlic, sautéing until garlic is brown. Take pan from heat, discard garlic. Pour clam juice, liquid from cans of clams and wine into pan. Place pan on medium heat and boil to reduce liquid by half. Stir in minced garlic and cook until soft; add clams. Bring sauce to a soft boil, remove from heat so clams don't toughen. Cook linguine, "al dente". Toss with butter, add clam sauce, toss again. Add parsley, toss again.

yield: Dinner for 4, or first course for 6

Serve with garlic bread and salad. My mouth waters just thinking about it.

PAT TIERNEY

PASTA WITH BROCCOLI

- 2 packages frozen, chopped broccoli or equivalent fresh broccoli
- ½ pound butter
- 2-3 anchovies, chopped
- ½ teaspoon anchovy oil
- 3 cloves garlic, pressed
- 1 1-pound box ziti macaroni

Sauce:
- 1 stick butter, melted
- ½ cup Parmesan or Locotelli cheese, grated
- ½ teaspoon dried red peppers

Sauté broccoli for 10 minutes in butter, anchovies, oil and garlic. Set aside in warm place. Boil pasta according to directions on box and drain. Mix together ingredients for sauce. Toss hot sauce with pasta. Add broccoli mixture and serve immediately.

yield: 6 servings

Delicious served as a side dish.

BETSY JONES

COLD SPAGHETTI

- 1 eggplant
- 1 cup olive oil
- 3 cloves garlic, chopped fine
- 1 onion, sliced
- 1 red or green pepper, sliced in julienne strips
- ½ pound mushrooms, sliced and sauteed in 1 tablespoon olive oil
- 1 pound spaghetti
- 12 black olives
- 3 tablespoons fresh parsley, chopped

Peel and dice the eggplant. Heat ½ cup of the olive oil in a large frying pan. Add the garlic and sauté until golden brown. Add the onion and sauté until golden brown. Add the pepper slices and sauté until lightly browned. Remove the pan from the heat and add the sautéed mushrooms.

In a large pot of water, cook the spaghetti until "al dente". Drain and toss immediately with remaining half cup olive oil, coating all the strands to prevent them from sticking.

Toss the spaghetti with the eggplant mixture and the black olives and let it cool completely. Just before serving, add the parsley and mix well.

yield: 4 to 6 servings
MIDGE CAVALIERI

NOODLE CASSEROLE

- 8 ounces small egg noodles
- ½ cup chives
- 1 pint sour cream
- 8 ounces small curd cottage cheese
- Salt and Pepper to taste
- 1 tablespoon butter

Pre-heat oven to 325°F. Cook noodles according to package directions. Drain. Mix chives, sour cream, cottage cheese, salt and pepper. Add to noodles and place in shallow buttered casserole. Bake for 25 minutes.

yield: 6 servings
PAT ATKINS

NOODLE PUDDING

1	pound broad noodles
½	pound butter or margarine, melted
5	eggs, separated
1	pint sour cream
8	ounces cream cheese, softened
½	cup sugar
	Corn flake crumbs

Optional:
- 1 cup raisins
- ½ cup chopped pineapple

Pre-heat oven to 350°F. Cook noodles and drain. Combine butter, egg yolks, sour cream, cream cheese, and sugar and toss with noodles. Beat egg whites until foamy and add to noodle mixture. Add fruit if desired. Pour into greased lasagna pan or large casserole. Shake on corn flake crumbs. Refrigerate for 2 hours or overnight if possible or bake 15 minutes, cool and freeze. When baking, bake for 45 minutes if casserole is at room temperature or 60 minutes if cold.

yield: 12 servings
NATALIE SOLFANELLI

POULTRY

CHICKEN PIE

1	roasting chicken, 4½ to 5 pounds
2½	quarts water
1	clove garlic, crushed
4	peppercorns
1	celery stock, chopped coarsely
1	large onion studded with 4 to 6 cloves
1	tablespoon salt
3	carrots, scraped, cut into 1 inch pieces
12	small pearl onions
½	pound mushrooms
12	tablespoons butter
⅔	cups flour
½	cup cooked peas (baby frozen best)
1	tablespoon chopped parsley
1	egg yolk
1	tablespoon heavy cream

Pie Crust:
1½	cups sifted flour
8	tablespoons butter, softened
1	egg yolk
1	tablespoon ice water

Pre-heat oven to 400°F. Rinse and dry chicken. Put chicken in large kettle, cover with water and add next five ingredients. Bring to a boil, reduce heat and simmer about 1 hour and 20 minutes or until chicken is tender.

Remove chicken from broth and cool. Remove celery and onion with spoon. Skim fat from broth and taste for chicken flavor. Bring broth to boil. Add carrots and onions. Cook for 20 minutes and remove. Add mushrooms, cook for 15 minutes and remove. Strain remaining broth and measure out four cups.

Prepare sauce. Melt butter in heavy skillet. Stir in flour. Cook for about 3 minutes, until bubbly but not brown. Gradually add four cups broth, stirring constantly until smooth. Remove the sauce from heat.

Remove chicken from bones. Remove skin and cut chicken into large pieces. There should be about four cups. Pour half of sauce into quart casserole. Arrange chicken and vegetables over sauce and add peas and remaining sauce. Sprinkle with parsley.

Crust: Place flour in center of pastry board. Cut in butter, egg yolk and ice water. Work mixture together with fingers until well blended. Form into ball. Refrigerate. You can use food processor with frozen butter and a pinch more water, if desired.

Cover chicken and vegetables with pie crust which has been rolled between wax paper. Cut steam vents and decorate with pastry trim. Combine egg yolk and cream and brush on pie. Bake for 45 minutes until crust is deep golden brown.

yield: 8 servings
JANET WRIGHTNOUR

LIGHTEST OF CHICKENS

Pre-heat oven to 350°F. Place cutlets in baking container. Squeeze lemon juice on each. Place green onion and pepper slices on each. Season with salt and fresh ground pepper. Bake for 35 minutes, covered. Add optional flavors as desired.

yield: Variable, depending on your need
SALLY E. PREATE

Boned chicken cutlets, 1 or 2 per person
Lemon juice
Green onions, chopped
Italian peppers, sliced lengthwise
Salt
Pepper

Optional:
Cherry tomatoes, halved
Thinly sliced lemon
Sliced carrots

CHICKEN IN CHIVES AND SOUR CREAM

Mix sour cream, chives, tarragon, salt, pepper, vinegar and sugar. Refrigerate several hours to blend flavors.

Pre-heat oven to 400°F. Melt 2 tablespoons butter in an 9" × 12" casserole. Put flour, salt and pepper into a paper bag. Place chicken breasts in bag, one at a time. Shake bag well. Dip floured chicken pieces in sour cream mixture. Coat well. Place chicken in buttered casserole. Sprinkle with paprika. Cover tightly. Bake for 30-40 minutes. Serve chicken over boiled rice accompanied by buttered sweet peas. Do not freeze.

yield: 4 servings
GUDRUN PICKERING

- 1 pint sour cream
- 2 teaspoons chopped chives
- 2 teaspoons tarragon
- ½ teaspoon salt
- ¼ teaspoon pepper
- 2 tablespoons white vinegar
- 2 tablespoons sugar
- 2 tablespoons butter
- ¼ cup flour
- Salt
- Pepper
- Paprika to taste
- 3 whole chicken breasts, split, boned and skinned

POULET AU CITRON

- 2 2½-pound chickens, quartered
- 2 tablespoons grated lemon peel
- ½ cup lemon juice
- 2 cloves garlic, crushed
- 2 teaspoons dried thyme leaves
- 1½ teaspoons salt
- 1 teaspoon black pepper
- ¼ cup butter or margarine, melted
- 3 lemons, thinly sliced
- ½ cup chopped parsley

Wash chickens. Dry well with paper towels. Arrange chicken in single layer in shallow baking dish. Combine lemon peel and juice, garlic, thyme, salt and pepper; mix well. Spoon over chicken, turning chicken to coat well. Refrigerate in marinade three to four hours, turning chicken several times.

Pre-heat oven to 425°F. Remove chicken and drain well on paper towels, reserving marinade. Brush chicken pieces with melted butter. Bake uncovered 25 minutes. Brush with reserved marinade. Bake, brushing occasionally with marinade, for an additional 25 to 35 minutes, or until chicken is browned and cooked thoroughly. Garnish with lemon slices and sprinkle with chopped parsley. Heat any remaining marinade to serve as sauce. Serve with rice.

yield: 6 to 8 servings
MIDGE CAVALIERI

CHINESE SESAME CHICKEN

- 2 pounds boneless breast of chicken, cut into thin slices
- Cake flour for dredging
- Vegetable oil for sautéing

Marinade:
- 1 egg white
- Dash of gin
- 1 garlic clove chopped fine
- ½ teaspoon paprika

Sauce:
- 4 tablespoons butter
- 1 garlic clove, pressed
- 2 tablespoons gin
- 1 teaspoon MSG
- 1 teaspoon salt
- 1 cup chicken broth
- 2 teaspoons cornstarch
- 2 tablespoons water
- 2 teaspoons sesame oil

Garnish:
- 2 tablespoons sesame seeds, toasted

Combine marinade ingredients and mix well. Marinate chicken for ½ hour. Remove and drain well. Dredge chicken in cake flour. Sauté in skillet in vegetable oil in batches. Keep warm. Make sauce: melt butter and sauté garlic clove. Add gin, MSG, salt and chicken broth. Dissolve cornstarch in water and add to liquid. Cook until clear. Add sesame oil and pour over chicken. Garnish with toasted sesame seeds.

yield: 4 servings
GERALD B. PAYNE

CHICKEN WITH BROCCOLI

3	whole chicken breasts, split
½	cup butter, melted
½	teaspoon salt
¼	teaspoon pepper
1	can cream of mushroom soup
¼	cup Cheddar cheese
¼	cup white wine
1	package frozen broccoli

Savory Toast Strips:

4	slices white bread, toasted
⅓	cup butter, melted
½	teaspoon onion salt
⅓	cup cornflakes, crumbled
¼	cup grated Parmesan cheese

Pre-heat oven to 350°F. Combine chicken with butter, salt and pepper and cook, covered, for 45 minutes. Debone and cut up into bite size pieces. Place soup, cheese and wine in pot, and warm until cheese is melted. Cook broccoli only half the time indicated in package directions. Place broccoli in bottom of casserole, layer cut chicken on top and pour sauce over all. Bake 1 hour.

Toast: Pre-heat oven to 400°F. Trim crusts from toast; cut each slice into 5 strips. Combine butter with onion salt. On a sheet of waxed paper, mix cornflake crumbs and cheese. Dip toast strips in butter mixture; then roll in crumb mixture, coating well. Place on ungreased cookie sheet, bake 5 minutes or until crisp. Serve at once with the casserole.

yield: 4 to 6 servings
LINDA CHURLA

CHICKEN-BROCCOLI CASSEROLE

4	cups cooked chicken, cubed
1	can cream of mushroom soup
1	can mushrooms, drained
1	can cream of chicken soup
1	cup Hellman's mayonnaise
1	teaspoon lemon juice
½	teaspoon curry powder
2	packages frozen broccoli, cooked
½	cup grated cheese or bread crumbs

Pre-heat oven to 350°F. Combine all ingredients. Place in large casserole. Sprinkle top with grated cheese or bread crumbs. Bake for 30 minutes.

yield: 10 servings

I received this recipe from a Mrs. Decker at a party at the Baptist Church when their women entertained the United Methodist women. It was delicious. This recipe may be halved for a family meal.

RUTH RICHARDS

STIR-FRIED CHICKEN AND VEGETABLES

- ½ cup corn oil
- 1 clove garlic, minced
- ¼ cup scallions, chopped
- 2 whole boneless chicken breasts, skinned and cut into small pieces
- ½ head broccoli, tender heads only
- ½ sweet red pepper, sliced
- ¼ pound mushrooms, sliced
- ¼ pound snow peas
- 2 tablespoons soy sauce
- 2 cups brown rice, cooked

Heat oil in wok or large frying pan. Add garlic and scallions and cook until brown. Add chicken and stir-fry until white all over. Add broccoli and red pepper, and stir-fry for two minutes. Add mushrooms and snow peas and stir-fry for a few more minutes. Add soy sauce. Serve over cooked brown rice.

yield: 4 servings
CORAL AND LT. GOVERNOR BILL SCRANTON

MEAT

GASCONY BEEF STEW

½	pound bacon
3	cups onions, chopped
3	cups carrots, cut in bite size pieces
4	cloves garlic, crushed
½	teaspoon thyme
½	teaspoon sage
2	bay leaves, crumbled
2	teaspoons salt
¼	teaspoon pepper
6	pounds beef chuck, cut into 1" cubes
1	cup all purpose flour
1½	cups white wine
¼	cup brandy
3	cups beef broth
2	16-ounce cans tomatoes, drained and chopped

Pre-heat oven to 325°F. Cook bacon in skillet over moderate heat until crisp. Drain and crumble. In large bowl combine bacon with onions, carrots, garlic, thyme, sage, bay leaves, salt and pepper. Line bottom of 8–10 quart oven-proof casserole or Dutch oven with 1 cup of vegetable mixture. Shake beef cubes in flour. Layer half the beef over vegetables in casserole, placing cubes close together. Strew half remaining vegetables over beef. Continue layering with remaining floured beef and vegetables, ending with vegetables. Pour wine, brandy, broth and tomatoes over stew. Add water, if necessary, to cover. Bring to simmer on top of stove. Cover, place in oven and bake for 3 hours.

yield: 16 servings

Can be made ahead of time. Cool and freeze up to 4 weeks. Thaw at room temperature for 4 hours. Reheat in 350°F. oven until bubbling, about 1½ hours.

JACQUELINE O'CONNOR

BEEF BOURGUIGNON

2	pounds beef, round, sirloin, or tenderloin, cut to bite size
1	tablespoon butter, or more
1	can small onions
1	can mushrooms
3	tablespoons flour
1	tablespoon sherry wine
1	cup red wine
1	cup beef consommé
2	teaspoons tomato paste
	Salt and pepper to taste

Pre-heat oven to 250°F. Sauté beef in butter. Add onions and mushrooms. Add flour and stir well. Add wines and other ingredients, stirring until well blended and simmering. Cook, covered, in oven for 3 hours.

yield: 6 servings

If using beef tenderloin or sirloin, reduce cooking time 1½ hours. Use over rice or noodles.

IRENE G. REID

BEEF STROGANOFF

- 1 pound lean chuck steak
- 2 small onions, finely chopped
- 4 tablespoons butter
- 1 cup mushrooms, sliced
- ½ teaspoon dried basil
- ⅔ cup beef stock
- 1¼ cups sour cream
- 2½ teaspoons finely chopped chives or parsley
- Salt, pepper and nutmeg to taste

Cut meat in slices, then in strips. Sauté onions in butter; add meat and brown over fairly high heat. Reduce heat; add mushrooms, basil and stock. Bring to a boil, cover and simmer 45 minutes. Add sour cream and re-heat but don't boil. Sprinkle with chopped parsley or chives. Season to taste.

yield: 4 to 6 servings

Serve over rice or noodles.

IRENE G. REID

BRISKET OF BEEF

- 1 whole beef brisket, approximately 8 pounds
- 2 large cloves garlic, minced
- 2 large onions, coarsely chopped
- 3 slices rye bread
- Pepper to taste
- 3 tablespoons Worcestershire sauce
- 2 packages onion soup mix
- 1 bottle chili sauce
- 1 can beer

Pre-heat oven to 350°F. Place brisket on a bed of garlic and onions in a roasting pan with tight cover. Tear bread into small pieces and scatter over meat. Cover meat and bread with pepper, Worcestershire sauce, soup mix, chili sauce, and beer. Cook for 1 hour. Reduce heat to 275°F. and cook for 3 hours longer. When cooked, let meat stand to cool, then slice. To make gravy, use bread, onions and liquid and blend in processor or blender until smooth. Re-heat meat in gravy, and pour extra gravy in gravy boat for passing.

yield: 12 servings

I serve this with carrots, mashed potatoes, tossed salad and garlic bread.

PAT TIERNEY

TERIYAKI

2 pounds sirloin steak

Marinade:
1 tablespoon finely chopped fresh ginger, or 2 teaspoons powdered
2 cloves garlic, chopped fine
1 medium onion, chopped fine
2 tablespoons sugar
½ cup soy sauce
1 cup water

Cut steak into ¼ inch strips. Mix marinade ingredients and pour over steak. Marinate overnight. May be refrigerated or frozen at this point. When ready to serve, bring to room temperature, place meat in shallow pan and broil 3 to 5 minutes on each side, basting with marinade.

yield: 6 servings

Serve with rice and steamed vegetables.

LETHA W. REINHEIMER

SLIMMEST OF BEEFS

3-5 slices cold rare roast beef per person, almost paper thin
Capers
Mushrooms, sliced
Fresh parsley, chopped
Oil
Lemon juice
Salt and Pepper

Arrange sliced beef on each platter; making each slice a petal around the imaginary center. Sprinkle with capers, mushrooms, and parsley to taste. Mix ⅔ oil and ⅓ lemon juice and pour generously on each. Sprinkle with salt and pepper to taste.

yield: Variable, depending on your need

SALLY PREATE

STUFFED MONTEREY JACK

1	cup onion, chopped
1	clove garlic, chopped
1	tablespoon oil
1¼	pounds ground beef
½	cup white wine
1	cup chicken stock
	Ground cumin
	Red Pepper
	Salt
½	cup green pepper, diced
½	cup red pepper, diced
½	cup seedless raisins
½	cup sliced almonds
1	cup cooked rice
1	tablespoon cornstarch
2	tablespoons water
1½	pounds Monterey Jack cheese
2	tablespoons bread crumbs

Pre-heat oven to 350°F. Sauté onions and garlic in hot oil until transparent. Add beef and brown. Pour off excess fat. Deglaze pan with wine. Add chicken stock and seasonings and simmer, covered, for 30 minutes. Stir in peppers, raisins, almonds and rice. Cook and stir five minutes or until most all liquid has evaporated. Blend cornstarch with water and pour over beef mixture and stir quickly. Cool. Line a 3-quart soufflé dish with slices of the cheese, overlapping slices by ¼ inch. Chop and reserve trimmings. Pour in beef mixture; press lightly. Combine cheese trimmings and bread crumbs and sprinkle on top. Bake in a water bath for 45 minutes. Remove from oven. Let stand at least 15 to 20 minutes before unmolding carefully onto pre-heated serving platter.

yield: 6 servings
PAT ATKINS

IMPOSSIBLE CHEESEBURGER PIE

1	pound ground beef
1½	cups chopped onion
½	teaspoon salt
¼	teaspoon pepper
1½	cups milk
¾	cup Bisquick baking mix
3	eggs
2	tomatoes, sliced
1	cup shredded Cheddar or Process American cheese

Pre-heat oven to 400°F. Grease 10" pie plate. Brown beef and onion; drain. Stir in salt and pepper. Spread in plate. Beat milk, baking mix and eggs until smooth: 15 seconds in blender on high, or 1 minute with hand beater. Pour into plate. Bake 25 minutes. Top with tomatoes; sprinkle with cheese. Bake until knife inserted in center comes out clean, 5 to 8 minutes. Cool 5 minutes. Serve.

yield: 6 to 8 servings

This is a delicious dish that looks and tastes almost like pizza.

CAROL COMSTOCK

ITALIAN MEATBALLS

2	pounds ground chuck
6	slices stale bread soaked in water
1½	teaspoons salt
1	clove fresh garlic, mashed
2	eggs
1	handful grated Parmesan or Romano cheese
½	teaspoon pepper
1	teaspoon dry basil
1	teaspoon parsley flakes
1	small onion, chopped

Mix all ingredients except onion well but gently in a large bowl. Shape into meatballs and sauté in cooking oil with onion until done.

Instead of sautéing meatballs, you can bake them in pre-heated 350°F. oven. Pour ⅛" oil in flat baking dish. Add meatballs and onions, cover with foil and bake 15 minutes. Turn meatballs, re-cover and bake 15 minutes. Uncover and bake approximately 15 minutes to brown.

yield: 3 dozen

They are also delicious if cooked directly in tomato sauce and not fried or baked beforehand. They freeze well. This recipe is a speciality handed down by my mother, Rose Grassi.

ESTELLE G. KELLY

VENISON STROGANOFF

- 1 large Spanish onion, sliced
- 2 tablespoons butter
- ½ pound fresh mushrooms, sliced
- 3 pounds venison steak, cut into 2" × 1" thin strips
- 2 bay leaves
- 1 teaspoon salt
- 1 teaspoon pepper or less
- 1 teaspoon Worcestershire sauce
- ½ cup beef bouillon
- 1 cup sherry
- 2 cups sour cream

Brown onions in butter; drain and save. Sauté mushrooms; set aside. Brown meat in same pot used for onions and mushrooms. Return onions to pot; add seasonings, bouillon, and ½ cup sherry. Cover and simmer gently for 1½ hours or until tender. During last half hour of cooking, add remaining sherry and mushrooms. If desired, gravy may be thickened with a paste of flour and water. When almost time to serve, add sour cream and reheat slowly. Do not boil.

yield: 6 servings

Serve with French bread, wild rice, and salad.

MARY GRAHAM

VENISON MEAT LOAF

- 1½ pounds ground venison
- Juice of ½ lemon
- 2 tablespoons butter, melted
- 1 cup cracker crumbs
- 1 teaspoon salt
- ¼ teaspoon pepper
- 1 small onion, chopped
- 1 egg, beaten
- ¼ cup milk
- 1 stalk celery, chopped
- ½ cup water
- 8 ounce can tomato sauce

Pre-heat oven to 325°F. Mix venison well with lemon juice. Mix butter, crumbs, salt, pepper, onion, egg, milk and celery together and combine well with venison. Pat into loaf pan and pour in water and then tomato sauce. Bake, uncovered, 1½ hours. Add more water if necessary.

yield: 4 servings
MARY GRAHAM

CORNED BEEF AND CABBAGE

1	4-pound brisket of corned beef, flat cut is preferable
	Cold water to soak beef
6	small onions, peeled
6	small carrots, peeled
6	small white turnips, peeled
6	potatoes, peeled and halved
1	large cabbage, cut into 6 wedges, core removed
2	tablespoons butter or margarine

Garnish:
   Horseradish
   Mustard pickles

Soak the corned beef in cold water for about an hour. Drain and cover with fresh, cold water. Gradually bring to a boil, and skim thoroughly. Simmer very gently for approximately 4 hours. To avoid toughness, do not let meat actually boil. Thirty minutes before beef is done, drop in the onions, carrots and turnips and cook until tender. In separate pan, boil the potatoes in plain salted water. In still another pan cook the cabbage 15–18 minutes. When tender, lift meat onto a large platter, rub over with butter. Slice thinly. Garnish platter with the cooked vegetables. Serve with horseradish and mustard pickles.

yield: 4 to 6 servings

Besides being delicious, this dinner is relatively simple and very impressive looking if the platter is arranged neatly and somewhat artistically. This is a real old fashioned Jigs and Maggie dinner.

ESTELLE G. KELLY

ARMENIAN SHISH KEBOB

1	5 to 6 pound leg of lamb
½	pound onions, sliced thin
1	tablespoon salt
½	teaspoon pepper
⅓	cup sherry
2	tablespoons olive oil
1	teaspoon oregano

Remove all fat and gristle from leg of lamb. Bone it and cut into 1 inch squares. Mix meat with sliced onions, seasonings and other ingredients. Let meat marinate in sauce at least one hour, preferably overnight. Put on skewers and broil over charcoal fire or oven broiler, basting with marinade.

yield: 8 servings

This recipe was given to me in my third year of marriage by dear friends, Mary and George Jayisian and wonderful "Grandmom". Up until this point I thought there was only one way to cook . . . . . "Italian"!

JEAN C. MORI

BARBECUED PORK CHOPS

- 12 pork loin chops, 1 inch thick
- 1 clove garlic, crushed
- ½ cup soy sauce,
- ¼ cup honey
- 1 large onion
- 3 tablespoons cooking oil
- 3 tablespoons cider vinegar
- 1 tablespoon brown sugar
- 1 cup catsup
- 1 tablespoon Worcestershire sauce
- ⅛ teaspoon charcoal seasoning
- 1 tablespoon prepared mustard
- 1 cup water
- ¼ cup lemon juice
- Garlic powder to taste

Garnish:
- Pineapple slices
- Parsley
- Cherries

Place chops in glass dish. Mix garlic, soy sauce and honey and pour over chops. Marinate chops several hours, turning occassionally. Remove chops from sauce. Place chops on grill over low to moderate heat; cook 10 minutes on each side. While chops are cooking, combine onion, oil, vinegar, brown sugar, catsup, Worcestershire sauce, charcoal seasoning, mustard, water, lemon juice, garlic powder. Place chops in pan; add sauce; cover. Place on grill over low heat and simmer 30 minutes. Serve chops on platter, garnish with pineapple, parsley and cherries if desired.

yield: 6 servings
BARBARA STEINBACH

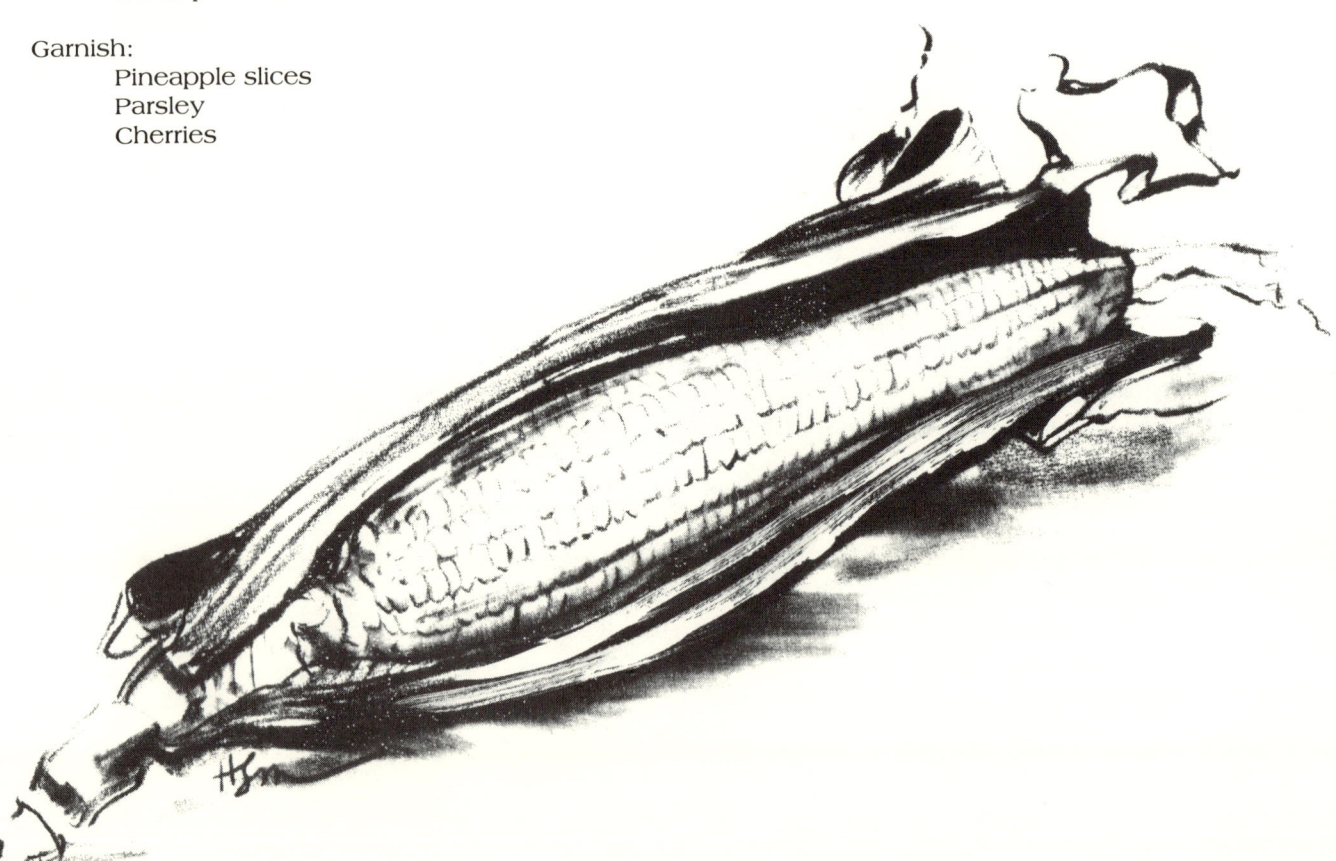

HAM AND PORK LOAF

Ham Loaf Mixture:
- 2 pounds lean ham, ground
- 1 pound lean pork, ground
- 1 cup bread crumbs
- 2 eggs
- 1 cup milk
- 1 teaspoon dry mustard
- ½ teaspoon powdered cloves
- pepper

Sauce:
- ½ cup water
- 2 cups brown sugar
- 1 teaspoon dry mustard
- ½ cup vinegar

Garnish:
- 4 pineapple slices

Pre-heat oven to 350°F. Mix ham and pork well. Add remaining ham loaf ingredients. Pat into 2 loaf pans. Combine sauce ingredients and simmer 3 minutes. Pour over loaves. Top with pineapple slices. Bake 2½ hours, basting frequently with sauce.

yield: 10-12 servings

This recipe was given to our family by Florence Westlake. The loaves freeze well with the sauce. You may want to substitute pineapple juice for the water in the sauce.

JUDSON W. BUNNELL

FISH

BAKED STUFFED SHRIMP

2	pounds large shrimp
3	tablespoons butter or margarine
2	tablespoons minced shallots
¼	cup minced onion
1	green pepper, seeded and finely chopped
1	cup soft bread crumbs
1	teaspoon salt
⅛	teaspoon pepper
1	egg, beaten
2	tablespoons melted butter
	Parsley sprigs

Pre-heat oven to 400°F. Shell and devein 6 shrimp. Set rest aside. Cook 6 shrimp in butter for 2 minutes or until pink. Remove; chop finely. Add shallots, onion and green pepper to fat left in skillet. Cook 3 to 4 minutes, stirring often. Remove from heat. Stir in crumbs, chopped shrimp, salt, pepper. Blend in egg.

Shell reserved shrimp, leaving tails on. Place shrimp, back down, on board. Make a slit along underside of each shrimp with knife, but do not cut through. Remove vein.

Mound stuffing mixture in hollow of each shrimp. Bring tail over stuffing. Put shrimp, tails up, in greased, shallow baking dish. At this point, dish may be covered and refrigerated. Drizzle shrimp with melted butter. Bake 10 to 12 minutes. Transfer to warm plates. Garnish with parsley.

yield: 6 servings
JEANETTE STAUFFER

RAINBOW SHRIMP STIR-FRY

¾	pound small-medium shrimp, shelled, deveined, washed and dried
½	egg white
1	teaspoon cornstarch
½	teaspoon salt
1	teaspoon dry sherry
½	carrot, sliced, parboiled for 3 minutes, drained
½	cup peas, frozen or fresh
4	ounces mushrooms, canned or fresh
½	cup diced bamboo shoots
½	teaspoon salt
3	tablespoons water
1	medium onion, diced in ½" pieces
2	slices fresh ginger root or powdered ginger
5	tablespoons oil
1	teaspoon cornstarch dissolved in 2 tablespoons water

Combine shrimp with egg white, cornstarch, salt and sherry. Refrigerate at least 15 minutes. Prepare vegetables. Heat wok or large frying pan with 2 tablespoons of oil over high heat until oil begins to smoke. Stir-fry carrots, peas, mushrooms, and bamboo shoots for 2 minutes with ½ teaspoon salt and 3 tablespoons of water, more if needed. Stir constantly. Remove and set aside. Heat wok or frying pan with 3 tablespoons oil. Add onion and ginger slices or 6–8 shakes of powdered ginger from dispenser. Stir for 30 seconds. Add shrimp, stirring constantly until shrimp is cooked and pink. Add liquid from vegetables and reduce heat to a medium setting. Return vegetables to the wok or pan and add the cornstarch mixture. Stir well. Add more water if desired to make a somewhat thick gravy. Serve immediately.

yield: 4 servings

This is a can't-miss recipe and a great introduction to stir-frying. Serve with rice.

BILL WARREN

LOBSTER NEWBURG

- 2 tablespoons cream
- 3 hard boiled egg yolks, finely mashed
- ¼ pound butter
- 2 tablespoons flour
- 1 cup cream
- 2 cups lobster meat, cooked
- 3 tablespoons sherry
- Salt and pepper to taste

Gradually add 2 tablespoons cream to finely mashed egg yolks. Melt butter in a double boiler and stir in flour. Add 1 cup cream gradually and stir until hot but not boiling. Add egg yolk mixture and lobster. Keep over hot water until thoroughly heated. Add sherry, salt and pepper.

yield: 4 servings
CAROLINE MORGAN

LOBSTER BOO

- 1 cup lobster, cooked and chopped
- 2 hard boiled eggs, yolks and whites separated
- 2 teaspoons parsley, chopped
- 1 cup white sauce
- ¼ cup sherry, depending on taste
- Salt and pepper to taste
- ⅓ cup buttered bread crumbs

Pre-heat oven to 350°F. Add lobster to egg yolks, which have been mashed to a paste. Add parsley, sauce, sherry, seasonings and chopped egg whites. Put in a small buttered baking dish. Cover with bread crumbs and bake 15-20 minutes or until brown.

yield: 2-3 servings

This recipe is from a Waverly School 4th Grade Fish Cook Book circa 1965! I've substituted Boo in the name of the recipe because I can't read what follows lobster in the original.

DONNA BELIN CLARKE

KING CRAB Au GRATIN

- 2 6-ounce packages frozen king crab
- 3 tablespoons butter or margarine
- 3 tablespoons flour
- 1 cup milk
- ½ cup light cream
- ½ cup chicken broth
- ¾ cup sharp Cheddar cheese, shredded
- ½ pound fresh mushrooms, sauteed
- 2 tablespoons onion, grated
- 1 teaspoon salt
- ¼ teaspoon paprika
- 2 tablespoons white wine
- ¼ cup dry fine bread crumbs

Pre-heat oven to 400°F. Defrost king crab. Melt butter or margarine in sauce pan. Stir in flour until smooth. Gradually stir in milk, cream and chicken broth until smooth again. Cook, stirring constantly over low heat until sauce is smooth and thick. Add cheese, mushrooms, onion, salt, paprika, and wine. Stir until cheese is melted. Stir in chunks of crab. Pour mixture into well-greased individual au gratin ramekins or 1-quart caserole. Sprinkle bread crumbs over top. Bake for 10 minutes for ramekins or 20 minutes for casserole.

yield: 6 servings
CASSANDRA DEVINE COVIELLO

BAKED BLUE FISH WITH ROSEMARY

- 1 3 to 4 pound bluefish
- Salt
- Freshly ground black pepper
- 1½ teaspoons rosemary, chopped
- ½ cup butter
- 1 tablespoon wine vinegar
- Lemon slices or wedges

Pre-heat oven to 400°F. Completely clean and scale fish or have cut into fillets. If whole fish is used, leave head and tail on. Rinse fish under cold water and pat dry with paper towels. Salt and pepper fish inside and out. Put fish in a baking dish; sprinkle the rosemary around the fish. Dot generously with butter. Bake whole fish about 30 minutes. If fillets, bake about 10–15 minutes. Baste with butter every 5 minutes. When fish flakes easily, transfer to a hot serving platter. Add vinegar to the baking dish. Heat through, stirring constantly. Pour the pan drippings over the fish. Decorate your serving plate with lemon slices or wedges.

yield: 3–4 servings depends on size of catch or how many fillets

Tastes best with fresh rosemary. Use half the amount if dry. The vinegar seems to remove the oily taste of bluefish.

MARY JOY HAVEY

BAKED FISH FILETS

2 medium tomatoes
½ cup buttered bread crumbs
   Cavenders Greek Seasoning
1½ pounds fish filets - yellow tail, snapper or flounder

Sauce:
½ cup white wine
¼ cup butter
1 teaspoon lemon or lime juice

Topping:
¼ cup grated Parmesan Cheese
   Paprika

Pre-heat oven to 500°. Peel and thinly slice tomatoes. Arrange in buttered baking dish large enough to hold filets in one layer. Toss bread crumbs with seasoning and sprinkle on tomatoes. Arrange fish filets on top.

Combine sauce ingredients and cook over low heat until butter melts. Raise heat to medium and simmer for 3 minutes. Pour sauce over filets and sprinkle with cheese and paprika. Bake for 10 minutes.

yield: 4 servings
ROSEMARY TRANE

JAMBALAYA

¾ pound hot Italian sausage, cut into cubes
¾ pound onion, diced
½ pound celery, diced
¼ pound red pepper, seeded and diced
¾ pound green pepper, seeded and diced
1½ tablespoons fresh garlic, chopped
1½ pounds ham, ½ inch thick, cut in strips
1 16-ounce can whole tomatoes
1 tablespoon fresh chopped thyme or ½ tablespoon dried
¼ teaspoon black pepper
3 bay leaves
¾ pound converted rice
2 cups clam broth
1¼ pounds large shrimp, peeled and deveined
¾ pound sea scallops
2 cups dry white wine
25 mussels
½ cup parsley, chopped

Pre-heat oven to 350°F. Sauté sausage. Remove from pan and set aside. Sauté onion, celery, red and green peppers and garlic in sausage drippings in same pan until tender. Transfer to large pot. Sauté ham and add to the pot. Drain tomatoes and save the juice. Add the tomatoes, thyme, pepper, bay leaves and rice to the pot. Stir over low heat. Add enough water to reserved tomato juice to measure 1¼ cups. Add clam broth and tomato juice to rice mixture. Bring to a boil, stirring often. Simmer over low heat 10 minutes and remove from heat. Set aside.

Poach shrimp and scallops separately, each in 1 cup wine over low heat until tender. Drain and add to the pot. Scrub and beard mussels and steam, covered, until open. Add to the pot. Cover pot and heat in oven for 15 minutes. Do not over-heat or shellfish will be tough. Serve immediately.

yield: 20 servings

The rice mixture may be made two days in advance and refrigerated. Bring to room temperature before proceeding with rest of recipe.

LETHA REINHEIMER

TUNA AND RICE

- ¼ cup onion, diced
- ½ cup celery, diced
- ¼ cup butter or margarine
- 1 can mushroom soup
- 1 6-ounce can tuna fish
- 2 cups rice, cooked
- Grated cheese, optional

Brown onion and celery slowly in butter in large skillet. Pour in soup and heat. Add tuna and heat thoroughly. Serve over rice. Cheese may be sprinkled on top.

yield: 4 servings
ELLEN CLENDENNING

TUNA SUPPER CASSEROLE

- 1 10-ounce package frozen spinach
- 1 6½-ounce can tuna
- 1 3 or 4-ounce can sliced mushrooms
- 2 tablespoons lemon juice
- 4 tablespoons butter or margarine
- 1 tablespoon onion, minced
- 2 tablespoons flour
- ½ teaspoon salt
- ⅛ teaspoon pepper
- 1 bay leaf, crushed
- 1 egg, slightly beaten

Pre-heat oven to 350°F. Cook spinach as directed on package. Drain well. Drain excess oil from tuna. Drain mushrooms, reserving liquid. To mushroom liquid, add lemon juice, then enough water to measure one cup liquid. In small saucepan melt 3 tablespoons butter or margarine. Stir in onion, flour, salt, pepper and bay leaf. Then blend in mushroom liquid mixture. Cook stirring, until thick and smooth. Beat sauce into egg and add mushrooms. Arrange spinach in buttered 1½ quart casserole. Top with tuna in big chunks; then top with sauce. Dot with 1 tablespoon butter. Bake 30 minutes.

yield: 4 servings
MARGE BLACK

SALMON LOAF

- 1 package lemon gelatin
- 1 cup boiling water
- ½ cup cold water
- 3 tablespoons vinegar
- ½ cup mayonnaise
- ¼ teaspoon salt
- 2 cups cooked salmon, fresh or canned, flaked
- ½ cup celery, chopped
- 2 tablespoons parsley, chopped
- ¼ cup onion, chopped

Dissolve gelatin in boiling water, stirring constantly. Add cold water, vinegar, mayonnaise and salt and beat well. Chill until almost firm; then beat until fluffy. Fold in remaining ingredients. Pour into 8½" × 4½" loaf pan. Chill until set. Unmold and garnish as desired.

YIELD: 6 servings
Emma L. Volpe

VEGETABLES

YUGOSLAVIAN VEGETABLE CASSEROLE

Pre-heat oven to 350°F. Combine potato, zucchini, eggplant, green pepper, carrot, onion, peas and parsley with ⅓ cup olive oil, salt, Tabasco and pepper. Line a greased 9" × 11" baking dish with ½ the vegetable mixture. Layer with half the tomato slices and sprinkle with rice. Add remaining vegetables and top with remaining tomato slices. Mix ½ cup olive oil with vinegar and pour over casserole. Bake covered for 1¾ hours. Sprinkle with cheese and place under broiler until cheese is melted.

yield: 12 servings
MARILYN COSTA

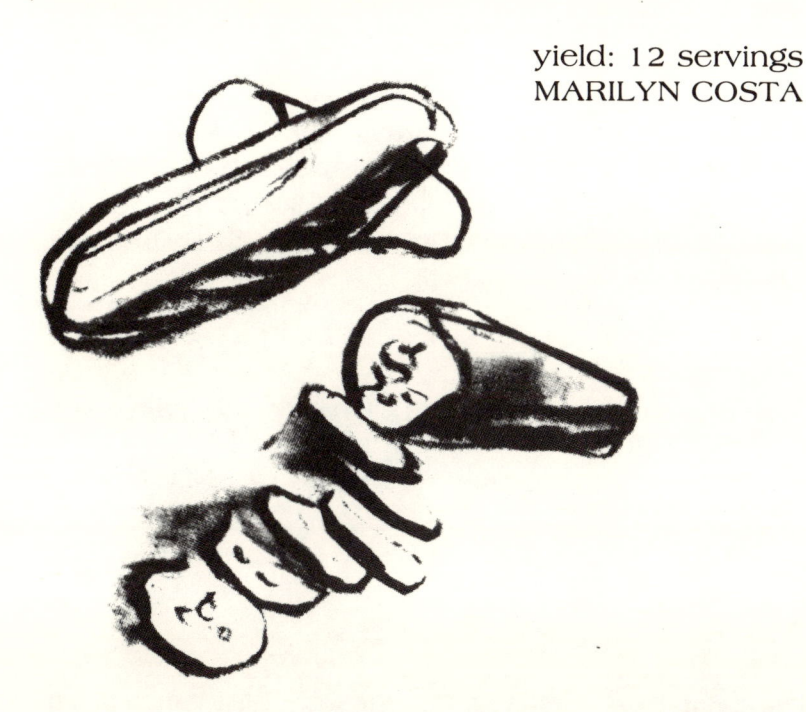

- 1 potato, diced
- 1 medium zucchini, diced
- 1 medium eggplant, diced
- 2 green peppers, diced
- 2 small carrots, quartered lengthwise and cut into 1" strips
- 1 Bermuda onion, corasely chopped
- ½ cup shelled peas
- 2 tablespoons chopped parsley
- ⅓ cup olive oil
- 1 tablespoon salt
- 1 teaspoon Tabasco sauce
- 1 teaspoon black pepper
- 4 large tomatoes, sliced
- ⅓ cup uncooked rice
- ½ cup olive oil
- 2 tablespoons white wine vinegar
- 1¾ cups cheddar cheese, shredded

ONION CASSEROLE

Pre-heat oven to 325°F. Sauté onions in butter until transparent. Cook rice in water 5 minutes. Drain well. Blend rice into onions with cheese and half and half. Taste for seasoning. Put into shallow 2-quart casserole and bake for 1 hour.

yield: 8 servings
PATTI SCHRECKENGAUST

- ¼ cup unsalted butter
- 7–8 large onions cut into chunks
- ½ cup uncooked rice
- 5 cups boiling, salted water
- 1 cup grated Swiss cheese
- ⅔ cup half & half
- Salt and pepper to taste

ONION AND APPLE CASSEROLE

- 1 quart small onions, peeled
- 3 tart apples, pared and diced
- Water
- Juice of ½ lemon
- ¼ cup sugar
- ¼ teaspoon cinnamon
- ¼ teaspoon nutmeg
- 2 tablespoons butter or margarine
- ⅓ cup bread crumbs

Pre-heat oven to 350°F. to 400°F. Parboil onions 20 minutes. Soak apples in water and lemon juice. Drain apples, mix with sugar and spices. Place apples and onions in layers in a greased casserole. Dot with butter and crumbs. Bake for 30 minutes covered and 30 minutes uncovered.

yield: 6 servings

This is a quick vegetable casserole to serve with ham.

MARY DOLBEAR

SUMMER SQUASH CASSEROLE

- 6 cups summer squash, grated
- ¼ cup onion, diced
- 1 cup carrots, diced
- 8 ounces prepared stuffing mix
- ½ cup butter, melted
- 1 can celery soup
- ¼ cup milk

Pre-heat oven to 350°F. Grease 1½ quart casserole. Parboil squash, onion, carrots. Drain. Mix squash mixture and stuffing. Put in baking dish. Heat soup with milk. Fold melted butter and soup mixture into vegetables. Bake until heated through, about 15 minutes.

yield: 6–8 servings

The carrots are optional, but make the casserole more colorful.

ELLEN CLENDENNING

ZUCCHINI CASSEROLE WITH SOUR CREAM

- 3 medium zucchini
- ¼ cup sour cream
- 1 tablespoon butter
- 1 tablespoon Cheddar cheese, grated
- ½ teaspoon salt
- ⅛ teaspoon paprika
- 1 egg yolk, beaten
- 1 tablespoon chopped chives

Topping:
- ½ cup bread crumbs
- 2 tablespoons butter
- ¼ cup Cheddar cheese, grated

Pre-heat oven to 375°F. Cut zucchini into small pieces. Simmer covered, in small amount of boiling water until tender, about 6–8 minutes. Drain and set aside. Combine all but last two ingredients. Stir over low heat until cheese is melted. Remove and stir in egg yolk and chopped chives. Add zucchini, place mixture in baking dish and top with bread crumbs. Dot with butter and sprinkle with cheese. Bake for 20 minutes. Brown for a few minutes under broiler.

yield: 4 servings

ANN CHAMBERLIN

EGGPLANT CASSEROLE

Pre-heat oven to 325°F. Boil eggplant in salted water 15 minutes and drain well. Sauté onions in oil until slightly golden. Combine all ingredients in a 2-quart casserole. Top with buttered bread crumbs. Bake for 1½ hours.

yield: 6 servings
JOANNE LEWIS TODD

- 1 large eggplant, peeled and cut into 1" cubes
- 4 large onions, sliced
- 2 tablespoons olive oil
- 4 large tomatoes, cut in large dice
- 2 green peppers, seeded, cut in strips
- 1 teaspoon basil
- 1 bay leaf
- Salt and pepper to taste
- Buttered bread crumbs

EGGPLANT CURRY

Sauté onions in hot oil until golden. Add garlic, green peppers, ginger, chili powder, and turmeric. Sauté spices for 3 minutes. Add eggplant cubes and sauté for several minutes to absorb spices. Stir and add water to cover eggplant. Simmer 5 minutes. Add chopped tomato and salt. Cook over medium heat, stirring occassionally, until eggplant is tender but not mushy. Add more water if necessary.

yield: 6 servings

I have served this recipe to both American and Indian guests and it has been well received by both. Not too hot and spicy for American taste. Rather, it seems more Italian flavoring than Indian.

MARY E. DEVANANDAN

- 2 medium onions, chopped fine
- 2 tablespoons oil
- 3 cloves garlic, crushed
- 2 tablespoons green pepper, finely chopped
- ½ teaspoon ginger powder or fresh ginger, grated
- ½ teaspoon chili powder
- ½ teaspoon turmeric
- 1 large eggplant, cut into 1" cubes
- 3 large tomatoes, chopped
- 1 teaspoon salt

EGGPLANT CASSEROLE

- 2 medium or 1 large eggplant
- 1½ medium onion, chopped
- 4 tablespoons butter
- 2 cups bread crumbs
- ½ cup milk
- 3 eggs, slightly beaten
- 2 tablespoons parsley, chopped
- 2 tablespoons celery, chopped
- Salt and pepper to taste

Pre-heat oven to 400°F. Peel and cut eggplant into small chunks. Boil until tender. Drain. Sauté onion in butter. Add to eggplant. Soak bread crumbs in milk, then add to eggplant and onion mixture. Blend in eggs, parsley, celery, salt and pepper. Pour into greased casserole. Bake until set, about 30 to 40 minutes.

yield: 6 servings

This mixture may be prepared the day before and put in refrigerator before baking. It is an excellent substitute for potatoes or dressing with any type meat. The celery is optional.

ANN CHAMBERLIN

SWEET AND SOUR STUFFED CABBAGE

- 1 large head cabbage
- 2 pounds ground beef
- 1 onion, chopped
- ⅓ cup raw rice
- 1 cup tomatoes canned
- 1 teaspoon of salt
- 1 teaspoon sugar
- Pinch of pepper

Sauce:
- 5 tablespoons maple syrup
- 2 cups canned tomatoes, drained
- 2 cups water
- ¼ teaspoon paprika
- Pinch of pepper
- 3 tablespoons sugar
- 1 teaspoon salt
- Juice of two lemons
- ¼ cup raisins

Pre-heat oven to 325°F. Boil cabbage for at least ten minutes and separate leaves. Mix together rest of ingredients for stuffing. Mix together all ingredients for sauce. Select 20 large cabbage leaves, and place 3 tablespoons of meat mixture on each. Fold cabbage leaves over meat and roll. Line bottom of large pot with the rest of the cabbage chopped up and add stuffed cabbage leaves and sauce. Cover and bake 2 hours. Add a little water if necessary to keep meat covered with liquid at all times. Taste, and adjust seasoning if needed before serving.

yield: 10 servings
MARILYN DWORKIN

CAULIFLOWER Au GRATIN SOUFFLÉ

1	pound cauliflower, cooked
2	tablespoons spicy brown mustard
1	whole egg
¼	cup grated cheese
1½	cup mayonnaise
⅛	teaspoon pepper
1	teaspoon salt

Pre-heat oven to 375°F. Place cauliflower or any cooked vegetable, such as broccoli, asparagus, etc. in casserole dish.

In mixing bowl, whip mustard with the egg and fold in rest of ingredients.

Pour over vegetables. Bake until golden brown on top, 10–15 minutes.

yield: 4 to 6 servings
MARWORTH

CARROTS, SCALLIONS AND MUSHROOMS

2	tablespoons margarine or butter
2	tablespoons oil
5	medium scallions, sliced
1	pound carrots, sliced
¾	pound mushrooms, sliced or quartered
1	tablespoon lemon juice
¼	teaspoon salt
¼	teaspoon freshly ground pepper

Heat oil and butter together. Lightly sauté the scallions, then add carrots and mushrooms and sauté until all are crisp-tender, about 8 minutes. Add lemon juice, salt pepper and stir thoroughly.

yield: 4 to 6 servings
MATTHEW MOONEY

PAILLASSON

3	cups potatoes, cut in julienne strips
2	cups turnips, blanched and cut in julienne strips
2	cups carrots, cut in julienne strips
¼	cup butter, melted
½	teaspoon salt or to taste
¼	teaspoon finely ground pepper
	Pinch of nutmeg

Pre-heat oven to 450°F. Combine all ingredients in large bowl and mix well. Turn into 10" non-stick skillet, pressing evenly with back of spoon. Cook over medium heat until bottom of vegetables begin to brown, about 10 minutes. Transfer to oven and bake until tender, about 25 to 30 minutes. Invert onto platter and serve.

yield: 12 servings

A great vegetable dish to accompany any main course. It is delicious and low in calories!

HILDA BARAKAT

SPINACH RICE BALLS

- 2 10-ounce packages frozen chopped spinach
- 1 package New England-style stuffing mix
- 1 small onion, chopped
- 5 eggs, well beaten
- ¾ cup grated Parmesan cheese
- ½ cup brown rice, cooked

Sauce:
- 3 tablespoons butter
- 1 tablespoon flour
- 1½ cups chicken broth

Pre-heat oven to 325°F. Cook spinach according to package directions. Drain and squeeze to remove excess moisture. Grind stuffing mix with onions in processor or pound mix until fine and add onions chopped fine. Combine spinach with onion and stuffing and the package of seasonings from the stuffing mix. Combine with eggs, cheese and rice. Shape into balls, 1½" or 2", as desired. Place in lightly greased cookie sheet. Moisten with small amount sauce. Bake for 20 minutes. Makes about 35 balls.

Sauce: Melt butter. Add flour, and stir over low heat. Add chicken broth. Simmer and stir until it begins to thicken.

yield: 35 balls

Can be frozen before baking and before adding sauce. Place on cookie sheets and freeze until firm. When frozen, remove and store in plastic bags.

DORA CIGARRAN

BAKED GOODS

OVEN PANCAKES

2	eggs
½	cup flour
½	cup milk
4	tablespoons butter

Pre-heat oven to 425°F. Beat eggs. Add flour and milk. Melt butter in black iron frying pan over medium heat. Pour in pancake batter. Bake in pre-heated oven for 15 minutes. Serve with maple syrup or stewed apples, or plums or rhubarb or fresh cranberry relish.

yield: One 12" pancake

It is like a giant popover, dramatic and super simple. Kids love to make it and eat it. Can be doubled and cooked in a large roasting or cake pan, be sure you double area of baking pan when you double the ingredients. To add great pizzazz, squeeze a little lemon juice over the top of the pancake when it is almost done and sprinkle with powdered sugar.

ROSAMOND PECK

CINNAMON POPOVERS

3	eggs
1	cup milk
1	cup all-purpose flour
3	tablespoons butter or margarine, melted
1	teaspoon ground cinnamon
¼	teaspoon salt

Pre-heat oven to 400°F. In blender container, combine all ingredients. Cover and blend 30 seconds or until combined. Fill 6 to 8 well greased popover or muffin pans ½ full. Bake for 40 minutes. Remove. Serve hot. Serve with butter and jelly.

yield: 6 to 8 servings

This makes a cream puff-type popover. Hollow in the center, crisp on the outside. May also be filled with apple pie filling and used as a dessert.

DON WRONA

JOHNNY CAKES

1	cup milk
1	cup buttermilk
1	teaspoon salt
1	teaspoon soda
1	tablespoon melted butter
1	tablespoon sugar
	Cornmeal

Pre-heat oven to 375°F. Mix ingredients together, adding enough cornmeal to make a thick batter. Spread in a buttered 15" × 11" baking pan. Bake for 40 minutes, or until done. Break apart to eat or slice into squares. Serve with butter.

yield: 8 servings
EMMA L. VOLPE

NEW ENGLAND GINGERBREAD

¾	cup Grandmas molasses
½	cup boiling water
¾	cup sugar
½	cup butter or margarine, melted
1	egg, beaten
¾	teaspoon cinnamon
½	teaspoon cloves
½	teaspoon nutmeg
1	teaspoon ginger
1	level teaspoon soda
1½	cups sifted white flour

Pre-heat oven to 350°F. Blend first 4 ingredients together over low heat. Stir constantly. Take off stove; cool. Add beaten egg. Add rest of ingredients and mix well. Bake in 8″ × 8″ × 2″ greased pan for 30 minutes.

yield:

This recipe is from my mother, Mrs. George M.D. Lewis.

JOANNE LEWIS TODD

NANA'S CHRISTMAS COOKIES

1	cup butter
2	cups sugar
2	eggs, separated
3	cups flour
1	teaspoon baking powder
½	teaspoon salt
2	teaspoons grated nutmeg
	Beaten egg white or milk for glaze

Pre-heat oven to 350°F. Cream together butter and sugar. Beat egg yolks and add. Sift dry ingredients together and add. Beat egg whites until stiff but not dry. Fold into dough. Chill several hours or overnight. Roll dough very thin and cut with Christmas cookie cutters. Paint with egg white or milk and decorate cookies with cherries, nuts or colored sugar. Bake 5 minutes.

yield: 3 dozen

BETTY HULL

WELSH COOKIES

4	cups flour
1	cup sugar
1½	teaspoon baking powder
½	teaspoon baking soda
½	teaspoon salt
2	teaspoons nutmeg
1	cup shortening
1	cup currents
2	eggs
6	tablespoons milk (scant half cup)

Pre-heat griddle to 350°F. Sift dry ingredients. Cut in shortening. Add currants. Beat eggs and milk together and add to mixture, mixing well. Roll dough on lightly floured surface and use round cookie cutter to form cookies, or roll dough into small balls and press between wax paper to form cookies. Cook cookies on grill for about 3 minutes on each side until puffed and lightly browned. Cool on paper towels.

yield: 40 cookies

This is a family recipe combined with friend's recipe. Additional baking powder may be used for puffier cookies.

MARTHA McGREGOR

OATMEAL LACE COOKIES

2¼	cups quick cooking rolled oats
1½	cups firmly packed dark brown sugar
1	cup butter or margarine, melted
½	teaspoon salt
1	tablespoon molasses
3	tablespoons all purpose flour
1	egg
1	teaspoon vanilla
2	ounces chocolate, melted

Put oatmeal in medium bowl with brown sugar, pour in the melted margarine or butter. Mix well. Let stand over night at room temperature. When ready to bake, pre-heat oven to 375°F. Add salt, molasses, flour, egg and vanilla extract to oatmeal mixture and mix well. Drop by half-measuring teaspoonful 2" apart on well greased cookie sheets. Bake one sheet at a time in preheated oven until golden brown. Let stand 1 minute. Remove with spatula to wire rack. When cool, brush cookie bottom with melted chocolate, let chocolate set. (It is best to use speciality chocolate used for molding or making candy.)

yield: 7 dozen

MARIA WRONA

BLUEBERRY MUFFINS

1½	cups sifted flour
½	cup sugar
2	teaspoons baking powder
½	teaspoon salt
¼	cup soft shortening
1	egg
½	cup milk
1	cup fresh blueberries
	Sugar for topping

Pre-heat oven to 400°F. Mix everything except berries just until all ingredients are blended. Carefully add berries. Line 12 muffin cups with paper liners and fill muffin cups ⅔ full. Bake about 20–25 minutes. Five minutes before done, sprinkle on granulated sugar and put back in oven.

yield: 12 muffins

These muffins have a very nice texture and are nice with the sugar sprinkled on top. The sugar is not necessary, just a nice touch.

CINDY WEEKS

DESSERTS

CREME de CACAO CHANTILLY

2 tablespoon gelatin
½ cup water
2 cups strong coffee
¾ cup Creme de Cacao
3 tablespoons sugar

Garnish:
    Chocolate Wafers
    Whipped Cream
    Creme de cacao
    Grated chocolate

Soften gelatin in water and add to hot coffee, stirring until dissolved. Add Creme de Cacao and sugar. Stir until sugar is dissolved. Pour mixture into a mold rinsed in cold water and chill until set. Dip mold in warm water and turn out on a chilled platter. Garnish with wafers of mocha chocolate and whipped cream, flavored with Creme de Cacao and a ring of finely grated chocolate.

yield: 6 servings
JEAN GERRARD

PEACH PIE

Pie Crust:
1½ cups flour
½ cup liquid shortening
½ teaspoon salt
2 tablespoons sugar
2 tablespoons milk

Filling:
½ cup sugar
3 tablespoons corn starch
1 cup water
2 tablespoons white corn syrup
3 tablespoons peach flavored gelatin
6 fresh peaches, peeled and sliced

Garnish:
    Whipped Cream

Pre-heat oven to 350°F. Combine pie crust ingredients and mix well. Press into 9" pie pan and bake for 15 to 20 minutes. Cool.
    Combine sugar, cornstarch, water and syrup. Boil until thick and clear, stirring constantly. Remove from heat and add gelatin. Cool. Add fresh peaches. Pour into crust and chill. Serve with whipped cream.

yield: 1 9" pie

A family favorite also made every year for the Labor Day Bull Roast at Church.

CINDY NEUBERT

MISSISSIPPI MUD CAKE

1	cup butter or margarine
2	cups sugar
4	eggs, slightly beaten
½	cup cocoa
1½	cups flour
¼	teaspoon salt
½	teaspoon baking powder
1	teaspoon vanilla
1½	cups chopped nuts

Frosting:
½	cup miniature marshmallows
1	cup chocolate icing

This cake is baked in a microwave oven. In 2 quart batter bowl, place butter. Cook on medium high for 1 to 2 minutes or till melted. Add sugar, eggs, cocoa, flour, salt, baking powder, and vanilla. Mix well with wire wisk. Add nuts and stir. Pour into 9" microwave bundt pan. Cook on medium for 11 to 13 minutes or until center no longer shakes like jello. Cook on high for 2 to 3 minutes or until toothpick inserted near center comes out clean. Let stand 5 minutes before turning out onto serving plate. Cool. Stir marshmallows into chocolate icing and frost cake before serving.

yield: One 9" bundt cake

A favorite from New Orleans.

LESLIE REID PATTERSON

SPANISH CREAM

3	cups milk
1	envelope plain gelatin
½	cup sugar
3	eggs, separated
¼	teaspoon salt
1	teaspoon vanilla
	Chocolate syrup

Pour milk in top of double boiler and sprinkle with gelatin. Add sugar and stir until dissolved. Add slightly beaten yolks and the salt. Cook until thickened. Stir constantly. Remove from heat, add vanilla and fold in the stiffly-beaten egg whites. Put in mold and refrigerate. To serve, remove from mold and pour a little chocolate syrup on top.

yield: 6-8 servings

This dessert is a nice light finish to a meal.

JANET DOBSON

QUEEN'S PUDDING

- 2 eggs, beaten
- 2 eggs, separated
- ⅓ cup sugar
- ¼ teaspoon salt
- ¼ teaspoon cinnamon
- 2 teaspoons vanilla
- 3 tablespoons melted butter or margarine
- 1 quart milk, scalded
- 2 cups day old bread, cubed
- ½ cup tart jelly
- ¼ cup sugar

Pre-heat oven to 350°F. Combine eggs, egg yolks, sugar, salt, cinnamon, vanilla and melted butter or margarine. Add milk, blend. Pour over bread cubes in a 1½ quart casserole. Let stand 20 minutes for bread to soak up custard mixture; stir. Set in pan of hot water (water should be 1" deep). Bake 1 hour and 15 minutes or until knife inserted 1" from edge comes clean. Remove from oven. Spread jelly over hot pudding. Beat egg whites until foamy, beat in ¼ cup sugar. Beat until meringue stands in stiff peaks. Cover pudding with meringue. Bake 15 minutes or until meringue is golden. Cool.

yield: 6 servings
JACQUELINE O'CONNOR

INDIAN PUDDING

- 3 cups milk
- 3 tablespoons yellow corn meal
- ½ cup dark molasses
- 1 egg
- ½ cup sugar
- 1 tablespoon melted butter
- ½ teaspoon ground ginger
- ½ teaspoon cinnamon
- ¼ teaspoon salt

Pre-heat oven to 300°F. Heat the milk in a medium size saucepan and when it comes to a boil, gradually stir in the corn meal with a wire whisk. Cook, stirring constantly until slightly thickened. Stir in the molasses. Beat the egg in a large bowl and add sugar, butter, ginger, cinnamon and salt. Pour the hot mixture in, stirring rapidly. When thoroughly blended, pour mixture into a medium sized greased baking dish. Bake 1 hour or until knife inserted in center comes out clean. Serve with heavy cream or vanilla ice cream.

yield: 6 servings

This recipe is from a book complied by Dee on the occasion of her sister Greta's marriage in 1975.

DEVEREUX CLARKE WELLES

HONEYCOMB PUDDING

Pudding:
- ½ cup sugar
- 1 cup flour
- ½ teaspoon soda
- ½ cup butter or margarine, melted
- ½ cup milk
- 1 cup molasses
- 4 eggs, well beaten

Floradora Sauce:
- 1 egg, separated
- ¼ cup confectioners' sugar, plus 2 tablespoons
- ¼ teaspoon vanilla
- ¾ cup heavy cream, beaten thick
- 1 tablespoon rum or sherry

Pudding: Pre-heat oven to 350°F. Mix sugar, flour and soda in mixing bowl. Mix butter with milk and add molasses. Beat thoroughly and add to dry ingredients. Add beaten eggs. Pour into greased 2-quart baking dish and bake for 45 minutes.

Sauce: Beat egg white and ¼ cup sugar until thick and stiff. Fold in beaten egg yolk, 2 tablespoons sugar and vanilla. Fold in beaten cream and flavor with rum or sherry.

YIELD: one–3" × 5" loaf or 2 quart casserole

Serve the pudding either hot or cold with Floradora Sauce, sour cream or ice cream. Leftover, it slices and travels well for picnics.

ROSAMOND PECK

DANISH RUM PUDDING

- 1 envelope unflavored gelatin
- ¼ cup cold water
- 5 egg yolks, beaten
- ¾ cup sugar
- 1 pint hot milk
- ½ cup white rum
- 1 cup whipped cream

Soak the gelatin in water until soft. Beat the egg yolks with the sugar until frothy and lemon colored. Slowly add the hot milk, stirring constantly. Pour the mixture into the top of a double boiler over boiling water and cook for a few minutes until smooth and creamy. Add the gelatin mixture to this. Blend well and cool. When the cream is cool, add the rum and whipped cream. Pour into a mold and chill for several hours.

yield: 6 to 8 servings
MARY JOY HAVEY

RICE PUDDING

- 2½ tablespoons rice
- ½ sugar
- ½ pint heavy cream
- 1 pint milk
- ½ teaspoon vanilla
- pinch of salt

Pre-heat oven to 275°F. Stir all ingredients together in 2 quart casserole until sugar is dissolved. Cook uncovered for about two hours, stirring a few times during first half hour.

yield: 4 to 6 servings
JANET HEALY

WALDORF RED "200"

Cake:
- ½ cup butter or margarine
- 1½ cups sugar
- 2 eggs
- 2 teaspoons cocoa
- ¼ cup red food coloring
- 1 cup buttermilk
- 1 teaspoon salt
- 2¼ cups sifted cake flour
- 1 teaspoon vanilla
- 1 teaspoon soda
- 1 teaspoon vinegar

Frosting:
- 1 cup milk
- 3 tablespoons flour
- 1 cup butter
- 1 cup granulated sugar
- 1 teaspoon vanilla

Pre-heat oven to 350°F. Cake: Cream butter or margarine, sugar and eggs together in large mixing bowl. Make a paste of the cocoa and food coloring. Add to the creamed mixture. Add buttermilk and salt, alternating with the flour. Add vanilla and soda. Add vinegar lastly. Spread in three greased 8½" round pans. Bake for 30 minutes or until toothpick comes out clean. Cool 10 minutes before removing from pans.

Frosting: Cook milk and flour until thick over medium heat, stirring constantly. Cool thoroughly. Cream butter, sugar and vanilla until fluffy. Blend into cooled mixture. Fill and frost cooled cake.

yield: 12 servings

Legend has it this recipe was long the private property of the Waldorf-Astoria. An admiring matron prevailed upon the head chef for the recipe long and loudly until he was instructed by hotel management to give the lady the recipe. Balking and angry the chef grudgingly obliged. However when the matron left the hotel that evening with the recipe in hand, the chef himself presented her with a bill for $200 for the recipe. She paid the bill, then evened the score when she allowed the recipe to be printed in several cookbooks, magazines and newspapers making a small fortune.

MOLLIE HEDGES

VERY RICH CHOCOLATE CAKE

- 6 eggs, separated
- ½ pound butter, softened
- 1 cup sugar
- 1 teaspoon vanilla extract
- 1 cup ground walnuts
- 10 ounces semi-sweet chocolate
- ½ cup flour, sifted

Chocolate Butter Icing:
- ⅓ pound butter
- 1 pound confectioners sugar
- 1 teaspoon vanilla extract
- 4 ounces semi-sweet chocolate
- Milk to moisten

Heat oven to 375°F. Beat the egg yolks, then add the butter and cream until smooth. Add the sugar, vanilla extract and the ground walnuts. Melt the chocolate in the top of a double boiler, and add to the mixture. Stir in the flour a little at a time until smooth. Beat the egg whites until stiff and fold carefully into the batter. Pour into a buttered and floured 9" cake pan and bake for 45 minutes. Remove the cake from oven when top is firm and inside not set. It should be creamy. Ice when cool with Chocolate Butter Icing.

Icing: Cream the butter until smooth and add the vanilla extract. Melt the chocolate in the top of a double boiler and add to mixture. Add the confectioner's sugar a little at a time, beating slowly. Add small amounts of milk a teaspoon at a time to keep icing smooth and creamy but not runny. Icing should have the consistency of beaten butter.

yield: 12 servings
DEMARIS FARRELL

CHOCOLATE ROLL

Cake:
- 5 eggs, separated
- 1 cup sugar
- 4 tablespoons cocoa
- ¼ cup confectioners sugar

Filling:
- 1½ cups heavy cream
- 1 teaspoon vanilla
- 2 tablespoons sugar

Pre-heat oven to 350°F. Beat egg yolks until light. Add sugar and beat well until creamy. Add cocoa and blend well. Beat egg whites until stiff but not dry. Fold into yolk mixture. Spread into buttered and floured 10½" × 15½" × 1" pan. Bake 18 to 20 minutes. While hot, turn out on clean towel which has been sprinkled with confectioner's sugar. Cover with slightly damp towel and cool.

Filling: Whip cream with vanilla and sugar and spread on cooled cake. Roll cake, gently shaking it loose from the towel. Place on serving platter, seam side down.

yield: 12 servings

You may substitute Cool Whip for heavy cream mixture, and you may wish to serve with chocolate sauce.

ROSEMARY TRANE

HOT MILK YELLOW CAKE

- 1 cup flour
- 1 teaspoon baking powder
- ¼ teaspoon salt
- 2 tablespoons butter or margarine
- ½ cup hot milk
- 2 large eggs
- 1 cup sugar
- 1 teaspoon vanilla

Pre-heat oven to 350°F. Sift together flour, baking powder and salt. Melt butter with milk and set aside. In electric mixer, beat eggs and add sugar, beating until thick. Add sifted dry ingredients and beat 1 minute on high speed. Add hot milk and butter mixture, along with vanilla. Beat on high speed 1 to 2 minutes until light and foamy. Pour into 9" round cake pan that has been buttered and lined with wax paper. Bake 30 minutes. Cool in pan 15 minutes. Remove from pan and cool completely.

yield: 1 9" cake

We've used this recipe for years - 43 to be exact - for all special occasions in our family. You can double the recipe if you want a two-layer cake.

LOUISE HULL

LEMON CURD FILLING

- 1 cup sugar
- ½ pound butter
- ¾ cup lemon juice, strained
- 1 teaspoon grated lemon rind
- 4 eggs, well beaten
- Individual tart shells or sugar cookies

Combine sugar, butter, lemon juice and rind in top of double boiler. Heat, stirring occasionally, until butter melts and ingredients are well blended. Add eggs and stir over simmering, not boiling, water until thick. Remove from heat and cool. Spoon into tart shells or onto sugar cookies when ready to serve.

yield: 1 pint filling

My mother used to send a jar of this filling to me while I was in college. My friends and I bought cookies or crackers and spread the filling on them for a special treat.

GERTRUDE SMITH PARKER

ILLUSTRATION NOTES AND REFERENCES

Before page 3— Spring—original painting by Bill Chickillo.

page 11— Waverly Community House as built in 1920.

page 19— Methodist Church, Church Street, Waverly; built in 1921.

page 25— Residence on north side of the Glenburn Road, one-half mile west of Clinton Street, Waverly; built in 1850 for Horatio Nicholson.

page 35— First location of Madison Academy, east side of Route 407, opposite Church Street, Waverly; existing building built in 1840 for Charles Bailey.

Before page 45— Summer—original painting by Karl Neuroth.

page 51— Hickory Grove Cemetery, facing south on west side of Miller Road between Route 407 and Carbondale Road, Waverly; established in 1807 as Baptist Burying Ground on hill above the homestead of Elder John Miller. Expanded and reorganized as Hickory Grove Cemetery in 1847 on one-and-one-half acres donated by Miller.

page 57— Barn and windmill of Joe Miller, east side of Miller Road, one-quarter mile north of Route 407, Waverly.

page 67— Residence on north side of Carbondale Road opposite Madison Lane, Waverly; built in 1854 for African Methodist Episcopal Church.

page 75— Residence on north side of the Glenburn Road, three-quarters of a mile west of Clinton Street, Waverly; built in 1878 for George R. Fuller.

page 83— Residence on east side of Route 407 opposite Cole Street, Waverly; built in 1830 for schoolhouse

Before page 95— Fall—original painting by Peter Hoffer.

page 101— Store building on northwest corner of intersection of Route 407 and Clinton Street, Waverly. First store in Abington Center (Waverly) built there in 1820 burned down and was rebuilt in 1850 with bricks made in the kiln on the Nathan Sherman farm on the flats along Carbondale Road.

page 111— Linair Farms buildings in the valley west of Route 407 one-half mile north of Community House square, Waverly; built in 1895 for James and Ann Blair Linen.

page 121— Residence on northwest corner of intersection of Beech and Church Streets, Waverly; built in 1856.

page 129— Residence on north side of Carbondale Road opposite Madison Lane, Waverly; built in 1850 by Lott Norris.

Before page 141— Winter—original painting by Ed Parkinson.

page 147— Residence on west side of Route 407 opposite end of Miller Road, Waverly; built in 1820 by Stephen Parker.

page 161— Lobby of Waverly Community House at Christmas.

page 173— Residence on west side of Route 407 (Abington Road) opposite Fairview Road, Clarks Green; built in 1811 by William and Sophie Clark.

page 183— Garage on west side of Route 407 opposite Carbondale Road, Waverly; built in 1890 as blacksmith shop for E. S. Calkins.

page 195— Lackawanna State Park, both sides of Route 407 along States Creek, five miles north of Waverly Community House.

Before page 207— Original painting by Gretchen Dow Simpson, looking west across Miller Road from hilltop on Carbondale Road.

page 211— Residence on east side of Waterford Road opposite Church Street, Glenburn; built in 1802 by Jonathan Hall.

These books were helpful for information and insight:
Carmer, Carl, *The Susquehanna,* Rinehart & Co., 1955.
Chapman, Isaac, *History of Wyoming,* 1830.
Folsom, Burton W., Jr., *Urban Capitalists,* John Hopkins University Press, 1981.
Galatian, Andrew B., *Scranton City Directory,* 1867-68.
Hollister, H., *History of the Lackawanna Valley,* 1900.
Kelley, Paul, *Anthracite,* Black Stone Press, 1981.
Kennedy, Rev. S.S., *Waverly News Scrapbook,* 1870-1895.
Miller, Elder John, *History of the Abingtons,* 1843 (portions).
Mumford, Mildred, *This is Waverly,* Waverly Women's Club, 1954.
Munsell, W.W. & Co., *History of Luzerne, Lackawanna and Wyoming Counties, Pennsylvania,* 1880.
Murphy, Thomas, *Jubilee History of Lackawanna County,* Historical Publishing Company, Topeka, Kansas, 1928.
Nicholson, Horatio W., *Scrapbook of Columns from the Scranton Herald,* 1853.
Parini, Jay, *Anthracite Country—Poems,* Random House, 1982.
Pierce, Stewart, *Annals of Luzerne County, Pennsylvania,* 1860.
and many documents and photographs lovingly collected and preserved by Bill Lewis, Norm Brauer and the Lackawanna Historical Society.

I offer heartfelt thanks for the invaluable help with the material of the historical narratives—in finding and selecting, sorting and paring, stewing and stirring, straining and tasting—to: Anderson Allen, Marge and Norm Brauer, Connie and Welles Belin, Rick Bell, Rhoda Bernstein, Helen Bourne, Wendy Burns, Bill Chickillo, Sue Clutter, Ned Connell, Pop Davis, Mary Linen Graham, Janet Healy, Nancy Hemmler, Peter Hoffer, Janet Holmgren, Helen Hyde, Bill Lewis, Emily Mastro, Kate Mennig, Joe Miller, Karl Neuroth, Gertrude Parker, Harold Parry, Ed Parkinson, Rebecca Peterson, Sally Preate, Alvie Reynolds, Kay Reynolds, Kenneth Rhodes, Barbara Rodes, Lou Roth, Dona Shuptar, Frances Stone, Peg Strom, Charles Welles, III, Michelle White, Janet Wrightnour, and to my understanding and encouraging family.

Rosamond Peck

HISTORIC INDEX

Abington Agricultural Society, 45, 108
Abington Baptist Association, 34
Abington Center Church, 15
Abington Players, 7, 10
Abington Township, xv
Abington-Waterford Turnpike, 181, 182
Abbot, 109
Ackerly Creek, 46, 98, 110
African Methodist Episcopal Church, 16, 64
Andrews, 9
Annual Fair and Agricultural Show, 8
Antiques Show, 97, 99
Articles of Confederation, xiii
Attic Shop, 118
Aylesworth Schoolhouse, 15

Bailey, 32, 33, 64, 98, 127
Bailey Hollow Church, 15
Bald Mountain, 72
Band of Hope, 23
Baptist Church, 8, 9, 15, 16, 118
Batchelor, 23, 64
Battle of Gettysburg, 50
Baylor's Lake, 110
Bedford, xiv, 22, 23, 32, 98, 99, 181, 182
Belin, xv, 7, 9, 10, 72, 73, 80, 110, 158, 194
Benton, xv, 128
Bergman, 119
Blair, 72
Bliss, 73, 98, 117
Boy Scouts, 49, 81
Briggs, 127
Brooks, 9
Brown, 181
Bull Roast, 48

Cadwallader, 180
Calkins, 98
Calvin, 49
Camp Archbald, 81
Capwell, 15, 49, 127
Carbondale, xiv, 15
Carpenter, 181
Cassandra Devine Dance Recital, 7
Chase, 64
Chickillo, 2

Chinchilla, xiv, xv, 48, 55, 127, 142
Civil War, 34, 50, 64, 117
Clark, xiv, 15, 49, 64, 108, 109, 127, 144, 171, 180, 182, 207, 208
Clarks Green, xiv, xv, 55, 172, 180, 181, 207
Clarks Summit, xv, 47, 73, 117, 118, 158, 182
Clymer, 180
Cobbs Gap Railroad, xiv
Cole, 73
Colvin, 49, 64
Comm; Community House—see Waverly Community House
Comm-Unity Club, 119
Connell, 80
Continental Congress, xiii
Copperhead, 127, 128
Corey, 55
Coursen, 9
Coviello, 159
Cowles, 98, 110
Cramer, 10
Crane, 23

Dalton, xv, 15, 46, 48, 110, 127, 128, 194
Davis, 73
Dean, 15, 49, 108, 110, 127, 194
Debozair, 32
Delaware Lackawanna and Western Railroad (DL&W), xiv, xv, 46
Delevan, 79
Decker, 80, 109
de Tocqueville, 128
Dixon, 9
Dorrance, 49
Drinker, 180
Dunmore, xiv
DuPont, 80

Easton, xiii
Edwards, 17
Elk Mountain, 194
Elm Park Church, 9
Erie Railroad, xiv
Estep, 158
Evans, 16, 80, 159

Factoryville, xv, 7, 15, 34, 127, 181

Fell, 23, 50, 64, 117
Field Day, 81
Finn, 127
Fireman's Carnival, 47
First Abington Baptist Church—see Baptist Church
Fleetville, xiv, 7, 48, 127
Floyd, 118
Fordham, 158
Foster, 55
Foundry, 98
Franklin Academy, 32
Free Methodist Church, 16
Freeland, 49
Fugitive Slave Law, 64
Fuller, 72, 73, 80, 194

GAR Post #307, 50, 118
Gardner, 15, 127
Garner, 64
Gearhart, 158
Girl Scouts, 49, 81, 158
Glen Oak Country Club, 127
Glenburn, xv, 72, 73, 106, 127, 128, 141, 181, 207
Glenburn Hotel, 128
Glenburn Manor House, 128
Glenburn Pond, 46, 110
Glenwood, xiv, 181
Godey's Lady Book, 72
Gorman, 32, 98
Grandma's Kitchen, 144, 145
Grange, 8
Grattan, 98
Graves, 80
Great Bend, xiv, 181
Green, 32, 98, 158, 193
Greenfield, xv, 181
Grey, 98
Griffin, 16
Gritman, 7, 127
Gunster, 17

Hall, 15, 17, 79, 80, 108, 127, 141, 207
Halloween, 95
Hallstead, 98
Hanyon, 17
Harford, xiv, 32
Hartford, 180
Healy, 7
Hickory Grove Cemetery, 16, 49, 50, 98, 141, 171
Hopkins, 119

259

Hull, 158
Humphrey, 110
Hyde, 119
Hyde Park, 55

International Order of Good Templars, 117
International Order of Odd Fellows, 117
Iroquois Confederacy, xii, 141

Jenkins, 9
Jermyn, 72
Johnson, 64
Jones, 9

Kendall, 49
Kennedy, 9, 22, 23, 45, 64, 72, 73, 97, 98, 193
Keystone Academy, 34
Knapp, 118
Knight, 79, 182
King's Daughters, 118

Lackawanna County, 17
Lackawanna County Fair and Grange Poultry Association, 46
Lackawanna River (Creek), xiii, 107, 109, 180
Lackawanna State Park, 46, 193
Lackawanna Valley, xiv, xv, 4, 34, 55, 142, 180
"Ladies Templar", 117
LaCoe, 46
Lake Winola, xv
Langstaff, 73
LaSorsa, 7
Leach, 49, 127, 142, 180
Leggets Creek, 142
Leggets Gap, 55, 117, 180
Leggets Gap Railroad, xiv, 72
Lenni-Lenape, xiii
Lennox, xiv
Lewin, 15, 127
Lewis, xv, 159
Liberty Bonds, 50
Light, 7, 79
Lily Lake, 55, 56, 194
Lily Lake Hotel, 55
Linair Farms, 65, 72, 109
Linen, 72
Luzerne County, xiv

Mackey, 17
Madison Academy, 17, 32, 33, 34, 80

Mahoney, 17, 97
Maitland Fair and Driving Company, 46
Manning, 109
Marworth Treatment Center, 23
Masons, 117
Maxey, 7
Mayer, 7
Mead, 98
Methodist Church, 7, 8, 16, 48, 97, 118, 206
Meredith, 180
Mershon, 99
Meyers, 46
Miller, 5, 15, 16, 32, 79, 80, 97, 107, 108, 127, 141, 144, 171, 181, 194
Miles, 99
Milkmaid's Convention, 206
Montage, 194
Montrose, xv, 64, 65, 181, 194
Moscow, xiv
Mount Pocono, xiii, 180
Mumford, 64

Nancy Light's Choral Readers, 7
Nanicokes, xiii
Neuroth, 44
New Salem Meeting House, 16
Newton, 46, 128
Nichols, 182
Nicholson, 3, 32, 33, 72, 98
Niles, 7
Norris, 64
North Abington, xv, 80, 81
North Abington Church, 15
Northern Electric Street Railway, xv, 46, 47
Northmoreland, 15
Northup, 79
Novak, 79

Oakford, 80
O'Malia, 182
Orchestra, Waverly, 9

Pallman, 46
Parker, 23, 80, 109, 110, 127, 144, 171, 172, 182, 208
Parini, 143, 180
Parkinson, Ed, 140
Patriotic Order of the Sons of America, 117
Peck, 9, 15
Pennsylvania Game Commission, 141
Perry, 98, 99
Philadelphia-Great Bend Turnpike, xiii, 10, 15, 23, 32,
 55, 79, 97, 127, 144, 145, 180, 181, 182
Phillips, 49, 127, 171
Pittston, 15, 172
Powell, 79
Presbyterian, 16, 79
Prickly Ash Flats, 46
Prohibition, 23
Providence, xiv, xv, 55, 172, 180, 181

Ransom, 46
Revolutionary War, xiii, 49, 180
Reynolds, 15, 49, 108, 127
Rice, 98
Rink, 117
Roaring Brook, 109, 142, 171

Saint-Exupery, 142
Saunders, 79
Scanlon, 182
Scott, xv, 127
Scranton, xiv, 128
Scranton (city), xiv, xv, 5, 46, 55, 65, 72, 73, 108, 144, 158
Scranton *Republican*, 64, 72, 97, 109, 193
Shannon, 109
Shaw, 98
Sherman, 97, 98, 127
Simpson, 9, 72
Singer, 97
Sisson, 32, 64
Slocum, 109, 171
Slocum Hollow, 142, 181
Smith, xiv, 7, 9, 32, 50, 118, 127, 180
South Abington, xv, 80
Spencer, 98
Sportsmen's Club, 7
Sproul, 7
Stanton, 49
States' Mill, 110
Stevenson, 17, 73, 80, 110
Stone, 17, 22, 23, 32, 33, 64, 98, 127, 144, 172, 181, 182, 207
Sturdevant, 15
Susquehanna County, xiv, 32
Susquehanna River, xiii, 81, 107, 171, 181
Susquehannocks, xiii

Temperance House, 23
Thompson, 46
Tillman, 64
Tillinghast, 64
Tinkham, 16, 98
Tobyhanna, xiv
Tory, xiii

260

Trenton Decision, xiii, 180
Tripp, 15, 32, 33, 108, 127, 180
Tunkhannock, 15
Tunkhannock Creek, 4, 107
Turnpike—see Philadelphia-Great Bend Turnpike

Underground Railroad, 64
Urica String Band, 9

Vail, 17
Van Fleet, 127
Van Sickle, 72, 99
Vanston, 9
Veterans of Foreign Wars, 118
Vipond, 158
Volstead Act, 23
Von Storch, 9, 158, 194

Walker, 33
Wall, 15, 108, 127
Wall Lake, 55
Wall's Store, 9
Wallsville, 46, 110
War Between the States, see Civil War
Warren, 158
Watkins, 72, 73
Waverly Community House, xvi, 7, 8, 9, 44, 48, 50, 63, 79, 97, 110, 118, 119, 141, 144, 145, 153, 159, 172
Waverly Cornet Band, 9
Waverly Country Club, 73
Waverly Grade School, 7
Waverly Hiller, 98
Waverly High School, 80
Waverly Hotel, 23, 182
Waverly Library, 119
Waverly Lodge #301, 117
"Waverly Magazine", 117

Waverly Plow, 98
Waverly School, 79
Waverly Woman's Club, 119
Wayside Inn, 182
Welles, 80
West Abington, xv
West Abington Church, 15
Whaling, 16, 98
White, 98
Wight, 16
Wilkes-Barre, xiv, 33, 65, 72, 108, 144
Winchell, 98
Women's League for Political Education, 8
Women's Social Club, 118
Woolworth, 73
Wyoming, Battle of, xiii
Wyoming Valley, 180

Yankee-Pennamite Wars, xiii

261

RECIPE INDEX

Appetizers
    Artichoke Hearts, Baked, 29
    Brie, Baked, 26
    Cheese Dreams, 29
    Chicken Wings, Red, 28
    Chicken Tib Bits, Curried, 31
    Clam Balls, 30
    Crab Casserole, 27
    Dips
        Artichoke, Hot, 26
        Cocktail Dip for Shrimp, 28
        Crab, Hot, 30
        Mexican Layered, 29
        Palmer's Edam, 27
    Salmon Mousse, 26
    Sausage and Beef, 30
    Spinach Balls, 27
    Shrimp Balls, 28

Apple
    Cake, 115
    Coffee Cake, 174
    Crabapples, Spiced, 157
    Crisp, Natural, 136
    Onion and Apple Casserole, 240

Artichoke
    Baked Hearts, 29
    Dip, Hot, 26
    Purée of Peas with, 13

Asparagus
    Caesar, 20
    Pork Slices with, 168
    Soup, 76

Avocado
    and Mushroom Salad, 169
    Mexican Layered Dip, 29
    Salad with Blue Cheese and Bacon, 93

Beans
    Black Bean Soup, 197
    Bourguinon, 133
    Chicken Green Bean Casserole, 87
    String Bean Casserole, 91
    Tuscan Bean Soup, 201

Beef
    Bourguignon, 225
    Brisket of Beef, 226
    Corned Beef and Cabbage, 231
    Flank Steak Orientale, Grilled, 52
    Gascony Beef Stew, 225
    Ground
        Impossible Cheeseburger Pie, 229
        Italian Meatballs, 229
        Montezuma Pie, 131
        Moussaka, 185
        Stuffed Monterey Jack, 228
        Sweet and Sour Stuffed Cabbage, 242
    Minute Steaks Parmesan, 86
    Oven Beef Barbecue, 85
    Richelieu with Madeira Sauce, 164
    Salad, Marinated, 58
    Slimmest of Beefs, 227
    Stroganoff, 226
    Teriyaki, 227

Biscuits
    Aunt Joe's, 40

Blueberry
    Muffins, 247
    Muffins, Jordan Marsh, 124
    Tarts in Nut Crust, 71

Bread
    Anadama, 203
    Brown, 41, 135, 153
    Cheese, Italian Crescia, 202
    Fruit and Nut, 122
    Herb, 198
    Lemon, 174
    Party Sandwich, 125
    Pita, Herb Toasts, 61
    Spoon, 136

Broccoli
    and Cheese Pie in Phyllo Pastry, 114
    and Chicken Casserole, 223
    Casserole, 89
    Marinated, and Carrots, 106
    Salad, 86

Cakes; see also Coffee Cakes
    Apple, 115
    Black Bottom Cupcakes, 203
    Carrot, 136
    Coconut Fruit Cocktail, 62
    Cheesecake
        Amaretto, 54
        Merry Cherry Bars, 126
        White Cloud with Peaches, 116
    Chocolate Bourbon, 137
    Chocolate, Moist and Delicious, 150
    Chocolate Roll, 253
    Chocolate, Very Rich, 253
    Ciambelloto, 179
    Mississippi Mud, 249
    Orange Pour, 151
    Waldorf Red "200", 252
    Yellow, Hot Milk, 254

Candies
    Never Fail Peanut Butter Fudge, 156
    Peanut Brittle, 154
    Terrible Truffles, 155
    Walnuts, Sugared, 156

Carrots
    and Broccoli, Marinated, 106
    Baby, Glazed, 91
    Cake, 136
    Creamed Soup, Cold, 212
    in Lemon Sauce, 77
    Paillasson, 243
    Soup, 213
    Timbales, 21

Cheese
    Bread, Italian Crescia, 202
    Brie, Baked, 26
    Dreams, 29
    Edam, Dip, 27

Cheese (continued)
    Ham and Onion Chowder, 197
    Strata, Sausage and Cheese, 38
    Swiss Scramble, 40

Chicken
    and Broccoli Casserole, 223
    Barbecued Legs, 90
    Ceci, 122
    Chicken Pie, 220
    Chinese Sesame Chicken, 222
    Cold Poached Breast with Green Peppercorn Sauce, 105
    Cordon Bleu, Poor Man's, 91
    Creole, 92
    Crepes, 102
    Curried Tib Bits, 31
    Great, 88
    Green Bean Casserole, 87
    In Chives and Sour Cream, 221
    Lightest, 221
    Livers and Ham with Grapes, 37
    Party Sandwich, 125
    Poulet au Citron, 222
    Salad, Ma Maison's, 215
    Saucy Stuffed, 189
    Stir-Fried and Vegetables, 224
    Tonnato, 69
    Wings, Red, 28
    with Broccoli, 223
    with Lemons, Artichokes, and Olives, 133

Chocolate
    Black Bottom Cupcakes, 203
    Brownies, Helen Gurley, 149
    Bourbon Cake, 137
    Chip-Rice Krispie Cookies, 151
    French Silk Pie, 53
    Hershey Bar Pie, 92
    Moist and Delicious Cake, 150
    Mousse, Layered, 166
    Peanut Butter Pie, 87
    Pecan Pie, Frozen, 192
    Roll, 253
    Tea Cookies, 176
    Very Rich Cake, 253

Coffee Cakes
    Apple, 174
    Coffee, 43

    Crumb, 149
    Krum Kuchen, 42
    Never Fail, 42
    Overnight, 38

Cookies, Bars, and Squares
    Almond Macaroons, 177
    Anzacs, 175
    Brownies, Helen Gurley, 149
    Celestial Squares, 61
    Cheesy Lemon Bars, 104
    Chewy Cookie Bars, 104
    Chocolate Chip-Rice Krispie, 151
    Chocolate Tea, 176
    Christmas Gingerbread Men, 152
    Christmas, Nana's, 246
    Cornflake Drops, 88
    Ginger, 177
    Lemon Squares, 123
    Linzer Bars, 175
    Merry Cherry Cheesecake Bars, 126
    Oatmeal
        Lace, 247
        Lacy, 204
    Orange, 176
    Peanut Butter, 150
    Pecan Pie Surprise Bars, 200
    Pepparkakor, 178
    Pumpkin Bars, 138
    Rice Krispie, 199
    Welsh, 151, 246

Corn
    Cheese Buttered, 87
    Soup, Red Pepper and Leek, 112

Curry
    Chicken Tib Bits, 31
    Cream of Pea Soup, 105
    Fruit Compote, 39
    Sauce, 102

Crepes
    Basic Recipe, 102
    Filling
        Chicken, 102
        Ham, 103
    Florentine Cups, 165
    Sauces for
        Curry, 102
        Mornay, 102

Desserts; See also cakes, candies, cookies, pies
    Apple Crisp, Natural, 136
    Apricot Cream, 106
    Apricot Mousse, 188
    Cerises au Port, 14
    Chestnut Roll, 170
    Chocolate Mousse, Layered, 166
    Chocolate Roll, 253
    Coffee Soufflé, Foolproof, 186
    Creme de Cacao Chantilly, 248
    Black Bottom Cupcakes, 203
    Fruit Compote, Curried, 39
    Fruit Compote, Summer, 104
    Gingerbread, New England, 246
    Ice Cream, Right Now Strawberry, 91
    Lime Soufflé, Chilled, 21
    Mandarin Dessert Mold, Frosty, 124
    Oranges, with Olive Oil and Pepper, 41
    Pavlova, 78
    Pistachio, 85
    Pudding
        Danish Rum, 251
        Honeycomb, 251
        Indian, 250
        Queen's, 250
        Rice, 251
    Spanish Cream, 249
    Swedish Cream, 70

Doughnuts, Real Maine, 179

Eggs
    Scramble for Fifty, 37
    Sausage and Cheese Strata, 38
    Spinach Casserole, 39
    Swiss Cheese Scramble, 40

Fish
    Baked Blue with Rosemary, 236
    Chowder, 200
    Clam Balls, 30
    Crab
        Casserole, 27
        Dip, Hot, 30
        King, au Gratin, 236
        Salad, 59
    Filets, Baked, 237

Jambalaya, 237
Lobster Boo, 235
Lobster Newberg, 235
Salmon Loaf, 238
Salmon Mousse, 26
Seafood Casserole, 187
Shrimp
    Baked Stuffed, 234
    Balls, 28
    Cocktail Dip for, 28
    Hostaria Del Orso, 167
    Rainbow Stir-Fry, 234
    Rockefeller, 132
Sole Filet, Dugleré, 20
Tuna and Rice, 238
Tuna Supper Casserole, 238

Fruit; see also Individual Fruit Names
and Nut Bread, 122
Compote, Curried, 39
Compote, Summer, 104
Salad
    Cranberry-Raspberry Mold, 125
    Oranges, with Olive Oil and Pepper, 41

Gingerbread, New England, 246

Ham
and Chicken Livers with Grapes, 37
and Pork Loaf, 233
Cheese and Onion Chowder, 197
Crepes, 103
Loaf, 42

Ice Cream
Apricot Cream, 106
Strawberry, Right Now, 91

Johnny Cakes, 245

Lamb
Armenian Shish Kebob, 231
Grilled Leg, 113
Moussaka, 185

Mayonnaise, Green, 103

Muffins
Blueberry, 247
Blueberry, Jordan Marsh, 124
Bran, 39
Swedish Limpa, 199
Zucchini, 152

Pancakes, Oven, 245

Pasta
Hay and Straw, 190
Lasagna, Tofu, 131
Linguine with White Clam Sauce, 217
Noodle Casserole, 218
Noodle Pudding, 86, 219
Spaghetti, Cold, 218
Tortellini Salad, 59
Tortellini Salad, Philharmonic, 216
Vegetable and Pasta Salad, 135
with Broccoli, 218

Peas
Purée of with Artichokes, 13
Soup, Curried, 105

Peach
Cheesecake, White Cloud, 116
Pie, 248
Torte, 93

Peanut
Brittle, 154
Butter Cookies, 150
Butter Fudge, Never Fail, 156
Butter Pie, 90
Salad, 85

Pies
Blueberry Tarts in Nut Crust, 71
Chocolate Peanut Butter, 87
Chocolate Pecan, Frozen, 192
Fluffy Peanut Butter, 90
French Silk, Chocolate, 53
Hershey Bar, 92
Lemon Curd Filling, 254
Lemon Meringue, 137
Peach, 248
Peach Torte, 93

Pita Toast, Herbed, 61

Pizza, Pesto, 217

Popovers, Cinnamon, 245

Pork
and Ham Loaf, 233
Chops, Barbecued, 232
Slices with Asparagus and Sorrel Sauce, 168

Puddings; see Desserts

Quiche
Broccoli and Cheese in Phyllo Pastry, 114
Crustless Brandied, 41
in Puffed Pastry, 60

Ratatouille, 60

Relishes
Jalapeño Jelly, 157
Pickled Peppers, 157
Spiced Crabapples, 157
Zucchini Pickles, 156

Rice
Brown, Confetti, 186
Pilaf, Armenian, 169
Ring, 216
Risotto, 13
Salad, 70
Wild with Mushrooms and Olives, 188

Rolls, 135

Salad
Avocado and Mushroom, 169
Avocado with Blue Cheese and Bacon, 93
Beef, Marinated, 58
Broccoli, 86
Broccoli and Carrots, Marinated, 106
Butternut Squash, Snow Pea and Endive, 191
Cabbage, Mimerer's, 214
Chicken, Ma Maison's, 215
Crab, 59
Cranberry-Raspberry, 125
Dig Deep, 123

265

Salad (continued)
    Greek, 186
    Layered Garden, 134
    Oranges with Olive Oil and Pepper, 41
    Peanut, 85
    Rice, 70
    Spinach, 134
    Summer, 43
    Tomato Aspic, 103
    Tortellini, 59
    Tortellini, Philharmonic, 216
    Vegetable and Pasta, 135
    Watercress with Lemon Vinaigrette, 165

Salad Dressings
    Ginger-Sesame, 191
    Mayonnaise, Green, 103
    Poppy Seed, 215
    Vinaigrette, Lemon, 165

Sauces
    Curry, 102
    Floradora, 251
    Madeira, 164
    Mornay, 102
    Peppercorn, Green, 105
    Salsa Verde, 14
    Sorrel, 168
    Tomato, 77

Sausage
    and Beef Appetizer, 30
    and Cheese Strata, 38

Soups
    Asparagus, 76
    Black Bean, 197
    Carrot, 213
    Cold Cream of Carrot, 212
    Corn, Red Pepper, and Leek, 112
    Curried Cream of Pea, 105
    Fish Chowder, 200
    Gazpacho, 68
    Ham, Cheese and Onion, 197
    Jamaica Pepperpot, 202
    Lentil, 214
    Mushroom and Vegetable, 198
    Potato and Spinach Balls, 214
    Senegalese, 212
    Spinach Egg Drop, 213
    Tomato and Celery Consommé, 163
    Tuscan Bean, 201

Spinach
    and Egg Casserole, 39
    Balls, 27
    Egg Drop Soup, 213
    Florentine Crepe Cups, 165
    Malfatti, 187
    Parmesan, 53
    Potato Soup and Spinach Balls, 214
    Rice Balls, 244
    Salad, 134

Streudel, 153

Tofu Lasagna, 131

Tomatoes
    and Celery Consommé, 163
    Aspic, Fresh, 103
    Broiled with Horseradish, 53
    Provençal, 115
    Sauce, 77

Veal
    Osso Bucco Milanese, 12
    Stuffed Roll with Fresh Tomato Sauce, 77

Vegetables
    Artichokes, Baked Hearts, 29
    Artichokes, Purée of Peas with, 13
    Asparagus Caesar, 20
    Beans Bourguignon, 133
    Broccoli
        and Carrots, Marinated, 106
        and Cheese Pie in Phyllo Pastry, 114
        Casserole, 89
    Cabbage, Sweet and Sour Stuffed, 242
    Carrots
        Baby, Glazed, 91
        In Lemon Sauce, 77
        Marinated with Broccoli, 106
        Paillasson, 243
        Scallions and Mushrooms, 243
        Timbales, 21
    Cauliflower au Gratin Soufflé, 243
    Cauliflower with Salsa Verde, 14
    Corn, Cheese Buttered, 87
    Eggplant, Casserole, 241, 242
    Eggplant, Curry, 241
    Elegant and Simple Vegetables, 21
    Mushrooms, Carrots and Scallions, 243
    Onion Casserole, 239
    Onion and Apple Casserole, 240
    Peas, Purée with Artichoke Bottoms, 13
    Potatoes
        Paillasson, 243
        Romanoff, 90
        Stuffed Baked, Brennan's, 52
        Stuffed Baked, Marworth, 89
    Ratatouille, 60
    Spinach
        Balls, 27
        Florentine Crepe Cups, 165
        Malfatti, 187
        Parmesan, 53
        Rice Balls, 244
    Squash, Summer Casserole, 240
    String Bean Casserole, 91
    Tomatoes, Broiled with Horseradish, 53
    Tomatoes Provençale, 115
    Turnips, Paillasson, 243
    Yugoslavian Casserole, 239
    Zucchini
        Baked, 114
        Casserole with Sour Cream, 240
        Grated in Cream, 78
        Soufflé, 69

Venison
    Meat Loaf, 230
    Stroganoff, 230

Walnuts, Sugared, 156

Zucchini
    Baked, 114
    Casserole with Sour Cream, 240
    Grated in Cream, 78
    Muffins, 152
    Pickles, 156
    Soufflé, 69